European Union and its Neighbours in a Globalized World

Volume 19

The series publishes monographs and edited volumes in the field of European and international law and policy. A special focus is put on the European neighbourhood policy, current problems in European and international law and policy as well as the role of the European Union as a global actor. The series supports the publishing and distribution of research results of cross-border research consortia. Besides renowned scientists the series is also open for publication projects of young academics. The series emphasizes the interplay of the European Union and its neighbouring countries as well as the important role of the European Union as a key player in the international context of law, economics and politics.

Gloria Fernández Arribas

Contemporary Challenges to the Fundamental Principles of International Law and EU Interaction

Springer

Gloria Fernández Arribas
Public International Law
University Pablo de Olavide
Sevilla, Spain

ISSN 2524-8928 ISSN 2524-8936 (electronic)
European Union and its Neighbours in a Globalized World
ISBN 978-3-031-75452-4 ISBN 978-3-031-75453-1 (eBook)
https://doi.org/10.1007/978-3-031-75453-1

This Springer imprint is published by the registered company Springer Nature Switzerland AG
The registered company address is: Gewerbestrasse 11, 6330 Cham, Switzerland

"When I use a word," Humpty Dumpty said in rather a scornful tone, "it means just what I choose it to mean—neither more nor less."
"The question is," said Alice, "whether you can make words mean so many different things."
"The question is," said Humpty Dumpty, "which is to be master—that's all."
Through the Looking-Glass, Lewis Carroll (1871)

"En todos los países hay dos morales, una dentro de la nación, otra internacional: según ésta, el deber *es la* conveniencia*; la* perfidia *se llama* habilidad*; del que abusa vilmente de la fuerza se dice que sabe* utilizar favorables circunstancias *y en fin, tiene una especie de* caló *que consiste, no en emplear palabras diferentes, sino en dar a las usuales diverso sentido, como quien pierde el moral."*
Ensayo sobre el Derecho de Gentes, Concepción del Arenal (1895)

Contents

1 Introduction 1
References 6

2 An International Community of Principles 7
2.1 Shaping the International Community and the Structural Principles of the International Legal Order 8
2.1.1 From International Society to International Community . . . 9
2.1.2 Structural Principles of the International Legal Order 12
2.2 History and Principles: Past and Present International Challenges 15
References 21

3 Sovereignty: The Cornestone of the International System 25
3.1 The Value of Sovereignty in the International Community 26
3.2 From International Organizations to Treaty Organs: Getting Sovereignty Back 31
3.2.1 The Proliferation of International Organizations 31
3.2.2 New Forms of Cooperation: A Threat to International Organizations? 33
3.3 New realms of sovereignty: shared sovereignty and the European Union 35
3.3.1 Framing Shared Sovereignty 36
3.3.2 Shared Sovereignty in Practice: Mixed Agreements 38
References 40

4 A Self-Determination Principle in the Twenty-First Century 45
4.1 The Role of Self-Determination in a Post-Colonial World 46
4.1.1 Unravelling the Concept: External Self-Determination and Internal Self-Determination 48
4.1.2 The Holders of the Right to Self-Determination and the Secession Dilemma 52

4.2 Three Advisory Opinions, Three Peoples Under Struggle: Western Sahara, Palestine and Chagos . . . 57
4.2.1 The Facts . . . 58
4.2.2 The Failed Role of the United Nations . . . 60
4.2.3 A Defence of the Right to Self-Determination by the International Community of States? . . . 63
4.3 Self-Determination in a Europe of Integration . . . 68
4.3.1 The European Union and Secessionism . . . 69
4.3.2 A Membership for Secessionist Territories? . . . 73
References . . . 76

5 An 'Optional' Principle of Non-Intervention? . . . 79
5.1 The 'Nebulous' Concept of Intervention . . . 80
5.2 How Human Rights Created a 'Right' to Intervene . . . 84
5.2.1 The Background of Humanitarian Intervention . . . 85
5.2.2 Legalising Intervention . . . 86
5.3 Intervention by Request: The Muddy Justification . . . 91
5.3.1 Consent: The Cornerstone of Intervention by Request . . . 92
5.3.2 On the Legality of the Intervention in Non-International Armed Conflicts . . . 95
5.4 Twenty-First Century Cyber-Interventionism . . . 97
5.4.1 The Link with International Law . . . 98
5.4.2 Cyber-Intervention in Electoral Processes and the Principle of Non-Intervention: Not an Easy Answer . . . 100
5.5 The European Union as a Paradigm of Intervention to Promote the Respect of Human Rights: A Practice-Based Approach . . . 105
5.5.1 Conditionality to Promote Respect for Human Rights . . . 106
5.5.2 Restrictive Measures: The Contentious Method . . . 107
References . . . 112

6 The Prohibition of the Use of Force Under Attack . . . 117
6.1 *Jus cogens* and the Prohibition of the Use of Force . . . 119
6.1.1 The Core Element of the Prohibition of the Use of Force . . . 119
6.1.2 The Risks of the Extensive Interpretations . . . 121
6.2 Anticipatory and Pre-Emptive Self-defence as an Expansionist Use of Force in Self-Defence . . . 123
6.2.1 Can Customary Law Be a Basis for Anticipatory and Pre-Emptive Self-Defence? . . . 124
6.2.2 Instrumentalising International Organizations to Expand the Concept of Self-Defence . . . 127
6.2.3 State Practice and Pre-Emptive Self-Defence . . . 128
6.3 The Unwilling or Unable Doctrine: International Terrorism as a Cover . . . 131

6.3.1 The Practice of Self-Defence Against Terrorist Groups 132
6.3.2 A Legal Practice? 135
6.4 Western Expansionist Theories on the Use of Force: A Backfire? The Russian Aggression Against Ukraine 137
6.4.1 Self-Defence Against Who? 139
6.4.2 The Humanitarian Intervention Wild Card 143
6.4.3 Bogus Military Assistance on Request 148
6.5 Does the European Union Have a Role in Protecting This Principle Against the New Interpretations? 151
6.5.1 The Position of the European Union Regarding the Use of Force Against Terrorist Groups 152
6.5.2 Military Assistance on Request and the European Union: Practice in the Field 155
References 157

7 Epilogue: Will the International Community and Its Principles Endure? 163

Abbreviations

ARSIWA	Articles of the Responsibility of States for Internationally Wrongful Acts
BIO	British Indian Ocean Territory
BIT	Bilateral Investment Treaties
BRICS	Brazil, Russia, India, China, South Africa
DARIO	Draft Articles on the Responsibility of International Organizations
COP	Conference of the Parties
ECJ	European Court of Justice
EU	European Union
ICJ	International Court of Justice
ICCPR	International Covenant on Civil and Political Rights
ICESCR	International Covenant on Economic, Social and Cultural Rights
ISIL	Islamic State of Iraq and the Levant
PCIJ	Permanent Court of International Justice
MEAs	Multilateral Environmental Agreements
MFN	Most Favoured Nation
NATO	North Atlantic Treaty Organization
NGO	Non-Governmental Organization
OSCE	Organization for Security and Co-operation in Europe
TWAIL	Third World Approaches to International Law
TEU	Treaty of the European Union
TFEU	Treaty on the Functioning of the European Union
UN	United Nations
US	United States of America
UNCLOS	United Nations Convention of the Law of the Sea
UNFCCC	United Nations Framework Convention on Climate Change

Abbreviations

Chapter 1
Introduction

More than 50 years have passed since the adoption of Resolution 2625 (XXV) on the Declaration of Principles of International Law concerning Friendly Relations and Cooperation among States.[1] A certain number of its fundamental principles appear to be in question today. This upheaval results not only from Russia's recent aggression against Ukraine, but also from years of a policy based on a biased interpretation and application of the fundamental principles that have weakened them.[2]

Resolution 2625 (XXV) entailed a milestone in international relations. It was adopted by the General Assembly without a vote and it established the framework for the international cooperation among states. In the words of the Resolution:

> The principles of the Charter which are embodied in this Declaration constitute basic principles of international law, and consequently appeals to all States to be guided by these principles in their international conduct and to develop their mutual relations on the basis of the strict observance of these principles.

The Resolution was the outcome of a process that had begun years before, when in 1961, twelve delegations submitted a proposal for a decision by the General

[1] UN General Assembly, *Declaration on Principles of International Law concerning Friendly Relations and Cooperation among States in accordance with the Charter of the United Nations*, 24 October 1970, A/RES/2625(XXV).

[2] Another issue that is also related to the threats to international law principles is the threats to Rules-Based International Order (RBO). It is necessary to clarify that the present work does not address the RBO threats analysis. The first reason is the controversial and undetermined nature of this concept, which has been regarded as a weakly legally-supported political creation. Moreover, it is perceived as a western concept that has not been accepted by all states, as manifested by Russia and China. Another implication is that the main threats to the RBO come from non-western countries. Conversely, this work addresses international law principles accepted by all states and the threats to those principles posed by states from different regions, not only non-western states. Finally, the RBO is sometimes considered to represent itself a "threat to the normative legitimacy and authority of international law". Jorgensen (2021), p. 13. See also Dugard (2023); Sloss (2022); Talmon (2019).

G. Fernández Arribas, *Contemporary Challenges to the Fundamental Principles of International Law and EU Interaction*, European Union and its Neighbours in a Globalized World 19, https://doi.org/10.1007/978-3-031-75453-1_1

Assembly. They proposed to include, in the following session's provisional agenda, the study of the principles that guarantee the peaceful coexistence of states. It is important to note that the Sixth Committee amended the name of the proposal, changing the words "peaceful coexistence" to "friendly relations and cooperation". As we shall examine later, this can be considered a manifestation, among others, of how the international society had evolved into a community, i.e., one in which the subjects do not only coexist, but also cooperate to achieve common goals. In 1963, it was finally decided to establish a special committee to study the topic and the latter presented the final document in 1970.[3]

The Declaration has been employed ever since as a set of normative standards that serve to analyse the legality of state actions, despite the non-compulsory character of the UN General Assembly resolutions. In this regard, the principles it enshrines have been included in other international instruments and are part of international customary law.[4] And they are recognised as such by the International Court of Justice.

The importance of this Resolution lies in the fact that it embodied the essential principles that allow a peaceful relationship, as established by all the states. Its survival and respect, therefore, are essential for the international community to endure over time.

However, as in all domains of law, complexities arise regarding the interpretation and application of the norms. In this case, the paradox is that it is the very states that should be promoting and creating the best conditions for their application that are jeopardising the existence of the principles as well as international peace and security. The whole construction of the system is based on concepts that need to be described, interpreted, analysed, and applied in each specific situation. And this is where the system fails, as some states are able to impose particular interpretations of concepts, such as self-defence or non-intervention, according to the particular interests at stake at each moment in time.

It is now necessary, over 50 years after its adoption, to approach the Resolution again and to review its content, interpretation, and application. We must determine the value and the role that the Resolution has played and may play in the future in

[3]See United Nations Audiovisual Library of International Law. Declaration on Principles of International Law concerning Friendly Relations and Cooperation among States in accordance with the Charter of the United Nations. New York, 24 October 1970. Procedural History. https://legal.un.org/avl/ha/dpilfrcscun/dpilfrcscun.html

[4]It is worth noting that some of these principles had already been included in the Bandung Conference final communiqué as principles that "would effectively contribute to the maintenance and promotion of international peace and security" since it was understood that they would guide the development of friendly co-operation. In any case, the conference focused on the problems and issues of special interest to Africa and Asian countries, and was marked by decolonisation. Indeed, it was established that "the Conference was convened empowered people in the colonized world to assert their own place in the world on their own terms". Eslava et al. (2017), p. 6. On the other hand, Resolution 2625 is universal in scope and was primarily designed to regulate international relations among states. The recognition of those principles at the Bandung Conference prior to their inclusion in Resolution 2625 also illustrates the "progressive development and codification" of the said principles, as stated in the Resolution preamble. See de Serpa Soares (2014); Wondam (2016).

guaranteeing a peaceful cooperation among states. It seems essential to determine whether the Resolution can continue to be the normative framework of international relations, and whether its principles have remained useful and valuable to regulate those relations, analysing, moreover, their legally binding character.

The analysis must consider a changing context. The world in which the declaration was adopted has evolved, together with the subjects and challenges. The potential harm that international actors, such as terrorist groups, can do today to state security and stability is far greater than that in 1970. The same applies to the digital revolution: not only has it created new weapons, but it has also shaped a new means to intervene in a state's internal affairs. There are other challenges that drafters in 1970 did not have in mind or could not foresee: the threat of climate change to a state's security or economy; or how economic interconnection and dependency on a planetary scale has led to a situation in which a pandemic or a regional conflict can affect the global supply chain.

In this context therefore, the proposed analysis will focus on the study of some of the fundamental principles enshrined in Resolution 2625 (XXV): sovereignty, self-determination, non-intervention, and prohibition of the use of force. In this regard, the latter are not the only principles included in the Resolution and they are not the sole fundamental principles that guarantee cooperation and friendly relations. Others, such as respect for human rights, principles of humanitarian law, or the prevention of environmental harm have also been regarded as essential.[5] However, the four principles referred to and the selected challenges[6] will contribute to understanding some of the main features of contemporary international law and the international community: the role of traditional subjects as well as the new ones; the sources of international law; issues of responsibility; new international threats; and the conflicting interests as well as the unity or fragmentation of the international community.

Moreover, a section will be devoted to the European Union's specific relationship with these principles. In this regard, the European Union exemplifies, as a subject and as a treaty-maker, the major evolution of international law. The Union illustrates how the international community has been institutionalised and contributes to the establishment of this concept. Therefore, exploring how the European Union has to

[5] See Viñuales (2020), p. 10; Cassese (2005), p. 47. The Millenium Declaration also enlarges the principles as it refers to: "respect for their territorial integrity and political independence, resolution of disputes by peaceful means and in conformity with the principles of justice and international law, the right to self-determination of peoples which remain under colonial domination and foreign occupation, non-interference in the internal affairs of States, respect for human rights and fundamental freedoms, respect for the equal rights of all without distinction as to race, sex, language or religion and international cooperation in solving international problems of an economic, social, cultural or humanitarian character". UN General Assembly, *United Nations Millennium Declaration* 18 September 2000, A/RES/55/2.

[6] As alluded to earlier, the present world faces numerous challenges, and analysing them all is beyond the scope of this work. The challenges selected and addressed here are therefore those allowing to understand the above-mentioned features of contemporary international law and the international community.

face the different approaches to those principles and how those principles can affect the grounds and values of the organization would allow us to appreciate another approach to the implementation and understanding of these principles by an evolving actor of the international community. In this regard, we must also remember that the Union is formed by western states that are considered to be the creators and defenders of those principles. The Union's position, therefore, may play a key role in the future analysis.

We shall adopt a mainly theoretical approach when studying the fundamental principles, analysing the concept and interpretations of major specialists in international law. In this regard, references to multiple works on each of the four selected principles will be included, and they will set the bases of the analysis. The theoretical approach is also essential to identify and analyse some of the main theories used to interpret the fundamental principles and also called on to legally justify breaches of international law.

Nevertheless, the study must be complemented with other perspectives. Indeed, if the goal is to understand the international community as well as its principles, and to analyse theories which are linked to state practices, we must pay attention to the practices of the main international subjects and actors. Practice also constitutes an element of customary law, so state practice is essential to determine the application of international principles, the breach of international law, or the theories that justify it. Yet state practice is also fundamental to pinpoint how the principles have evolved regarding their interpretation, implementation as well as content, and the concepts themselves. Such an exploration may even lead to conclude on the existence of new principles.

Finally, a political approach to the study of the fundamental principles enshrined in Resolution 2625 (XXV) will focus on the national or regional interests that led the states or international organizations to define their position regarding the interpretation and application of international law and its principles. These positions can be observed in meetings of international organizations, statements, or national documents, which will be useful to compare the practice and official states opinions. The latter will be contradictory at times, and at other times will help to confirm the specific way the law is interpreted.

This approach to the study of the international community and its principles will focus mainly on questions about the fundamental principles and its main challenges. But to analyse the principles, it is first necessary to understand the concept of international community, its value in the contemporary system, and its link with the fundamental principles. Once the international community has been defined, the principles underpinning it will be studied, starting with the principle of sovereignty. This principle is the cornerstone of a state-based system, even though the rise of international organisations as the main form of cooperation may have affected its content and meaning. We shall explore how states seem to have lost or shared their sovereignty in favour of cooperation and the consequences of this for the content and application of this principle.

However, one of the most demanding analyses is to disclose the role of the principle of self-determination in a century in which colonialism seems to have been overcome. In fact, the key word is 'seems' because, as we delve deeper, we continue to encounter territories and peoples still awaiting decolonisation or the exercise of their right to self-determination. The evolution of the international community and the rise of new interests and movements have also led to contested interpretations of the principle. Some of them confront the principle of sovereignty or territorial integrity, such as remedial secession. Yet some also affect the interests of international organizations such as self-determination as grounds for secession inside the European Union.

One the criticisms expressed against the European Union owing to its leader's declarations regarding the mentioned secessionist movements focused on intervention in internal affairs. This principle has been considered by some as 'dead and buried',[7] and lacking any application in today's international community. The blurred content of the principle, the difficulties to agree on a definition, and the inconsistent practice of the states has led to question its scope of application and its effectiveness. The principle must also be analysed in the context of a community in which common interests, such as human rights, have reduced states' spheres of independence. But in addition, in a community in which the very values that states claim to defend are used to circumvent the law, and in which it is difficult to differentiate when states are pursuing common objectives or defending individual interests to the detriment of the principle of non-intervention. The difficulties in determining the breach of this principle have gone one step further with the capabilities that have come with the digital revolution. Cyber interventionism in the democratic process has shown how the digital world can expand the impact of intervention. In addition, perpetrators are difficult to identify making it harder, therefore, to respond to such a violation.

The European Union has also contributed to reviewing the concept of non-intervention in the twenty-first century. In this regard, the Union has set itself up as a promoter of human rights in third countries, which has led the organization to adopt measures that border at some point on intervention in internal affairs. They could, however, find a place in the new and related interpretations of non-intervention and human rights.

Nevertheless, do expansive interpretations of the principle of the prohibition use of force represent the most dangerous threat to the international community? The violation of the prohibition of the use of force entails the violation of the principle of sovereignty, non-intervention, and in most cases, the principle of self-determination. But it mainly entails the greatest threat to international peace a security. Accepting these facts, it is worth asking why the principle is challenged, undermined, and disregarded by states. To answer this question, the most contested expansive theories on the use of force must be examined in the context of a society facing great challenges and threats, but unable to come up with valuable ideas to face those threats while respecting the fundamental principle of the prohibition of the use of force. Those fears and inability have also dragged the European Union into a blurred

[7] See Kohen (2012), p. 158.

position regarding the expansive interpretations of the use of force, despite its commitment to the respect of international law and the promotion of a peaceful relationship with third actors.

Finally, this book aims to provide a comprehensive view of the fundamental principles, relating all of them and addressing the complexities that arise when the application of some clash with that of others. Today's international panorama calls for an analysis that delves into the system's origins, or foundations. We need to ask whether the rules-based international order that emerged after World War II will continue to govern international relations.

References

Cassese A (2005) International Law. Oxford University Press, Oxford

Dugard J (2023) The choice before us: International Law or a 'rules-based international order'? Leiden J Int Law 36:2

Eslava L, Fakhri M, Nesiah V (2017) The spirit of Bandung. In: Eslava L, Fakhri M, Nesiah V (eds) Bandung, global history, and international law. Critical pasts and pending futures. Cambridge University Press, Cambridge

Jorgensen M (2021) The jurisprudence of the rules-based order: Germany's Indo-Pacific guidelines and the South China Sea code of conduct. KFG Work Pap Ser 49:13

Kohen M (2012) The principle of non-intervention 25 years after the Nicaragua Judgment. Leiden J Int Law 25(1):157–164

Serpa Soares M (2014) Editorial comments keynote speech at the international colloquium on the five principles of peaceful co-existence and the development of International Law. Chin J Int Law 13(3):481–484

Sloss DL (2022) Introduction: preserving a rules-based international order. In: Sloss DL (ed) Is the international legal order unraveling? Oxford University Press, Oxford

Talmon S (2019) Rules-based order v International Law?. German Practice in International Law, available at www.gpil.jura.uni-bonn.de/2019/01/rules-based-order-v-international-law

Viñuales JE (2020) The fundamental principles of International Law – an enduring ideal? In: Viñuales JE (ed) The UN Friendly Relations Declaration at 50. Cambridge University Press, Cambridge

Wondam P (2016) The 60th anniversary of the Bandung Conference. Asia Inter-Asia Cult Stud 17(1):148

Chapter 2
An International Community of Principles

The Russian war of aggression against Ukraine has shocked all who believed that the international legal order and international community were effective enough to prevent World War II scenarios from occurring again. Yet such spectacles were already unfolding outside Europe.

The revelation has led scholars and experts to examine the solidity of the principles of the international community, including an essential one: the prohibition of the use of force. If scholars promptly reacted by analysing these principles, it is because the international coexistence of states rests on norms and principles, the latter having created a community, and the fading of those principles and norms may therefore entail the disappearance of the international community. Indeed, if one main actor or state abandons its principles, what happens next?

To understand the international legal order, it is essential to grasp the essence of the international community, a community in which states forge and organise their relationships. To conceive the system's future, it is also necessary to comprehend how states have evolved. Driven perhaps by the evolution and complexity of international relations, they have shifted from a state of mere coexistence, in which they acted individually to achieve their goals, to a system in which collective action is key to face common challenges.

In the same vein, the international community—as any society or community—needs its norms: those that guarantee the coexistence of its subjects, as well as those that provide legal certainty and allow the shaping of common goals. In addition, communities also need principles, which constitute a higher stage, and at the same time, the foundation on which norms take root, providing confidence in the system. In this chapter, we will build an understanding of today's international system and examine how international society evolved into an international community. International principles will be a prominent part of the analysis, as they constitute the main component of the community, that is, they represent the driving force of the creation of the international community.

G. Fernández Arribas, *Contemporary Challenges to the Fundamental Principles of International Law and EU Interaction*, European Union and its Neighbours in a Globalized World 19, https://doi.org/10.1007/978-3-031-75453-1_2

Nevertheless, to understand those principles, it is also necessary to review the historical context and challenges that international society was facing when they were adopted.

The objective is thus to analyse the roots of the present system and its challenges. The intention of the analysis is not, however, to upend the system, or to suggest abandoning current principles and norms, and elaborating new ones adapted to present and future centuries. We are not advocating either some form of stagnation of our international rules-based order. The question is rather how to improve the system, so that it provide an answer to the challenges awaiting all states, especially those for which the present setup has not led to full development, security and independence.

2.1 Shaping the International Community and the Structural Principles of the International Legal Order

References to an international society or to an international community are at the centre of international law analysis. They determine the foundations of international law and the object of its application. In this regard, different positions can be found regarding the existence of a genuine international community, a contrary position being to merely consider the existence of an international society.[1] The concepts, however, of international community and international society are sometimes used interchangeably.[2] These debates are rooted in the very concept and meaning of both terms as well as in the sorts of relationships that can be established between them.

A combined interpretation of the statements of both Friedman and Cassese helps us to understand how the identified elements can be linked. In this regard, Cassese held that in an international society, each member is more 'prone to pursuing its own interests than those of the whole group'; while in a community we find 'a homogeneity view, common bonds, closeness and mutual aid'.[3] For his part, Friedman considered that international law was shifting from a law of coexistence to a law of cooperation.[4] Therefore, if coexistence refers merely to different entities existing

---

[1]See those individualistic approaches referred by Koskennimi and regarding the absence of common values or interests. Koskenniemi (2005), p. 480.

[2]Paulus (2009), p. 45. Charlesworth and Chinkin for example refer how Grotious articulated the notion of international society considering that states form a community. Charlesworth and Chinkin (2000), p. 23. And Anzilotti affirms that solidarity between interests and the civilization give birth to a Society of Sates or an International Community. Anzilotti (1935), p. 40.

[3]Cassese (2012), p. 651, In the same vein, Pérez-Prat establishes that the international community concept emphasizes the unity of its components, prioritizing representation of common interests over individual ones, the existence of rules, principles and procedures. Pérez-Prat Durbán (2004), p. 94.

[4]See Hakimi (2017a), p. 8.

without any common links, we can affirm that Friedman's 'law of coexistence' regulates international society, which 'is grounded in the mere juxtaposition of its subjects'.[5] On the other hand, the 'law of cooperation' would be the law of the community. We could thus consider that we have today shifted from an international society to an international community.[6]

2.1.1 From International Society to International Community

In his 1970 General Course on Public International Law at The Hague Academy, Tomuschat clearly exposed how international society evolved into an international community. Addressing the complexity of the international legal order, he established various milestones: the first was the law of coexistence, at the origin of the international legal order; the second stage was cooperation; a third stage was that in which social law was present; to finish, he concluded with reflections and questions on the current existence of an international community.[7]

Added to these contemporary positions, references to the existence of an international community have been made since the beginnings of international law, perhaps not using its specific terminology, but advancing similar conceptions at least. In this sense, in the seventeenth century, Francisco Suarez considered that 'the human race (...) always preserves a certain unity, not only as a species, but also a moral and political unity (as it were) enjoined by the natural precept of mutual love and mercy'.[8]

Not only did scholars refer to the international community but so did treaties or judgements. A major illustration of this is Art. 53 of the Vienna Convention on the Law of Treaties,[9] which establishes that: 'For the purposes of the present Convention, a peremptory norm of general international law is a norm accepted and recognized by the international community of States as a whole'.

The International Court of Justice (ICJ) also mentioned the existence of an international community and its significance in the adoption of norms and principles. The leading case is perhaps *Barcelona Traction*,[10] in which the Court elaborated the concept of *erga omnes*, establishing that 'in particular, an essential distinction should be drawn between the obligations of a state towards the international community as a whole, and those arising vis-à-vis another state in the field of diplomatic

[5] Weil (1983), p. 441; Cassese (2012), p. 648.

[6] Abi-Saab (2020), p. 15.

[7] Tomuschat (1999).

[8] See Ibid. p. 74.

[9] United Nations, Vienna Convention on the Law of Treaties, 23 May 1969, United Nations, Treaty Series, Vol. 1155, p. 331.

[10] ICJ, *Barcelona Traction, Light and Power Company, Limited*, (Baelgium v. Spain), Judgment of 5 February 1970: I.CJ. Reports, 1970.

protection'.[11] In addition, the Court referred to the international community when analysing the *jus cogens* norms in the *Jurisdictional Immunities of the State* case. It thus established that:

> it is difficult to see that international law contains a rule requiring the payment of full compensation to each and every individual victim as a rule accepted by the international community of States as a whole as one from which no derogation is permitted.[12]

Together with these references to the international community, when analysing the main principles of international law, the Court has also referred for example to the importance of the principles governing diplomatic and consular relations for the international community as a whole.[13] However, the most relevant case regarding the international community concept would probably be *Reparations*. In that case, in 1949, the Court considered that fifty states represented 'the vast majority of the members of the international community'.[14] Previously, the Permanent Court of International Justice (PCIJ) had referred to the 'community of Sates' when it interpreted the phrase 'principles of international law' included in Article 15 of the Convention of Lausanne.[15]

Therefore, the international community concept has been present in the minds of treaty-makers as well as interpreters for a long time, but perhaps not in accordance with the concept we referred to at the beginning of this section. In those ICJ references, the international community could be considered as an element that agglutinates the group of states[16] and, therefore, as synonymous with international society, or perhaps as a *desideratum* or first recognition of the emergence of the notion of international community. We must highlight in any case that the Court refers to it when analysing international law principles and values, *jus cogens* and *erga omnes*, regarded as the common concepts or principles that push international society towards the condition of international community.[17]

Be that as it may, international society or, in its most advanced form, the international community is governed by norms that regulate its members' behaviours,[18] and these norms constitute international law: the legal order of the

---

[11] *Ibid.* para. 33, emphasis added.

[12] ICJ, *Jurisdictional Immunities of the State* (Germany v. Italy: Greece intervening), Judgment of 3 February 2012: I.C.J. Reports 2012, para. 94.

[13] ICJ, *United States Diplomatic and Consular Staff in Tehran* (United States of America v. Iran), Judgment of 24 May 1980: I.C.J. Reports 1980, para. 92.

[14] ICJ, *Reparation for injuries suffered in the service of the United Nations*, Advisory Opinion of 11 April 1949: I.C. J. Reports 1949, p. 185.

[15] PCIJ, *The Case of S.S. Lotus* (France. v. Turkey.), Judgement, 1927 P.C.I.J. Series A-No. 10, p. 16.

[16] Tomuschat (1993), p. 231.

[17] Hakimi (2017b), p. 318; Weil (1983), pp. 423–427; Cassese (2012), p. 654; Carrillo Salcedo (1996), p. 132; Sreenivasa Rao (2008), p. 93.

[18] Vid. Sreenivasa Rao (2008), p. 86; Anzilotti (1935), p. 4.

community of states.[19] In the realm of strict positivist theories,[20] these norms are the main expression and major elements that regulate such a behaviour. On the other hand, other scholars, such as Tomuschat, have also referred to the principles and values that form part of the international legal order.[21] This latter position prompts a different approach to international law in which historical, political, as well as social circumstances are considered and, according to Truyol y Serra, lead to a hierarchy of values.[22]

This understanding of the international legal order as a system of norms and principles is common among scholars, though they differ regarding the role played by those principles or their origin and nature. According to those closest to natural law theories, the principles originate in a universal legal conscience that is independent of a state's authority.[23] Others accept the superior nature of these principles but consider that states play a role in their conception, thereby respecting the consent-based structure[24] and regarding them as general values accepted by the international community as a whole.[25]

When analysing those principles, one option is to understand that they merely inform the adoption of norms playing a role in the content of those norms and filling the lacuna in the interpretation of a specific issue.[26] This group of principles includes not only those referred to, for example, in Article 38 of the ICJ Statute,[27] but also principles pertaining to different domains or legal regimes of international law.[28] Friedman divides these types of principles into three categories:

> principles of approach and interpretation to legal relationships of all kinds, minimum standards of procedural fairness and substantive principles of law sufficiently widely and firmly recognized in the leading legal systems of the world to be regarded as international legal principles.[29]

---

[19] Anzilotti (1935), p. 42. Pérez-Prat considers that while analysing international law it is also necessary to look at it not only a normative order, but also to open the analysis to the power dimension and moral justification. Pérez-Prat Durbán (2004), p. 46.

[20] See Weil (1983); García-Salmones Rovira (2020), pp. 87–91.

[21] Tomuschat (1999), p. 28. This position could be considered contrary to the traditional positivist theories in which consent replaces universal values as the basis of obligation and closer to the liberal international legal theory in which states consent to the principles of international law. See Charlesworth and Chinkin (2000), pp. 27–29.

[22] Truyol y Serra (1957), p. 438.

[23] Galisonga Jordá (2005), pp. 648–649.

[24] Tomuschat (1999), p. 28.

[25] Andrés Saenz de Santamaria (2012), p. 25 et seq.

[26] Lauterpacht (2011), pp. 85 *et seq*.

[27] See International Law Commission, *First report on general principles of law by Marcelo Vázquez-Bermúdez, Special Rapporteur*, A/CN.4/732, 5 April 2019; International Law Commission, *Second report on general principles of law by Marcelo Vázquez-Bermúdez, Special Rapporteur*, A/CN.4/741, 9 April 2020.

[28] For example, principles applicable to international investment or principles of Humanitarian Law.

[29] Friedman (1963), p. 287.

Nevertheless, other principles can be regarded differently to the extent that they are constitutional, structural, or fundamental principles of the international community. Indeed, they reflect unity as well as common values and they govern not only coexistence but also cooperation.[30]

According to natural law theories, the latter principles are characterised by stability and persistence.[31] However, it is now widely accepted that principles evolve with historical times,[32] and this could affect their existence and especially their interpretation as well as application. In this regard, Cassese established that modern principles 'are a typical expression of the present world community'.[33]

2.1.2 Structural Principles of the International Legal Order

Having established the existence of principles as part of the international legal order, we must focus on the existence of the previously mentioned group of structural principles, which constitute the constitutional[34] or normative[35] framework of international law. These principles have been regarded as necessary to guarantee hierarchy, stability, and legal certainty. They express the states' commitment to representing the international community's various interests.

It is commonly understood[36] that the principles established in Resolution 2625 (XXV)[37] constitute the structural principles of international law. Distinct positions, however, have been adopted regarding the principles included in that declaration. For example, Cassese affirms that not all of them are universal and fundamental since cooperation and good faith would only be political guidelines.[38] On the other hand, Cassese and others consider that they are not the only fundamental principles

[30] Tomuschat (1999), p. 78; Abi-Saab (2020), p. 19; Abellán Honrubia (2005), p. 63.

[31] Galisonga Jordá (2005), p. 651

[32] Andrés Saenz de Santamaria (2012), p. 25

[33] Cassese (2005), p. 64.

[34] Diez de Velasco (2013), pp. 79–81.

[35] Jiménez Piernas (2011), p. 62.

[36] Mainly among Spanish scholars. See Cassese (2005), p. 47; Andrés Saenz de Santamaria (2012), pp. 25–26; Jiménez Piernas (2011), p. 62; Diez de Velasco (2013), p. 80; Abellán Honrubia (2005), p. 59; Pérez González (2005), p. 1030; Roldán Barbero (2018), p. 87.

[37] UN General Assembly, *Declaration on Principles of International Law concerning Friendly Relations and Cooperation among States in accordance with the Charter of the United Nations*, 24 October 1970, A/RES/2625(XXV).

[38] Cassese (2005), p. 47; On the other hand, Koskenniemi considers as fundamental principles: sovereignty, non-interference, self-determination and he includes state immunity, Koskennimi (1985), p. 121.

and that the protection of human rights,[39] of the environment,[40] or democracy[41] must also be included.

According to the most widespread positions, the structural or fundamental principles would be the prohibition of the use of force, peaceful settlement, non-intervention, sovereign equality of states, self-determination and outside Resolution 2625 (XXV), respect for human rights. Therefore, we have before us a set of principles which are not given, but created by the states, yet no individual acceptance is necessary to make them compulsory or to consider their existence as universal. The principles that comply with these features can be inferred from state practices, but they do not simply correspond to customary law or treaty law. These principles are hierarchically superior and inform the adoption of international norms. Consequently, the principles would not only set limits to state actions, they also need to drive, and must always drive state actions towards representing common values deriving from those principles. The principles must therefore also inform international political decisions.

The fact that these principles are recognised means that we should acknowledge the existence of an international community.[42] Indeed, from that moment onwards, we begin to refer to a group of states with common values and objectives, acting within a framework of common goals when pursuing their own objectives.

It has also been stated that denying these principles can undermine the structure of the international legal order,[43] or that it is not possible to legitimise illegal action which violates these principles.[44] Practice, however, has led to different conclusions regarding this latter statement for example. In this regard, Zappala[45] analysed how the consequences of the 2001 intervention in Iraq, which violated Article 2.4 of the United Nations Charter prohibiting the use of force, was finally legitimated through various means: the states' involvement in reconstructing the country; through the acceptance of special tribunals; or through the legitimation of the new Iraqi government, justifying all these actions with the protection of other principles such as self-determination or human rights.

---

[39] Andrés Saenz de Santamaria (2012), p. 26; Tomuschat (1999), p. 70; Abellán Honrubia (2005), p. 59. Cebada Romero focuses on human rights as constitutional principles in order to analyze the consitutionalization of the international legal order and the birth of a global international law. See Cebada Romero (2013).

[40] Andrés Saenz de Santamaria (2012), p. 26.

[41] Diez de Velasco (2013), p. 80.

[42] The origin of the principles can be traced back to 1945—some of them even earlier—when the community started to form. The community did not come into being on an exact date, e.g., on the day of the 1970 Declaration, or any other. It is rather the result of an evolving process marked by a number of milestones among which the 1970 Declaration, in which the majority of the states put the principles governing their relationships into writing.

[43] Pérez González (2005), p. 1030. See also Aznar Gómez (2007).

[44] Diez de Velasco (2013), p. 114.

[45] Zappalà (2012).

This example leads us to examine the very content of these principles and how they can give rise to different or contradictory interpretations. We must reflect in any case on whether these disturbances can affect the existence itself of these principles or the structure of the international legal order, the function of international law or the existence of the international community. In this regard, we can refer to Weil's statement that 'ill-defined values might well destabilize the whole international normative system and turn into an instrument that can no longer serve its purpose'.[46] But what is the purpose of international law and its principles?

Hakimi affirmed that the most widely accepted function of international law is to guarantee cooperation and coexistence among states, which she calls the cooperation thesis.[47] The same function was previously recognised by the PCIJ in the *Lotus* case in 1927, which affirmed that international law was established 'in order to regulate the relations between these co-existing independent communities or with a view to the achievement of common aims'.[48] This main function can be divided into other functions such as: preserving peace and security;[49] establishing rights and obligations of states;[50] protecting and achieving general interests;[51] integration;[52] or reducing anarchy.[53] All are based on the idea that international law must reduce disputes and look for consensus. Koskenniemi holds a particular view in that he considers that the 'objectives of International law cannot be dissociated from the objectives of the members of the international society', which leads him to consider that peace or security concepts are as they have been agreed upon and understood by the system's members.[54]

This conception regarding the purpose of international law is grounded in the features of the international community that has some common values and principles but is also characterised by conflicting interests and fragmentation.[55] It is thus necessary to regulate cooperation. According to some views, conflicts are thus at the core of the international society as well as of international law and they hinder the achievement of a truly international community. However, from a more benevolent viewpoint, conflicts can be understood to promote discussion and improve the

---

46 Weil (1983), p. 133.

47 Hakimi (2017a), p. 1. This idea is also line with the function of law, according to Casanovas y La Rosa: "toda regla jurídica tiene su origen en una motivación de orden práctico consistente en dar una cierta solución a un conflicto de intereses". Casanovas y La Rosa (2011), p. 57.

48 PCIJ, *The Case of S.S. Lotus*, p. 18.

49 Jiménez Piernas (2011), p. 48.

50 Andrés Saenz de Santamaria (2012), p. 19.

51 Abellán Honrubia (2005), pp. 63–64.

52 Diez de Velasco (2013), p. 82

53 Weil (1983), p. 128.

54 Koskenniemi (2011), p. 243.

55 Paulus goes further and considers that "fragmentation rather than community has become the key to describe contemporary international society". Paulus (2009), p. 50. See the leading study on the theory of fragmentation: Koskenniemi (2006).

international community together with international law;[56] in Chaumont's words, '*le progès ne résulte pas de l'ordre formel mais doit partir du désordre réel, dans la mesure où ce dernier peut être dépassé*'.[57]

Without entering the realm of critical legal studies and their core notions of contradiction[58] and indeterminacy, we must accept that contradiction or confrontation of norms, principles and values are present in the international community.[59] The reason for this may be the existence of different interests and, therefore, interpretations. Or it may owe to the fact that the very nature of the principles makes their coexistence difficult, or perhaps to the evolution of the international community and international law. Be that as it may, as Koskenniemi stated, the matter is not about choosing between contradictory ideas but about choosing all of them; in his words, 'law is not about peace or justice, freedom or security, stability or change, but always about both one and the other simultaneously'.[60]

In sum, we can affirm that structural or fundamental principles of international law underlying an international community exist and that they contribute to the stability of the international legal order, placing them at a superior level. At the same time, however, these principles can be object of confrontation, diverging interpretations, evolution, transformations, or contradictions, whether among themselves or among the norms that implement them.

Therefore, it is necessary to analyse whether those conflicts lead to the transformation or erosion of the fundamental principles, diminishing their importance or even making them disappear, while affecting the content and purpose of international law and the existence of the international community. Finally, we need to focus that analysis on whether we have before us different interpretations or true breaches.

2.2 History and Principles: Past and Present International Challenges

In the previous section, we referred to the origins, the evolution, interpretations and application of international law principles. We must now therefore describe the social and political situation that gave rise to the origin and understanding of these

[56] See Hakimi (2017b); Charlesworth (2002).

[57] Chaumont (1970), p. 346.

[58] M. Koskenniemi and D. Kennedy can be pointed as the main representatives. According to Chaumont there are three big contradictions: cooperation versus national independence, international legal order versus revolution; and delf-determination versus "areas of influence", Chaumont (1970), p. 348. In the same line Casanovas y La Rosa establishes, while analyzing the existentialism theories, that Sates invoke international law to achieve fully opposite interests. Casanovas y La Rosa (2011), p. 56.

[59] Remiro Brotons (1994), p. 29.

[60] Koskenniemi (2011), p. 256.

main structural principles. In this way, to understand how the interpretation and application of the principles have evolved, we need to compare past situations with our current state of affairs.

The historical and political situation in which Resolution 2625 (XXV) was adopted was marked by decolonisation. With the rise of new states came the questioning of the international legal order that had been ruling state relationships for decades. The new states challenged a law that was considered European and Christian,[61] a legal order that had been created without them and that supported the interests of imperialist states,[62] thus prompting a necessary change.

The enlargement of the number of states introduced new interests and objectives in the international arena. New subjects of international law emerged whose economic, political and social situation[63] differed from that of the colonial or Western states. The position of these new states regarding the international norms and principles was therefore linked to their specific situation,[64] focusing on the norms that could contribute or ensure their survival and consolidation.

In this regard, their support or acceptance of international norms varied according to the content of those norms. They greatly mistrusted, however, customary law since it had been created by the practice of the European states and therefore, 'the new States cannot be expected to accept the thesis that practice of a norm by a group of States may create rules of international law binding upon all States'.[65]

An element that influenced the new states' position in international law was economic development linked to natural resources. This factor led them to support and strengthen a major principle of international law: sovereignty. And sovereignty was therefore linked to sovereignty over natural resources.[66] However, since the means and know-how for the development and exploitation of natural resources was in the hands of Western states and companies,[67] sovereignty over natural resources was never completely achieved. In any case, sovereignty was also linked to self-determination, a principle that governed the access of these states to the world community and protected their own existence.

The period during which Resolution 2625 (XXV) was negotiated was also characterised by a more complex world, in which wars were multiplying in the

[61] Moyn and Özsu (2020), p. 28.

[62] Prakash Sinha (1965), p. 121.

[63] There was a tendency to refer to those no western or soviet states as 'third world', a concept according to Fatourus 'tendentious'. In any case, he considered that geographically, 'third world' included most the Asian, African and Latin American states, but not existing total cohesion among them, having different policies but tending to follow 'similar lines with respect to a number of important topics'. Fatourus (1964), p. 784. They also acted trough informal coalitions as the Bandung Conference, the Group of 77, and the Non-Aligned Countries. McWhinne (2012). https://legal.un.org/avl/ha/ga_2131-xx/ga_2131-xx.html

[64] Fatourus (1964), p. 785.

[65] Prakash Sinha (1965), p. 122.

[66] Moyn and Özsu (2020), p. 31.

[67] Fatourus (1964), pp. 795–796.

former colonies. It was the time of the wars in Congo, Biafra, Palestine, Algeria, Rhodesia, Vietnam or Cambodia among others. Western or socialist countries intervened in some of them, transforming those wars into proxy wars. This dramatic situation led the new states to strongly support the prohibition of the use of force,[68] yet, at the same time, controversies arose about the use of force to guarantee the right of self-determination.[69] Finally this principle became the "pivotal norm"[70] of their demands and the basis for the new system.

In addition, the principle of non-intervention was also linked to decolonisation and self-determination. It thus shows how deeply that process marked the development of the international legal order that emerged during the mid-twentieth century. In this regard, given the weakness of these new states, the definition of intervention was also under discussion, but not only regarding the use of force. Even though the new states were aware of how much they needed the economic and financial support of the former colonies and Western states, they also sought to prohibit economic and financial coercion. Balancing that complicated relationship was therefore a difficult task. The controversy gave rise to Resolution 2131 (XX),[71] which was not accepted by Western states as 'a definitive statement of the principle at issue'.[72] A proposal was made to include a paragraph stating that assisting people under colonial domination could not be defined as intervention.[73] But despite this, the outcome of the Resolution was a declaration demanding the respect of the right to self-determination with no foreign pressure.

Yet, decolonisation was not the only factor driving the system's evolution during that half of the twentieth century: the cold war also left its mark. The two blocks confronted each other regarding the international legal order, focusing on the interpretation and content of the main principles.[74] In the same vein, both blocks attempted to approach the new states. Understandably, the Soviet Union was probably the most successful player in this venture, given its absence in the colonial race and the support it gave to the interests of the new states.[75]

The Soviet Union's close position to that of the new states is visible in its interpretation of the mentioned principles. For example, it was favourable to a

---

[68] Moyn and Özsu (2020), p. 37; Fatourus (1964), p. 790.

[69] Two options to justify the use of force were formulated: self-defence or customary law. And even though the mentioned mistrust of new state regarding customary, this last option was the favourite one for those states that have been under colonial domination. Moyn and Özsu (2020), p. 42; Houben (1967), pp. 708–709.

[70] Abi-Saab (1998), p. 254.

[71] UN General Assembly, *Declaration on the Inadmissibility of Intervention in the Domestic Affairs of States and the Protection of Their Independence and Sovereignty*, 21 December 1965, A/RES/21231(XX).

[72] Fatourus (1964), p. 717.

[73] Ibidem.

[74] Dupuy (1998), p. 364

[75] Since the death of Stalin neutralist or not aligned nations started to be considered by the Soviet Union, no as potential enemies, but as potential friends. Fatourus (1964), p. 795

broad definition of the coercion concept in the case of the principle of non-intervention,[76] and it supported the demands of the new states, including their definition of economic or financial coercion that was different from that of the Western states. The communist states, as in the case of the new states, considered that they had not sufficiently participated in the creation of international law either,[77] and that they were therefore acting within a system that did not consider their own interests.

Nevertheless, the Soviet Union and its allied countries tried to defend their interests and their concept of the international relations and international order through intense diplomatic activity.[78] In this regard, they also participated in international fora in order to negotiate and introduce their point of view and ideology, for example in discussions on including war propaganda in the definition of the use of force.[79]

This activity did not always go hand in hand with the new states' interests. Indeed, interventions in civil wars in support of certain factions or the nuclear race—whose consequences could affect the whole community, as exposed by the Cuban missile crisis—were contrary to the positions adopted by these states. The latter even rejected the cold war as 'the most important factor in international relations'.[80]

This international situation was categorised as 'peaceful co-existence',[81] and according to the previous analysis of the 'law of coexistence', we must acknowledge that international society was simply a group of subjects without any common objectives. On the other hand, this international society concept did not stop a large number of treaties and international norms from being adopted in this regard. The post-World War II period can be considered as flourishing times for international law-making. Peaceful co-existence and its necessity for regulation led to the adoption of a number of essential international law treaties,[82] such as the Convention on the prohibition of Genocide,[83] the Convention relating to the status of Refugees,[84] the Diplomatic and Consular Vienna Conventions,[85] or the Convention on

[76] Moyn and Özsu (2020), p. 28.

[77] Fatourus (1964), p. 703

[78] Dupuy (1998), p. 364. According to Sinclair this concept "bore the hallmarls of the Soviet ideology", Sinclair (1994), p. 2.

[79] Houben (1967), pp. 707–708

[80] Fatourus (1964), p. 795

[81] Dupuy (1998), p. 363

[82] In any case the Covenant on Civil and Political Rights and the Covenant on Economic, Social and Cultural Rights exemplified what Dupuy referred as "radically incompatible political principles" Dupuy (1998), p. 364.

[83] UN General Assembly, *Convention on the Prevention and Punishment of the Crime of Genocide*, 9 December 1948, United Nations, Treaty Series, vol. 78, p. 277.

[84] UN General Assembly, *Convention Relating to the Status of Refugees*, 28 July 1951, United Nations, Treaty Series, vol. 189, p. 137.

[85] United Nations, *Vienna Convention on Consular Relations*, 24 April 1963, United Nations, Treaty Series, vol. 596, p. 261.

the Law of Treaties,[86] and lastly, the achievement of Declaration 2625 (XXV). We can observe a change in this latter Declaration as the term 'cooperation' is included in its title. It is worth noting that the cold war continued together with opposite interests and principles until the late 1980s, yet it coexisted with an emerging international community.

The new states also had a prominent role in these developments. Indeed, despite their mistrust in the existing international legal order, they supported and actively participated in the adoption of new treaties. The new states also became parties to pre-existing treaties, and were actively involved in international fora, such as at the United Nations: an international organisation created by Western states but that also served the interests of the new states.[87]

The international circumstances described above marked by decolonisation and the cold war led to the adoption of Resolution 2625 (XXV). We shall examine its principles according to recent state practices later, and as we analyse the principles in the following chapters, we shall also consider international challenges. We will, however, first briefly present some of these issues together with today's state of affairs. This will allow us to compare the conjuncture with the historical momentum in which the Resolution was adopted.

Discussing international law today may seem to equate to studying an old issue that is today in crisis. It appears that realists have imposed their views on the ineffectiveness of international law.[88] Critical scholars have also instilled doubts about the present 'liberal international order'.[89] Moreover, both left- and right-wing politicians criticise the neoliberal economic agenda of international law and how it serves, according to the former, the struggle of the Global South countries,[90] or, according to the latter, how it is instrumental to attack state sovereignty.[91]

Together with this common goal of discrediting international law, we have found that far from disappearing, the new states' former mistrust of the established international legal order has in fact simply taken on new forms and fresh supporters. The wounds of colonisation have not healed, and the 'threat of recolonization'[92] is present, as shown by the rise of a second generation of Third World Approaches to International Law (TWAIL) scholarship.[93] The latter entails a rejection of the entire

---

[86] United Nations, *Vienna Convention on the Law of Treaties*, 23 May 1969, United Nations, Treaty Series, vol. 1155, p. 331.

[87] Fatourus (1964), pp. 792–793.

[88] See Hakimi (2020), p. 1283.

[89] Staggs Kelsall (2022), pp. 729–730. According to Staggs the critics of the liberal international legal order argue that "International law masks its sanctioning of hegemony, its colonial predilections, its allegiance to capitalism and its aversion towards gender non-conformity". Ibid, p. 734.

[90] Hakimi (2020), p. 1288.

[91] Ibid, p. 1288 and 1295–1297. Hakimi refers to the America First doctrine of Trump administration, which has been a model to follow by the right-populist politicians.

[92] Chimni (2006), p. 3.

[93] See Thuo Gathii (2011), p. 26.

international legal order since 'the economic and political independence of the third world is being undermined by policies and laws dictated by the first world and the international institutions it controls'.[94]

Just as the Soviet Union often supported the new states' interests during the decolonisation process and the cold war era, China is now an ever-greater detractor of the Western hegemony of international law.[95] Both Russia and China have on their agendas the objective of reinforcing their international status and changing their territorial status quo as well, supporting Global South claims in order to simultaneously destabilise today's international legal order.

However, as commented by Hathaway and Shapiro, the states 'that failed at Versailles but succeeded in Paris, Yalta, San Francisco and Bretton Woods, are the ones now placing the international order they created under the greatest stress'.[96] Therefore, the United States, France or the United Kingdom are also contributing to discrediting the international legal system, together with Russia or China. The former has launched a war of aggression against Ukraine, and the latter is maintaining a policy of occupation of contested territories in the South China Sea.

As we shall see in the following sections, the expansive interpretation of the exception to the use of force, resulting in the 'erosion of the United Nations authority',[97] or the use of the international institutions for national interests, applying 'egoistic policies which defy the very essence of international law of co-operation',[98] have contributed to questioning the value and efficiency of the international legal order. The above has also been fuelled by nationalist as well as populist movements and leaders, who consider international law as a threat to national interests, sparing no efforts to diminish its importance and effectiveness.[99]

This stress undergone by the international legal system is also taking place in a complex and changing world, in which the international legal order seems to be struggling to keep up with the new challenges it has to face. In this regard, such challenges or threats include: the rise of new actors, also linked with international terrorism; technological evolution, which has led to cyberattacks or targeted killing; climate change and conflicts over natural resources; new forms of confrontation, such as hybrid wars or the grey zone; the rise of interrelated upheavals, such as the financial, climate, food security and refugees crises, and the capacity of international law to cope with them[100]; or globalisation, which, as described by Dupuy, is

---

[94] Chimni (2006), p. 3.

[95] Staggs Kelsall (2022), p. 748.

[96] Hathaway and Shapiro (2019), p. 14

[97] Dupuy (1998), p. 279

[98] Abi-Saab (2020), p. 21.

[99] The America First policy run by the Trump administration is a prominent example of this practice. See. Hakimi (2020), pp. 1295–1299.

[100] Staggs Kelsall (2022), p. 738.

unfolding not as a project, as universalism did in the 60s and 80s, but as an inevitability.[101]

It seems that as Abi Saab averred in 1998:

> The end of Cold War, far from pushing international society towards a more integrated global international community, has introduced new dangers together with new bones of contestation among the members of this society, which create the risk of making it evolve in the opposite direction.[102]

We shall examine how valid this statement is today in the following chapters.

References

Abellán Honrubia V (2005) Sobre el método y los conceptos en Derecho Internacional Público. In: Urritia VG et al (eds) Soberanía del Estado y Derecho Internacional: Homenaje al Profesor Juan Antonio Carrillo Salcedo. Universidad de Córdoba, Córdoba; Universidad de Sevilla, Sevilla; Universidad de Málaga, Málaga

Abi Saab G (1998) Whither the international community? Eur J Int Law 9:254

Abi-Saab G (2020) The system of the friendly relations declaration. In: Viñuales J (ed) The UN Friendly Relations Declaration at 50: an assessment of the fundamental principles of International Law. Cambridge University Press, Cambridge

Andrés Saenz de Santamaria P (2012) Sistema de Derecho Internacional Público. Civitas, Cizur Menor

Anzilotti D (1935) Curso de Derecho Internacional. Editorial Reus, Madrid

Aznar Gómez M (2007) En torno a la unidad sistémica del Derecho Internacional. Rev Esp Derecho Int 59(2):563–594

Carrillo Salcedo JA (1996) Droit international et souveraineté des états: cours général de droit international public. In: Recueil des Cours. Collected courses of the Hague Academy of International Law, vol 257

Casanovas y La Rosa O (2011) Aproximación a una teoría de los regímenes en Derecho Internacional Público. In: Rodrigo Hernández AJ, Gacría i Segura C (eds) Unidad y pluralismo en el derecho internacional público y en la comunidad internacional. Tecnos, Madrid

Cassese A (2005) International Law. Oxford University Press, Oxford

Cassese A (2012) Gathering up the main threads. In: Cassese A (ed) Realizing Utopia. The future of International Law. Oxford University Press, Oxford

Cebada Romero A (2013) El Derecho Internacional Global: Una retórica útil para una transformación necesaria. Rev Esp Derecho Int 65(1):15–42

Charlesworth H (2002) International Law: a discipline of crisis. Mod Law Rev 65(3):377–392

Charlesworth H, Chinkin C (2000) The boundaries of International Law. A feminist analysis. Manchester University Press, Manchester

Chaumont C (1970) Cours Général de Droit International Public. In: Recueil des Cours. Collected courses of the Hague Academy of International Law, vol 129

Chimni BS (2006) Third world approaches to International Law: a manifesto. Int Comm Law Rev 8:3

Diez de Velasco M (2013) Instituciones de Derecho Internacional Público. Tecnos, Madrid

[101] Dupuy (1998), p. 282.

[102] Abi Saab (1998), p. 265.

Dupuy P-M (1998) International law: torn between coexistence, cooperation and globalization. General conclusions. Eur J Int Law 9:364
Fatourus A (1964) International Law and the third world. Va Law Rev 50(5):784
Friedman W (1963) The uses of 'general principles' in the development of international law. Am J Int Law 57(2):287
Galisonga Jordá A (2005) El reconocimiento de los principios jurídicos en el Derecho Internacional contemporáneo y el desarrollo de la conciencia jurídica universal. In: Urritia VG et al (eds) Soberanía del Estado y Derecho Internacional: Homenaje al Profesor Juan Antonio Carrillo Salcedo. Universidad de Córdoba, Córdoba; Universidad de Sevilla, Sevilla; Universidad de Málaga, Málaga
García-Salmones Rovira M (2020) What is positivism today? AJIL Unbound 114:87–91
Hakimi M (2017a) The work of International Law. Harv Int Law J 58(1):8
Hakimi M (2017b) Constructing an international community. Am J Int Law 111(2):318
Hakimi M (2020) Why should we care about International Law? Mich Law Rev 118(6):1283
Hathaway OA, Shapiro SJ (2019) The international law and its transformation through the outlawry of war. Int Aff 95(1):14
Houben P-H (1967) Principles of international law concerning friendly relations and co-operation among states. Am J Int Law 61(3):708–709
Jiménez Piernas C (2011) Introducción al Derecho Internacional Público: Práctica de España y la Unión Europea. Tecnos, Madrid
Koskenniemi M (2005) From apology to Utopia. The structure of international legal argument. Cambridge University Press, Cambridge
Koskenniemi M (2006) Fragmentation of international law: difficulties arising from the diversification and expansion of international law: report of the Study Group of the International Law Commission
Koskenniemi M (2011) The politics of International Law. Hart Publishing, Oxford
Koskennimi M (1985) General principles: reflexions on Constructivism Thinking in International law. Eripainos, Oikeustiede-Jurisprundentia 18:121
Lauterpacht H (2011, first published 1933) The function of law in International Community. Oxford University Press, Oxford
McWhinne E (2012) General Assembly Resolution 2131 (XX) of 21 December 1965 declaration on the admissibility of intervention in the domestic affairs of the States and the protection of the independence and sovereignty. United NationsAudiovisual Library of International Law
Moyn S, Özsu U (2020) The historical origins and setting of the friendly relations declaration. In: Viñuales J (ed) The UN Friendly Relations Declaration at 50: an assessment of the fundamental principles of International Law. Cambridge University Press, Cambridge
Paulus A (2009) International Law and international community. In: Amstrong D (ed) Routledge Handbook of International Law. Routledge, New York
Pérez González M (2005) Apuntes sobre los principios generales del Derecho en Derecho Internacional. In: Urritia VG et al (eds) Soberanía del Estado y Derecho Internacional: Homenaje al Profesor Juan Antonio Carrillo Salcedo. Universidad de Córdoba, Córdoba; Universidad de Sevilla, Sevilla; Universidad de Málaga, Málaga
Pérez-Prat Durbán L (2004) La provincia en el Derecho Internacional. Dykinson, Madrid
Prakash Sinha S (1965) Perspective of the newly independent states on the binding quality of international law. Int Comp Law Q 14(1):121
Remiro Brotons JA (1994) Civilizados, bárbaros y salvajes en el Nuevo Orden Internacional. Curso de Derecho Internacional y Relaciones Internacionales de Vitoria y Gasteiz
Roldán Barbero J (2018) El principio de prohibición de uso de la fuerza armada y la posverdad. In: Diez-Hochleitner Rodríguez J (ed) Principios y justicia en el derecho internacional libro homenaje al profesor Antonio Remiro Brotóns. Dykinson, Madrid
Sinclair I (1994) The significance of the friendly relations declaration. In: Vaughan L, Warbrick C (eds) The United Nations and the principles of International Law. Routledge, London

Sreenivasa Rao P (2008) The concept of International Community in International Law: theory and reality. In: Buffard I et al (eds) International Law between universalism and fragmentation. Festschrift in Honour of Gerhard Hafner. Martinus Nijhoff Publichers, Leiden
Staggs Kelsall M (2022) Disordering International Law. Eur J Int Law 33(3):729–730
Thuo Gathii J (2011) TWAIL: a Brief History of its Origins, its Decentralized Network, and a Tentative Bibliography. Trade Law Dev 3(1):26
Tomuschat C (1993) Obligations arising for states without or against their will. In: Recueil des Cours. Collected courses of the Hague Academy of International Law, vol 241
Tomuschat C (1999) International Law: ensuring the survival of mankind on the eve of a new century. In: Recueil des Cours. Collected courses of the Hague Academy of International Law, vol 281
Truyol y Serrra A (1957) Nota sobre el Derecho Internacional Público como disciplina científica y materia docente. Rev Esp Derecho Int 10(3):438
Weil P (1983) Towards relative normativity in International Law? Am J Int Law 77:441
Zappalà S (2012) Can legality trump effectiveness in today's International Law? In: Realizing Utopia. The future of International Law. Oxford University Press, Oxford

Chapter 3
Sovereignty: The Cornerstone of the International System

State sovereignty is one of the principles enshrined in Resolution 2625 (XXV)[1] and is linked to the concept of equality. It determines perhaps in this way the ultimate objective of this principle in the contemporary world: promoting peaceful coexistence and cooperation rather than recognising and guaranteeing traditional state prerogatives.[2] In this regard, the Resolution refers to equality while simultaneously recognising 'differences of an economic, social, political or other nature'.[3] The question is therefore: How can we address sovereign states, which are regarded as both equal and unequal at the same time?

Sovereignty has been considered an ambiguous[4] and malleable[5] term, and for Henkin, an 'unfortunate mistake'.[6] There are as many definitions of sovereignty as there are ways in which scholars have approached the issue. Definitions typically refer to state capabilities or limitations with respect to other states (external sovereignty).[7] This understanding has led to the presentation of sovereignty as a negative attribute in the sense that no legal power can be exercised over the sovereign state.[8] Therefore, the concept of sovereignty has been linked to the notion of

[1] UN General Assembly, *Declaration on Principles of International Law concerning Friendly Relations and Cooperation among States in accordance with the Charter of the United Nations*, 24 October 1970, A/RES/2625(XXV).

[2] On the evolution of sovereignty see Schrijver (1999).

[3] On inequality see, Kinsbury (1998).

[4] Koskenniemi (2005), p. 242.

[5] Alvarez (2012), p. 31.

[6] Henkin (1989), p. 24.

[7] On the contrary, internal sovereignty has been understood by Kokenniemi as self-determination. Koskenniemi (2005), p. 240. Also, it can be described as the capacity to exercise public authority in the territory of the State. See ICJ, *Case concerning Right of Passage over Indian Territory*. Dissenting Opinion Judge Fernandes, Judgment of 12 April 1960: I.C.J. Reports 1960, p. 124.

[8] Combacau and Sur (2004), p. 23.

G. Fernández Arribas, *Contemporary Challenges to the Fundamental Principles of International Law and EU Interaction*, European Union and its Neighbours in a Globalized World 19, https://doi.org/10.1007/978-3-031-75453-1_3

independence.[9] In this regard, Judge Huber, in the *Isla of Palmas* case, established regarding territorial sovereignty that 'sovereignty in the relations between states signifies independence. Independence in regard to a portion of the globe is the right to exercise therein, to the exclusion of any other state, the functions of a state'.[10] Along the same lines, Schiemann adopted a general and basic understanding of sovereignty centring on the internal manifestation of sovereignty. The author stated that sovereignty 'includes an alleged right of a state to organize affairs within its borders as it pleases, and an alleged right to be free from interference by other states'.[11]

These definitions correspond to a general and ambiguous concept of sovereignty, but other definitions focus on the content of sovereignty. In this regard, it has been linked to 'competences', stating that sovereignty was the set of powers attributed to a state by international law, exercisable on a plane of independence and equality with respect to other states.[12] Such state competences would constitute the factors that determine the extension of sovereignty.[13] Therefore, based on the mentioned definitions, sovereignty could be understood as the freely and independent exercise of the state competences attributed by international law, within the state's territory as well as in its relations with third states. Sovereignty therefore presents an *ad intra* and *ad extra* component.

3.1 The Value of Sovereignty in the International Community

Given that independence is a key component of sovereignty, should we regard sovereignty as an impediment to our progress towards an international community of common values? For Henkin, sovereignty is undoubtedly an obstacle: though the existence of international law is not questioned today, states continue to use sovereignty as an argument against agreements or international institutions and the concept should therefore be eliminated.[14] Pellet likewise referred to the misuse of the concept, stating that

[9]Koskenniemi (2005), p. 240.

[10]Isla of Palmas case, (Netherlands, USA), 4 April 1928, Reports of International Arbitral Awards, Vol. II, p. 838.

[11]Schiemann (2007), p. 475.

[12]Remiro Brotons et al. (2007), p. 127.

[13]Koskenniemi (2005), p. 268.

[14]Henkin (1989), p. 25. Alvarez analyses the different position of globalists, in favour of international institutions and regulations, and sovereigntists, in favour of states sovereignty. Alvarez (2012). p. 27.

> it is becoming (or reverting to being) an instrument for contesting existing legal rules; and, when invoked carelessly, it aims to flatter the populist and "sovereigntist" instincts of the populations at the same time as being largely deprived of any conceptual utility.[15]

Nevertheless, sovereignty does not imply the non-applicability of law, nor that states should set the law aside as they please,[16] which could be the main obstacle to the existence of the international community. At first sight, sovereignty entails the absence of a superior entity[17] and the existence of a consent-based system.[18] Such a view, however, is simplistic, because the whole concept of sovereignty, rights and obligations, together with the emergence of international organizations present contradictions.

It has been argued that a state's acceptance of international law is a manifestation of sovereignty, as established in the well-known *Wimbledon* case,[19] in the sense that states are free to limit their competences. The latter was summarised by Combacau and Sur, who commented that sovereignty '*suggère la possibilité pour un État d'aliéner aussi largement qu'il le juge opportun sa liberté future, pourvu qu'il le fasse en usant de sa liberté actuelle'*.[20] In this way, it is through the acceptance of duties and obligations that states exercise their sovereignty, deciding to limit or to cede sovereign rights.

Nonetheless, sovereignty not only entails rights or competences that can be freely disposed of by states, but also obligations.[21] It is in the realm of obligations that we encounter contradictions between the voluntarism and sovereignty concepts. According to Resolution 2625 (XXV), sovereignty entails the duty to respect another state's personality or independence or to live at peace with other states, and, contrary to the case of rights, these obligations cannot be freely disposed of by the states. If an entity wishes to be considered a sovereign state, it has to accept those obligations, which means that there is no sovereignty without obligations, and there is no state without sovereignty.[22] Therefore, the whole concept of sovereignty entails from its very beginning a limit on the states and, in the contemporary system in which the

---

[15] Pellet (2021). https://esil-sedi.eu/esil-newsletter-autumn2021/

[16] Carrillo Salcedo (1996), p. 44.

[17] *Ibidem.*

[18] See the developments of Tomuschat (1993), p. 168; Brownlie (2012), p. 290; Combacau and Sur (2004), pp. 246–248; Remiro Brotons et al. (2007), p. 146; Cassese (2005), p. 52.

[19] 'No doubt any convention creating an obligation of this kind places a restriction upon the exercise of the sovereign rights of the State, in the sense that it requires them to be exercised in a certain way. But the right of entering into international engagements is an attribute of State sovereignty'. PCIJ, *Case of S.S. Wimblendom* (United Kingdom and ors. v. Germany), Judgement, 1923 P.C.I.J. Series A-No. 01, p. 25.

[20] Combacau and Sur (2004), p. 250.

[21] Pellet (2021); Schwarzenberger (1995), p. 225.

[22] Koskennimi refers to the different approaches regarding the origin of sovereignty, from Kelsen's view considering that the legal order pre-exist the sovereignty of states and delegates the quality of statehood, to Schmitt's view who considers that sovereignty precedes law. Koskenniemi (2005), pp. 229–231.

main objective of international law is peaceful coexistence and cooperation, the limits and restrictions on sovereignty is what guarantee the avoidance of conflicts. As Schwarzenberger established, with the adoption of fundamental principles of international law, sovereignty is reduced, linked with other principles and is an abandonment of anarchy.[23]

Therefore, even though state sovereignty is acknowledged to be at the core of the international legal system,[24] the contemporary tendency, especially after World War II, has been to limit sovereignty in favour of international regulations and institutions: 'the more international order grows the less room is for independent decisions'.[25] Moreover, the reasons for these limitations may lie in what Henkin called the excesses and excrescences of sovereignty,[26] as well as in the individualism and purpose of achieving particular goals[27] that, in the end, may affect peaceful coexistence.

In any case, we must acknowledge that there has never been such a thing as absolute sovereignty[28] or complete independence, not even during the revolutionary period. At that time, the figure of absolute sovereign was proclaimed but it was limited at the same time by the concept of non-superior authority that emerged from the collective security alliance for mutual protection.[29] Neither did such absolute sovereignty exist at the beginning of the twentieth century. In fact, Woolf stated in 1916 that 'complete independence today is a legal fiction'.[30] Nevertheless, after World War II, the concept of sovereignty followed[31] continued to undergo new and persistent limits, some of which were accepted and proposed by states, while others were imposed by globalisation.[32] Examples abound of how modern international law has come to restrict state's exercise of sovereignty. Classic illustrations include human rights and the emergence of international organizations.

In addition, as mentioned earlier, some changes have been imposed by economic globalisation. While economic deregulation was initially attempted, more recently, it is the need to achieve some stability by applying some form of regulation that has been recognised.[33] A significant example could be that of the Bilateral Investment

---

[23] Schwarzenberger (1995), p. 215.

[24] Koskenniemi cites Rosalyn Higgings' inaugural lecture. Koskenniemi (2005), p. 236.

[25] Tomuschat (1993), p. 184.

[26] Henkin (1989), p. 25. In any case, Henkin considers that some elements of sovereignty must be identified because they constitute the 'characteristics and indicia of statehood today' as 'independence, equality, autonomy, "personhood", territorial authority, integrity and inviolability, impermeability and privacy'. Ibid. p. 26.

[27] Carrillo Salcedo (1996), p. 53.

[28] Ibid. p. 61.

[29] Grewe (2000), p. 416.

[30] Schermers and Blokker (2011), p. 2.

[31] Carrillo Salcedo (1996), p. 56.

[32] Tomuschat (1999), p. 66; Pérez-Prat Durbán (2004), p. 110.

[33] Pérez-Prat Durbán (2004), pp. 31–32 and 110.

Treaties (BIT) through which states grant non-state actors—international companies—the capacity to bring claims against them in international tribunals.[34] They contain advantageous clauses for companies which, strikingly, constrain a state's capacity to exercise internal sovereignty. The tribunal decisions mentioned above are issued in an international context, with a minority of international law experts as arbitrators and with an international subject as party. They centre on purely economic and contractual issues, setting aside the main elements of international law and diminishing state prerogatives. As Professor Stern brought to light in her masterful concurring and dissenting opinion in the *Impregilo v. Argentina* case,[35] they also abandon the *favorem soveranitatis*.[36]

Nevertheless, the process of ever-increasing restrictions on sovereignty does not entail that states and their sovereignty are close to disappearing.[37] Despite the existence of multiples actors, and nowadays also multiple subjects, the international community is an inter-state society:[38] states are still at the centre of the international system and the consent-based system, with some exceptions, is still one of the main features of international law. This allows states to recover, for example, lost domains of sovereignty, as in the case of BITs in which big defenders such as the United States 'are now back-tracking from the strong investment protections'.[39] In addition, sovereignty and states continue to be essential, even for the entities and forces that

[34] According to Alvarez the international investment regime is the most sovereignty-intrusive regime. Alvarez (2012), p. 31.

[35] International Centre for Settlement of Investment Disputes, Impregilo S.p.A. v. Argentine Republic, (ICSID Case No. ARB/07/17). Concurring and Dissenting Opinion of Professor Brigit Stern. The subject-matter of this decision was the application of the Most Favored Nation (MFN) clause to the dispute settlement mechanism included in a Bilateral Investment Agreement (BIT). According to Professor Stern, the decision of the tribunal entailed the creation of a *sui generis* clause mixing the requirements established in the Argentina-Italia BIT and Argentina-US BIT. But the opinion of Professor Stern goes further analyzing why the MFN clause should not be applied to dispute settlement procedures, making a difference between rights (substantive and jurisdictional) and access to rights, and focusing on the *ratione voluntatis* condition to have access to rights. In this regard, in international law rights do not entail automatic access to jurisdictional protection, it is always needed the consent of the state, the 'consent in the cornerstone of ICSID arbitration'. As Stern stated: 'Unless specifically stated to the contrary, the qualifying conditions put by the State in order to accept to be sued directly on the international level by foreign investors cannot be displaced by an MFN clause, and a conditional right to ICSID cannot magically be transformed into an unconditional right by the grace of the MFN clause. The access to the right as provided in the basic treaty cannot be modified through an MFN clause. Any other solution presents in my view great dangers. The "umbrella clause", which was included in the Argentina-US BIT and incorporated into the case through the MFN clause, has started to be abandoned. This has led to a drop in the number of BITs included in that clause since 2000 and a reduction of state exposure to ISDS claims. See Investment Policy Hub, Mapping of IIA Clauses, UNCTAD, https://investmentpolicy.unctad.org/pages/1031/mapping-of-iia-clauses

[36] Tomuschat (1993), p. 170.

[37] Tomuschat (1993), p. 161; Pérez-Prat Durbán (2004), pp. 31–32 and 120.

[38] Carrillo Salcedo (1996), p. 58; Torrecuadrada García Lozano (2011), p. 13.

[39] Alvarez (2012), p. 3.

have been considered as threats to states. In this regard, it has been stated that there is no alternative to sovereignty in the short or medium term: it is the most appropriate system taking into account the historical and political development of the contemporary 'worlds'; it is adaptable; and it is the only repository of democratic legitimacy.[40]

Therefore, sovereignty will continue to exist and to encounter limits in the contemporary world. The classical reasons for limiting sovereignty include those related to the coexistence of different sovereignties and the maxim 'the sovereign of one State ends where sovereignty of another begins'.[41] However, other reasons must be added, such as the necessity to limit sovereignty in order to guarantee peace and security. Another reason is the sovereign states' inability to face the challenges of a more interdependent world alone, in which globalisation has become one of the main threats to sovereignty,[42] being this the key word: globalisation of the economy, globalisation of terrorism, globalisation of misinformation, globalisation of nationalisms, globalisation of diseases, etc.

Finally, it has been said that sovereignty is being eroded,[43] international organizations being one of the major causes of the process.[44] In most analyses of sovereignty in the modern world, international organizations appear to be the main international agents of erosion of sovereignty, but at the same time, they seem to embody a new way of expressing and realising sovereignty.[45] The rising number of transnational challenges and the need for common approaches and solutions has led to transferring functions, rights, and powers to international institutions. The institutionalisation of the international community is a fact, and the proliferation of international organizations characterises the phenomenon.[46] Institutionalisation could be presented as a point of no return and as the future of the international community. Yet, the same developments previously referred to regarding the BITs backtracking can also be observed in relation to international institutions. The system may have reached its peak: Will the next step be a back-tracking?

---

[40] Pérez-Prat Durbán (2004), p. 117.

[41] Tomuschat (1993), p. 195.

[42] Kinsbury (1998), p. 78.

[43] Tomuschat (1993), p. 195; Koskenniemi refers to a reduction of the domestic jurisdiction. Koskenniemi (2005), p. 250.

[44] The international organizations considered to contribute to the possible eroding of sovereignty are not exclusively integration organizations but also cooperation ones, even though they are based on sovereignty. In this regard, the establishment of an international organization entails the conferring of powers, thus affecting sovereignty. See Sarooshi (2005); Martín Martinez (1996).

[45] Pérez-Prat Durbán (2004), p. 124; Torrecuadrada García Lozano (2011), p. 17.

[46] Schermers and Blokker (2011), p. 3.

3.2 From International Organizations to Treaty Organs: Getting Sovereignty Back

The twentieth century was characterised by major transformations of the international society. The proliferation of subjects and actors, as well as international rules, led to the birth of a new worldwide legal order based on multilateralism, the rule of law, and legal certainty. In addition, in this new world order, international organizations began to act as fresh and effective forums in which states could act collectively to achieve common objectives and defend shared interests, multiplying the opportunities for dialogue and negotiation.[47]

The fact of transferring functions to international organizations in order to undertake new transnational challenges has also been related to the need to work in the international arena under some kind of public order.[48] Therefore, international organizations have fully contributed to making international society evolve into an international community. In addition, institutionalisation helps to constitutionalise the international community.[49] As Wessel stated,

> The proliferation and law-making, or even legislative, functions of many international organizations made us aware of the existence of—perhaps not the emergence of a world government—but at least of global governance 'beyond the state' in what is sometimes normatively framed in familiar "communitarian" terms: a "world community[50]

3.2.1 *The Proliferation of International Organizations*

The proliferation of international organizations[51] reached its peak in the second half of the twentieth century when the newly founded United Nations set states onto a path of cooperation, searching for new international and regional spheres in which to act jointly. This proliferation of international organizations confirms one of the features of the international community: interdependence,[52] and the maxim that states cannot exist autonomously.[53] In this regard, state sovereignty is among the concepts primarily affected by the proliferation of international organizations and the transfer of functions. Indeed, it is not possible to affirm anymore that sovereign states are not subordinated to any other entity. A major example could be the United

[47] Pérez-Prat Durbán (2004), p. 123.

[48] Tomuschat (1993), p. 167.

[49] See Peters (2010). Also Klabbers et al. (2009). Carrillo Salcedo refers to the constitutionalization of the international society. Carrillo Salcedo (1996), pp. 125–126.

[50] Wessel (2018), p. 11.

[51] See Blokker and Schermers (2000).

[52] Pérez-Prat Durbán (2004), p. 101; Schermers and Blokker (2011), pp. 1–4; Carrillo Salcedo (1996), p. 51.

[53] See sociological criticism to sovereignty. Koskenniemi (2005), p. 234.

Nations, which has the capacity to reduce state sovereignty to a minimum.[54] We could say that the United Nations Charter and the institutional system generally may have transformed and eroded the sovereign states system,[55] or even that international organizations have changed the nature of international society and the states.[56] The latter, however, have not been displaced: they have preserved their main role and even have the capacity to reverse the system.

The emergence of international organizations has also led to the birth of a new discipline: international institutional law.[57] Therefore, in general terms, we can consider that international law is not only a law for coordinating states but also international organizations.[58] This discipline had to gain a foothold as an autonomous domain from the very start,[59] since differences among international organizations could have made it difficult to elaborate a set of rules applicable to all of them. In practice, the work of this new discipline has resulted in the establishment of a similar or even identical set of rules for all international organizations.[60] Nonetheless, today, after years of analysis,[61] there are different theoretical positions[62] and studies on the theory of international organizations. The latter shows that they represent a 'living organism', evolving, adapting to changes, and attracting the interest of scholars.

However, with the turn of the century, the international organization model seems to have taken a step back, since the creation of regional organizations during the 90 s has been accompanied by a growing tendency to resort to informal forms of cooperation.[63] We could say in this regard that while 'during and after the World War II, many international organizations were created almost automatically as soon as some new international problem was identified, almost the opposite is true

[54] Tomuschat refers to sanctions adopted by the Security Council against Iraq because of the Iraqi aggression against Kuwait. Tomuschat (1993), p. 172. A different position is that of Pellet, who considers that Sovereignty is a holistic concept that cannot be limited; therefore, we can inferred that the competences of the states are those to be limited. Pellet (2021).

[55] Carrillo refers to the two opposites conceptions of international order, the classical one regarding sovereignty of states, and the new one established by the UN Charter. Carrillo Salcedo (1996), p. 131.

[56] Pérez-Prat Durbán (2004), p. 119.

[57] Schermers (2004), pp. 6–7.

[58] Carrillo Salcedo (1996), p. 121.

[59] Schermers and Blokker (2011), p. 7; Klabbers (2008), p. 170.

[60] Schermers and Blokker (2011), p. 4.

[61] Ibid. pp. 8–22.

[62] See Klabbers (2016); Klabbers (2008).

[63] According to Schermers 'at the end of the twentieth century a certain aversion developed against the creation of new IOs', Schermers (2004), pp. 6–7. Pérez Prat considers that rather than a decline, a realignment of international organizations is taking place. Pérez-Prat Durbán (2004), p. 127. In addition, it has been claimed that during the first decade of the twenty-first century, "the formation of IGOs has decreased by 20% compared to the previous decade". Abbott et al. (2013), p. 3

today'.[64] An explanation for this backtracking could be that the proliferation of international organizations has started to show its drawbacks: excessive bureaucracy[65] together with factors relating to the well-known theory of the fragmentation of international law. As Koskenniemi stated, 'fragmentation becomes struggle for institutional hegemony'.[66] To these reasons we could add a renewed interest in preserving sovereignty in sensitive domains that require, nevertheless, common accomplishments. States have witnessed how international organizations such as the United Nations have 'extended its jurisdiction by referring to its "purposes and principles',[67] in the same way as the European Union, but in this latter case based on implied competences and with the helpful support of the European Court of Justice (ECJ), as well illustrated in the case of the *ERTA* judgement.[68]

3.2.2 New Forms of Cooperation: A Threat to International Organizations?

In this context of suspicion regarding international organizations, the new century brought new models of cooperation and law-making outside the sphere of international organizations. As affirmed by Blokker and Wessel, 'times change, and IOs with them'.[69] And these new models include, among others, soft law,[70] soft organizations,[71] such as the G20 or Kimberly process, and the treaty organs.[72]

Treaty organs are difficult to characterise, but we could describe them as a set of organs that are similar to that of international organizations and established by an international treaty. These organs are assigned functions enabling them to implement the treaty, but they do not have a proper entity encapsulating the organs and to which they appertain. In sum, the organs are visible but not the organization. These organs may or may not have implied legal personality, but in any event, their competences and functions are more limited than those of international organizations.[73]

Climate change has been regarded as a field in which international regulation and institutionalisation need to be implemented since unilateral actions are ineffective at

---

[64] Blokker and Wessel (2019) p. 145.

[65] Ulfstein (2012), p. 430.

[66] Koskenniemi (2007), p. 8.

[67] Koskenniemi (2005), p. 250.

[68] Judgment of the Court 31 March 1971, Commission v. Council, C-22/70, ECLI:EU:C:1971:32.

[69] Blokker and Wessel (2005), p. 1.

[70] See Ellis (2012); Chinkin (1989); Boyle (1999). Boyle (2010).

[71] Klabbers (2001).

[72] On treaty organs see Churchill and Ulfstein (2000); Desai (2010); Röben (2015); Rodley (2013); Szasz (1999); Ulfstein (2012); Ulfstein (2011); Ulfstein (2008); Fernández Arribas (2020).

[73] See Fernández Arribas (2020), p. 478.

addressing this major global challenge.[74] Yet, paradoxically, treaty organs have developed extensively in this domain through Multilateral Environmental Agreements (MEAs).

The reluctance to create international organizations can be traced back to the beginning of these regulations. In this regard, the 1902 Convention for the Protection of Birds Useful for Agriculture was the precedent of the International Ornithological Committee that was created many years later in 1978. The delay was due to the state parties' rejection of the 'possibility of establishing a regulatory body and institutionalization of their cooperation, dreading any restraint on their sovereignty'.[75]

This principle of sovereignty[76] appeared again in the United Nations Framework Convention on Climate Change (UNFCCC), the preamble of which reaffirmed 'the principle of sovereignty of states in international cooperation to address climate change'. Therefore, the respect of the sovereignty principle and the states' fear of losing sovereignty in such a sensitive area has to be considered as a reason—along with flexibility, less bureaucracy or fewer costs—to avoid the establishment of international organizations to regulate climate change.

The UNFCCC is, as its name indicates, a framework convention. This means that the text establishes very limited substantive obligations for the state parties but identifies the subject matters for future regulations and establishes the bases, structures, and legislative techniques for those regulations.[77] According to the system established by the UNFCCC, the main substantive obligations are adopted by means of various techniques and via different organs or bodies.[78] Therefore, the protection of sovereignty can be observed throughout the whole system's structure. Regarding this system, when contemplating treaty organs and environmental agreements, the first treaty organ to come to mind is the Conference of the Parties (COP), which appears in most treaties and is naturally included, or rather established, in the UNFCCC.[79] However, the UNFCCC's organic structure goes much further than that of the rest of the MEAs since over twenty treaty organs have been established.

---

[74] AG 70/1 Transforming our world: the 2030 Agenda for Sustainable Development. Resolution adopted by the General Assembly on 25 September 2015. Report of the Secretary-General on the 2019 Climate Action Summit and the forward in 2020, 11 December 2019.

[75] Menkes and Menkes (2009), p. 118.

[76] According to Sarooshi the international organizations are the 'real-world' manifestation of the contested concept of sovereignty. Sarooshi (2004), p. 1110. In any case, as Schermers and Blokker state, 'The fact that, since the early twentieth century, public international law has increasingly imposed substantial limitations upon the freedom of States does not take away their legal status as sovereign entities, as long as the essence of State functions is retained'. Schermers and Blokker (2011), p. 5.

[77] See Merkouris and Perreaut (2017), p. 378; Menkes and Menkes (2009), p. 121; Boyle and Ghaleigh (2016), p. 29. On the contrary, Sands considers that to call the Climate Change Convention a 'framework' is a mistake since the Convention establishes different commitments, subsidiary bodies, guiding principles and dispute settlement mechanisms. Sands (2012), p. 276.

[78] It must be noted that the UNFCCC system refers to bodies to address treaty organs. See Fernández Arribas (2022).

[79] Article 7.1 ('A Conference of the Parties is hereby established').

These treaty organs or bodies, as they are named on the UNFCCC's website, can be grouped into three different categories: supreme bodies, subsidiary bodies, and constituted bodies. We can thus say that the UNFCCC may be the most elaborate and complex example of a treaty organ system.

These forms of cooperation share similarities with international organizations,[80] which could lead us to believe that international institutional law could be applied to regulate them. This option, however, would probably contradict the states' initial intention when creating the system, namely, pursuing some kind of flexibility and safeguarding sovereignty. Nevertheless, the UNFCCC system shows that some of the desired objectives of avoiding the establishment of international organizations to regulate climate change—such as flexibility, less bureaucracy, or fewer costs—are not completely achieved through the treaty organs.

Therefore, we have before us an international institutional system—constituted by the treaty organs—which is acting in very sensitive areas within the international arena and to which no legal status has been assigned for the sake of sovereignty, flexibility, and broad adherence. Nevertheless, the UNFCCC is also a system with multiple institutions or bodies and norms, which bring it closer to traditional legal systems. And, as in any legal system, legal certainty is essential for its functioning. This situation calls for a specific regulation since it can no longer operate within a legal vacuum.

Treaty organs illustrate how sovereign states can revert the system or at least weaken it in such a way that one of the main state sovereignty intruders, international organizations, are depreciated and set aside, prioritising new forms of cooperation that are less invasive with respect to national sovereignty. Nevertheless, the large number of international organizations existing today confirms that these entities are indeed major instruments of international cooperation. They have competences in almost all domains of international concern and they are affirming their competences, power and necessity against attempts to discredit them.

3.3 New realms of sovereignty: shared sovereignty and the European Union

According to Grewe, two tendencies regarding the application and interpretation of international law could be observed in the second half of the twentieth century. The first, belonging to communist and new states, was the preservation of national

[80] In the case of UNFCCC, we can find of organs that are similar to those of the IOs, but to which some capacities have been assigned, such as the COP and the Secretariat's treaty-making capacity or the Secretariat's rights and immunities. In addition, some of these organs, such as the Compliance Committee, can adopt decisions that are binding to the Member States, which constitutes another element that is typical of International Organizations.

sovereignty,[81] considering that sovereignty is a 'bulwark against perceived Western neo-colonialism'.[82] The second tendency is that of the established nation states and is oriented 'towards the containment and gradual dismantling of national sovereignty',[83] in which the European Union could be framed. This tension between nation states and integration is at the core of the European Union's development,[84] and its evolution has also been understood as a manifestation of the crisis of states.[85]

The European Union has been regarded as the 'most far reaching institutional project for divided sovereignty',[86] and given the transfer of sovereign powers from member states to the Union, references to shared sovereignty within the European Union frequently occur, the concept being widely accepted. However, a closer analysis raises questions as to whether member states are genuinely transferring sovereignty to the European Union and whether the European Union can be considered a sovereign entity.

3.3.1 Framing Shared Sovereignty

Based on the analysis of sovereignty above, 'shared sovereignty' could be regarded as an oxymoron,[87] and discussing shared sovereignty in a state's relationship with the European Union or other international organizations can be particularly difficult if one considers that the sovereignty attribute belongs exclusively to states.[88] Nevertheless, definitions of this concept are typically associated with the sharing of sovereignty with an international organization. In this context, sharing sovereignty 'deals with how states willingly cede part of their sovereignty to intergovernmental organizations or supranational bodies',[89] and 'shared sovereignty involves the creation of institutions for governing specific areas within a state'.[90] More broadly, Schiemann stated that 'developments in commercial and political life, which have in fact resulted in a loss of power by the state to regulate what is going on inside that state, have been described as sharing sovereignty'.[91]

[81] Later on, the former socialist states decided to join to those west European institutions which entail the limits to sovereignty. Wallace (1999), p. 504.

[82] Charlesworth and Chinkin (2000), p. 37.

[83] Grewe (2000), p. 654.

[84] Wallace (1999), p. 506.

[85] Carrillo Salcedo (1996), p. 55

[86] Kinsbury (1998), p. 82

[87] Ibid. p. 476

[88] See Eckes and Wessel (2017), p. 16; Pellet (2021).

[89] Mamudu and Studlar (2009), p. 77.

[90] Krasner (2005), p. 76.

[91] Schiemann (2007), p. 476.

We can thus conclude, according to these characterisations, that member states lost sovereignty, powers, or competences[92] (in this case) in the process of founding the European Union. For example, the direct effect and supremacy principles allow the European Union to penetrate member state's domestic legal order more deeply than those of other international institutions.[93]

This conclusion does not necessarily lead us to question member states sovereignty,[94] or that this loss created a new sovereign entity,[95] but raises a question regarding the potential exercise of sovereignty by international institutions and, thus, by the European Union. As a result, while certain scholars are convinced that the European Union may exercise sovereignty,[96] others have adopted a more cautious position. They substitute the sovereignty concept with autonomy, thereby noting that the European Union only exercises the sovereign rights conferred on it by its member states. The concept of practical sovereignty[97] suggested by Eckes and Wessel could thus be more appropriate when examining the domains in which the organization performs the activities of a sovereign entity, that is, when the European Union acts 'as a (quasi-) sovereign'[98] entity, thereby limiting the member states' ability to operate in those areas.

The domains affected by shared sovereignty are extensive,[99] and some of them are linked to the hard core of state sovereignty, as in the case of external relations, which continue to be unalienable. However, despite the member states' reluctance to cede external relations competences, it is a fact that the European Union has increased its activities and competences in that field.[100] The EU has progressed from its initial commercial competences to accomplishments of a more political nature, a process described as 'external hyperactivism'.[101]

This joint exercise of sovereign powers by the European Union and its member states in specific areas of international law has been the object of ongoing disputes between member states and the European Union, leading to extensive jurisprudence created by the European Court of Justice.[102] The European Union's increased activity has not only had an impact on member state sovereignty but also on

[92] Tomuschat (1999), p. 173.

[93] Marquardt (1994), p. 634.

[94] Ibid, p. 174.

[95] Wallace notes that with the Treaty of Amsterdam, the European political system 'has moved far beyond traditional concepts of sovereignty without developing a consensus on what is emerging in its place', Wallace (1999), p. 517.

[96] See Tokár (2001).

[97] Eckes and Wessel (2017), p. 20.

[98] Ibid. p. 17.

[99] A clear and particular example about the shifting of sovereign that increase the European Union competences has been elaborated by Mamudu and Studlar, regarding tobacco control and its links with cross-border advertising, marketing, and smuggling. Mamudu and Studlar (2009), p. 77.

[100] Eckes and Wessel (2017), pp. 4 et seq.

[101] Pérez-Prat Durbán (2004), p. 119.

[102] See Butler and Wessel (2022).

international law itself, given the European Union's active role in developing international law and the international community.[103]

3.3.2 Shared Sovereignty in Practice: Mixed Agreements

In order to illustrate the statement above, the issue of mixed agreements and dispute settlement can be instructive. Mixed agreements are 'agreements which include among their parties the Union and all or some of its member states, and which fall partly within the competence of the Union and partly within the competence of the member states'.[104] This is one of the results of the member states' transfer of sovereign powers to the European Union, which, in relation to specific competences with external aspects, has led to situations in which the states must share the representation, the competence to negotiate, or the competence to adopt international agreements, thereby ceding sovereign competences.

The complexity of mixed agreements has been the subject of numerous studies. These studies focus on identifying the competencies corresponding to each party and that have resulted in the well-known declarations of competence.[105] Nevertheless, scholars have also centred on representation in negotiations, the role of Member States when implementing such agreements, and setting up the participation of the European Union and its Member States (and their corresponding powers and functions) in cases where the European Union is party to an international institution.[106]

Among the mixed agreements, multilateral mixed agreements should be mentioned as a category that includes international conventions[107] to which the European Union is a party and that also occasionally grant membership to international institutions,[108] the European Union acting in some of them 'on equal footing with states'.[109] In this regard, the European Court of Justice has played an essential

[103] See Hoffmeister (2008); Barrett (2023). In addition, on "ILC (outside) view on the relevance of EU practice for the identification, codification, and development of rules of general international law", see Cabrita (2021).

[104] Heliskoski (2001), p. 6.

[105] Casteleiro Delgado (2012); Heliskoski (2011); Lijnzaad (2014).

[106] See Hillion and Koutrakos (2010); O'Keeffe and Schermers (1983),; Odermatt and Wessel (2018).

[107] We consider 'conventions' to be those treaties that 'lay down for the parties to them a whole regime', Thirlway (2014), p. 95.

[108] Among others: the United Nations Convention on the Law of the Sea, the Kyoto Protocol and the Paris Agreement adopted under the United Nations Framework Convention on Climate Change, the Convention on International Trade in Endangered Species of Wild Fauna and Flora, the United Nations Convention against Corruption, the Convention on the Conservation of Antarctic Marine Living Resources, the Convention on the Rights of Persons with Disabilities, the 2006 International Tropical Timber Agreement, the Constitution of the Food and Agriculture Organization of the United Nations or the Agreement Establishing the World Trade Organization.

[109] Eckes and Wessel (2017), p. 3.

role in defining the different competencies of the European Union and its member states, taking both the content of the European Union treaties and the principle of sincere cooperation or duty of cooperation as bases for its extensive body of case law.[110] This has resulted in significant restrictions on the member states' ability to act in the domains regulated by mixed agreements, constituting, therefore, a restriction on sovereignty.

The international agreements referred present different dispute settlement mechanisms, and the question is whether EU member states can make use of these procedures. The latter represents one of the manifestations of international sovereignty: the freedom to choose the peaceful dispute settlement mechanism to solve international treaty conflicts. Various options exist in this regard. They range from the creation of permanent arbitral tribunals (such as the United Nations Convention of the Law of the Sea[111] or the United Nations Convention against Corruption[112]) to the referral of disputes to treaty organs (such as the 2006 International Tropical Timber Agreement[113]). The availability of such options could raise doubts as to whether a member state's capacities and capabilities to defend its own interests may change according to the type of dispute settlement mechanism used.

Among the extensive ECJ case law mentioned, the *MOX Plant* case[114] represents an increase in shared sovereignty, and the constraints placed on member states may have consequences beyond the scope of the European Union. In this case, the ECJ established that when disputes arise between European Union member states regarding the content of an international treaty to which the European Union is also a party, the Court will have exclusive competence to solve the dispute, provided that the matter appertains to an area in which the Union has exclusive or shared competence, having exercised such powers in the latter case. In addition, in the *MOX Plant* case, the ECJ exercised this competence[115] despite the advantages of the Convention's dispute settlement system.[116] Therefore, the ECJ granted itself exclusive jurisdiction in resolving disputes between member states that are parties to mixed agreements. Such self-granting of jurisdiction allows, under certain conditions, to set aside the dispute settlement mechanism established in the treaty.[117]

In the *MOX Plant* case, the ECJ determined that this exclusive competence was justified because the treaties signed by the European Union were considered as an

[110] Cremona (2008); Heliskoski (1996); Hillion (2010). See also "EU Statements in multilateral organisations - General Arrangements", Council of the European Union, 24 October 2011.

[111] Article 287 UNCLOS.

[112] Article 66 United Nations Convention against Corruption.

[113] Article 31 International Tropical Timber Agreement.

[114] Judgment of 30 May 2006, Commission v. Ireland, C-459/03, ECLI:EU:C:2006:345.

[115] Govaere (2010), p.199; C-459/03, *Commission v Ireland*, paras. 92–120.

[116] Govaere (2010), p. 20; C-459/03, *Commission v Ireland*, para. 137.

[117] *Ibid* paras. 121–130.

integral part of European Union law.[118] In addition, as established in Article 344 of the Treaty on the Functioning of the European Union (TFEU), member states are obliged to submit disputes to the ECJ relating to treaty interpretation and application. Lastly, the dispute settlement system of the treaty involved in the *MOX Plant* case, namely the United Nations Convention of the Law of the Sea (UNCLOS), allowed the parties to choose an agreed means of dispute settlement.[119]

Therefore, the implications for state sovereignty are unequivocal. The consequences of sharing sovereignty would be to forbid the provisions of an international treaty regarding dispute resolution from being fully implemented by European Union member states. This case illustrates how international organizations increase their jurisdiction and powers, thereby limiting state sovereignty and, in this case, imposing a specific settlement mechanism in a dispute in which the European Union was not a party and in which the states had, according to international treaties, different dispute settlement options.

References

Abbott K, Green J, Keohane R (2013) Organizational Ecology in and Organizational Strategies in World politics. Discussion Paper 13/57, The Harvard Project on climate agreements

Alvarez JE (2012) State sovereignty is not withering away: a few lessons from the future. In: Cassese A (ed) Realizing Utopia. The future of International Law. Oxford University Press, Oxford

Barrett K (2023) International Law developed through the European Union. In: Oxford research encyclopedia of international studies. Oxford University Press, Oxford

Blokker NM, Schermers HG (eds) (2000) Proliferation of international organizations. Legal issues. Kluwer Law International, Leiden

Blokker NM, Wessel RA (2005) Editorial: updating international organizations. Int Org Law Rev 2(1):1

Blokker NM, Wessel RA (2019) Revisiting questions of organisationhood, legal personality and membership in the OSCE: the interplay between law, politics and practice. In: Steinbrück Platise M, Moser MC, Peters A (eds) The legal status of the OSCE. Cambridge University Press, Cambridge

Boyle AE (1999) Some reflections on the relationship of treaties and soft law. Int Comp Law Q 48(4):901–913

Boyle AE (2010) Soft law in International Law-making. In: Evans MD (ed) International Law. Oxford University Press, Oxford

Boyle A, Ghaleigh NS (2016) Climate change and International Law beyond the UNFCC. In: Carlane CP et al (eds) The Oxford handbook of international climate change. Oxford University Press, Oxford

Brownlie I (2012) Principles of Public International Law. Oxford University Press, Oxford

[118] Judgment of the Court of 30 April 1974, C-181/73, *R. & V. Haegeman v Belgian State*, ECLI: EU:C:1974:41, para. 5; Judgment of the Court (Fourth Chamber) of 25 February 2010, C-386/08 Brita GmbH v. Hauptzollamt Hamburg-Hafen, ECLI:EU:C:2010:9, paras. 41–42.

[119] Article 282 UNCLOS.

Butler G, Wessel R (eds) (2022) EU external relations law. The cases in context. Hart Publishing, London

Cabrita T (2021) The integration paradox: an ILC view on the EU contribution to the codification and development of rules of general international law. Eur World Law rev 5(1):1–15

Carrillo Salcedo JA (1996) Droit international et souveraineté des états : cours général de droit international public. In: Recueil des Cours. Collected courses of the Hague Academy of International Law, vol 257

Cassese A (2005) International Law. Oxford University Press, Oxford

Casteleiro Delgado A (2012) EU Declarations of competence to multilateral agreements: a useful reference base? Eur Foreign Aff Rev 17(4):491–509

Charlesworth H, Chinkin C (2000) The boundaries of International Law. A feminist analysis. Manchester University Press, Manchester

Chinkin CM (1989) The challenge of soft law: development and change in International Law. Int Comp Law Q 38(4):850–866

Churchill RR, Ulfstein G (2000) Autonomous institutional arrangements in multilateral environmental agreements: a little-noticed phenomenon in International Law. Am J Int Law 4(4): 623–659

Combacau J, Sur S (2004) Droit international public. Montchrestein, Paris

Cremona M (2008) Defending the community interest: the duties of cooperation and compliance. In: Cremona M, De Witte B (eds) EU foreign relations law: constitutional fundamentals. Hart Publishing, London

Desai BH (2010) Multilateral environmental agreements. Legal status of the secretariats. Cambridge University Press, Cambridge

Eckes C, Wessel R (2017) The European Union from an international perspective: sovereignty, statehood, and special treatment. Amsterdam Law School Legal Studies Research Paper No. 2017-33

Ellis J (2012) Shades of grey: soft law and the validity of Public International Law. Leiden J Int Law 25(2):313–334

Fernández Arribas G (2020) Rethinking international institutionalisation through treaty organs. Int Org Law Rev 17(2):457–483

Fernández Arribas G (2022) Unravelling the UNFCCC'S institutional system: halfway between treaty organs and international organization. Spanish Yearb Int Law 26:25–44

Govaere I (2010) Beware of the trojan horse: dispute settlement in (mixed) agreements and the autonomy of the EU Legal Order. In: Hillion C, Koutrakos P (eds) Mixed agreements revisited. Hart Publishing, London

Grewe WG (2000) The epochs of International Law. Walter de Gruyter, Berlin, Boston

Heliskoski J (1996) The 'Duty of Cooperation' between the European community and its member states within the World Trade Organization. Finnish Yearb Int Law 7:59–133

Heliskoski J (2001) Mixed agreements as a technique for organizing the external relations of the European Community and their member states. Kluwer Law International, Leiden

Heliskoski J (2011) EU declarations of competence and international responsibility. In: Malcolm DE, Koutrakos P (eds) The international responsibility of the European Union: European and international perspectives. University of Bristol, Bristol

Henkin L (1989) International Law: politics, values and functions. General course of Public International Law. In: Recueil des Cours. Collected courses of the Hague Academy of International Law, vol 216

Hillion C (2010) Mixity and coherence in EU external relations: the significance of the 'duty of cooperation'. In: Hillion C, Koutrakos P (eds) Mixed agreements revisited. Hart Publishing, London

Hillion C, Koutrakos P (eds) (2010) Mixed agreements revisited. The EU and its member states in the world. Hart Publishing, London

Hoffmeister F (2008) The contribution of EU practice to International Law. In: Cremona M (ed) Developments in EU external relations law. Oxford University Press, Oxford

Kinsbury B (1998) Sovereign and inequality. Eur J Int Law 9(4):599–625
Klabbers J (2001) Institutional ambivalence by design: soft organizations in International Law. Nordic J Int Law 70(3):403–421
Klabbers J (2008) The paradox of International Institutional Law. Int Org Law Rev 5(1):170
Klabbers J (2016) The transformation of International Organizations Law: a rejoinder. Eur J Int Law 26(4):975–977
Klabbers J, Peters A, Ulfstein G (2009) The constitutionalization of International Law. Oxford University Press, Oxford
Koskenniemi M (2005) From apology to Utopia. The structure of international legal argument. Cambridge University Press, Cambridge
Koskenniemi M (2007) The fate of Public International Law: between technique and politics. Mod Law Rev 70(1):8
Krasner SD (2005) The case for shared sovereignty. J Democr 16(1):76
Lijnzaad L (2014) Declarations of competence in the law of the sea, a very European affair. In: Lodge M, Nordquist MH (eds) Peaceful order in the world's oceans: essays in honor of Satya N. Nandan. Brill, Leiden
Mamudu HHM, Studlar DT (2009) Multilevel governance and shared sovereignty: European Union, Member States, and the FCTC. Govern Int J Policy Admin Inst 22(1):77
Marquardt P (1994) Subsidiary and sovereignty in the European Union. Fordham Int Law J 18(2): 634
Martín Martinez M (1996) National sovereignty and International Organization. Kluwer Law International, The Hague/Boston
Menkes J, Menkes M (2009) International Organisations, climate change expectations, and the reality of institutionalisations - an analysis of the United Nations Framework Convention on Climate Change. Polish Yearb Int Law 29:118
Merkouris P, Perreaut MA (2017) United Framework Convention on Climate Change 1992. In: Fitzmaurice M et al (eds) Multilateral environmental treaties, Elgar encyclopedia of environmental law, vol 5
O'Keeffe D, Schermers HG (eds) (1983) Mixed agreements. Kluwer Law and Taxation Publishers, Deventer
Odermatt J, Wessel RA (2018) Multilateralism under strain: the challenge of the EU's engagement with international institutions. City Law School (CLS) Research Paper No. 2018/01
Pellet A (2021) Guest editorial. The proper use of sovereignty. ESIL Newsletter. https://esil-sedi.eu/esil-newsletter-autumn2021/
Pérez-Prat Durbán L (2004) La provincia en el Derecho Internacional. Dykinson, Madrid
Peters A (2010) Constitucionalismo compensatorio: las.funciones y el potencial de las normas y estructuras internacionales. In: Peters A, Aznar Gómez M, Gutiérrez I (eds) La Constitucionalización de la Comunidad Internacional. Tirant Lo Blanch
Remiro Brotons A et al (2007) Derecho Internacional. Tirant Lo Blanch, Valencia
Röben V (2015) Environmental treaty bodies. In: Wolfrum R (ed) Max Planck encyclopedia of public international law
Rodley N (2013) The role and impact of treaty bodies. In: Shelton D (ed) The Oxford handbook of international human rights law. Oxford University Press, Oxford
Sands PJ (2012) Principles of International Environmental Law. Cambridge University Press, Cambridge
Sarooshi D (2004) The essentially contested nature of the concept of sovereignty: implications for the exercise by International Organizations of Delegated Powers of Government. Mich J Int Law 25(4):1110
Sarooshi D (2005) International organizations and their exercise of sovereign powers. Oxford University Press, Oxford
Schermers HG (2004) The birth and development of International Institutional Law. Int Org Law Rev 1(1):6–7

Schermers HG, Blokker NM (2011) International Institutional Law. Martinus-Nijhoff/Brill Publishers, Leiden
Schiemann K (2007) Europe and the loss of sovereignty. Int Comp Law Q 56(3):475
Schrijver N (1999) The changing nature of state soverignty. Br Yearb Int Law 70(1):65–98
Schwarzenberger G (1995) The fundamental principles of International Law. In: Recueil des Cours. Collected Courses of The Hague Academy of International Law, vol 87
Szasz PC (1999) The complexification of the United Nations System. Max Planck UNYB 3:57
Thirlway H (2014) The sources of international law. In: Evans MD (ed) International Law. Oxford University Press, Oxford
Tokár A (2001) Something happened. sovereignty and the European Integration. In: Dawson S, Mistry J, Schramme T, Thurman M (eds) Extraordinary times. IWM junior visiting fellows conferences, p 11
Tomuschat C (1993) Obligations arising for states without or against their will. In: Recueil des Cours. Collected courses of the Hague Academy of International Law, vol 241
Tomuschat C (1999) International Law: ensuring the survival of mankind on the eve of a new century. In: Recueil des Cours. Collected courses of the Hague Academy of International Law, vol 281
Torrecuadrada García Lozano S (2011) Normas Universales para una Sociedad Universal. Revista de Relaciones Internacionales de la UNAM 110:13
Ulfstein G (2008) Treaty bodies. In: Bodansky D, Brunnée J, Hey E (eds) The Oxford handbook of international environmental law. Oxford University Press, Oxford
Ulfstein G (2011) Reflections on institutional design – especially treaty bodies. In: Klabbers J, Wallendahl Å (eds) Research handbook on international organizations. Edward Elgar, Cheltenham
Ulfstein G (2012) Treaty bodies and regimes. In: Hollis DB (ed) Oxford guide to treaties. Oxford University Press, Oxford
Wallace W (1999) The sharing sovereignty: the European paradox. Polit Stud 47(3):504
Wessel RA (2018) Studying International and European Law: confronting perspectives and combining interests. Grotius Centre Working Paper Series, No. 2018/071-PIL

Chapter 4
A Self-Determination Principle in the Twenty-First Century

On 21 February 2022, President Vladimir Putin signed two Presidential Decrees on the recognition of the Donetsk and Lugansk People's Republics as independent states, based on the will expressed by the people of the Republics.[1] It was followed by the President's well-known 24 February address[2] launching the special operation, using the doctrine of humanitarian intervention among others as a ground for intervention, and linking the recognition of independence to the doctrine of remedial secession. In this regard, 'the feelings and pain of these people that were the main motivating force behind our decision to recognise the independence of the Donbass people's republics'.[3] A year later, in a speech before the Duma, President Putin addressed the residents of Donetsk and Lugansk: 'you, my friends, determined your future at the referendums'.[4] Based on these facts, to consider today that the principle of self-determination is a principle linked mainly to the process of decolonization is to ignore the evolution, manipulation and politicization of one of the fundamental principles of international law, which, according to Kohen, is 'the most important fundamental principle of contemporary international law'.[5] In addition, certain situations and people are still awaiting the exercise of the right to self-determination in the twenty-first century. We will come back to some of them in the next section. The cases of the Sahara, Palestine and Chagos for their part, are addressed in the sections that follows.

---

[1] Signing of documents recognising Donetsk and Lugansk People's Republics. February 21, 2022. http://kremlin.ru/events/president/news/67829

[2] Address by the President of the Russian Federation. February 24, 2022. http://en.kremlin.ru/events/president/news/67843

[3] Ibid.

[4] Presidential Address to Federal Assembly. February 21, 2023. http://en.kremlin.ru/events/president/news/70565

[5] Kohen (2020), p. 133.

G. Fernández Arribas, *Contemporary Challenges to the Fundamental Principles of International Law and EU Interaction*, European Union and its Neighbours in a Globalized World 19, https://doi.org/10.1007/978-3-031-75453-1_4

4.1 The Role of Self-Determination in a Post-Colonial World

The sin of the principle of self-determination seems to reside in the lack of definition of some of its main components. It also seems to lie in the different approaches adopted by the two blocks during negotiations on the instruments to implement this principle. Those negotiations were based mainly on diverging political interests and understandings that led to a vague definition with a large amount of *travaux préparatoires*[6]—certainly illustrating the variety of states positions.

For example, the undefined concept[7] of self-determination has led Cassese to analyse Article 1.2 of the UN Charter negatively, that is, determining what it 'did not mean'.[8] On the other hand, Kohen considers that, as in the case of any legal obligation, it is possible to infer legal consequences from the principle of self-determination and to shape its main features as: (a) the holders of the right is the people; (b) it can be invoked *erga omnes*; (c) it is a *jus cogens* norm; (d) it is applicable to all, not only to colonial or alien domination; and (e), it entails the right to freely determine its internal and international political status.[9]

However, even if we accept those elements as main features of the principle, its content and meaning also differ across scholars, states, and practices. In this regard, there are different understandings of the concept of 'peoples', of what outside the colonial context means, or of the meaning of internal self-determination. Interpretations of all these elements have evolved in accordance with the development of the international community, mainly from the mid-twentieth century onwards. They have also followed the evolution of treaty law as well as states and international organisation practices relating to this principle. Therefore, the purpose of this section is to clarify what can be understood by self-determination, and why this principle is still applicable today even though it probably reached its peak during the decolonization process.[10]

The self-determination concept has been defined based on two components: external self-determination and internal self-determination, the latter being the most controversial due to the different understandings of the contents and implementation of internal self-determination.

Regarding external self-determination, Resolution 2625 (XXV)[11] defines the content of this right, establishing peoples' right to freely 'determine, without external

---

[6] See Cassese (1995), p. 37.

[7] See Hofbauer Jane (2016), pp. 68 et seq.

[8] Cassese (1995), p. 42.

[9] Kohen (2007), p. 964. Sparks (2023), pp. 215–219; Orakhelashvili (2006), pp. 133–134; Hilpold (2022), p. 204.

[10] Craven and Parfitt (2018), p. 227.

[11] UN General Assembly, *Declaration on Principles of International Law concerning Friendly Relations and Cooperation among States in accordance with the Charter of the United Nations*, 24 October 1970, A/RES/2625(XXV).

interference, their political status'. Therefore, as Hofbauer states, it means to choose 'how they wish to be regarded by the international community'.[12] Resolution 2625 (XXV) also included the different political status to which the peoples could accede: independent State; free association[13] or integration with an independent State;[14] or emergence of any other political status. These options were previously included in the 1960 General Assembly Resolution 1541 (XV),[15] linking them to non-self-governing territories and the process of decolonization,[16] as did the General Assembly Resolution 1514 (XV) on the Declaration on the Granting of Independence to Colonial Countries and Peoples.[17]

Moreover, Resolution 1541 (XV) clarifies the procedure to opt for alternative political statuses, establishing the need to express the will of the peoples through an 'informed and democratic'[18] process in the case of association. It was also added that, in the case of integration, the process should be 'impartially conducted and based on universal adult suffrage'.[19] The lack of reference to this kind of process in the case of independence has led to regarding it unnecessary to obtain the express will of the peoples through a democratic process.[20] In any case, as the ICJ stated in the *Western Sahara* advisory opinion, 'self-determination requires a free and genuine expression of the will of the peoples concerned'.[21]

---

[12] Hofbauer Jane (2016), p. 70.

[13] This was the option adopted by Palau and other Ocean Island which formed a free association with the United States. Raic (2002), p. 210.

[14] The option adopted for example by the British colony of Cameroon since some part merged with the French colony of Cameroon creating the new state of Cameroon and the other part joined to the existed state of Nigeria. Ibid, pp. 209–210.

[15] UN General Assembly, *Principles which should guide Members in determining whether or not an obligation exists to transmit the information called for under Article 73 e of the Charter*, 15 December 1960. A/RES/1541 (XV).

[16] The ICJ refers in its Western Sahara advisory opinion to the 'policies of the General Assembly regarding the decolonization of non-self-governing territories'. ICJ, *Western Sahara*, Advisory Opinion of 16 October 1975: ICJ Reports 1975, para. 31.

[17] UN General Assembly, *Declaration on the Granting of Independence to Colonial Countries and Peoples*, 14 December 1960. A/RES/1514 (XV).

[18] A/RES/1541 (XV), Principle VII a).

[19] A/RES/1541 (XV), Principle IX b).

[20] See Raic (2002), pp. 212–214; Cassese (1995), p. 124.

[21] ICJ, *Western Sahara*, para. 55

4.1.1 *Unravelling the Concept: External Self-Determination and Internal Self-Determination*

Though closely linked to decolonization and self-government processes,[22] external self-determination can also be applied outside the colonial context and in present situations.

First, according to Resolution 2625 (XXV), the principle of self-determination is applicable to peoples subjected to alien subjugation, domination, and exploitation, since the Resolution considers that these actions violate the principle. Therefore, any foreign occupation of a state entails a violation of the principle, and it is thus applicable outside the colonial context and in situations of occupation today.[23] In this sense, the concepts of foreign subjugation, domination, or exploitation, which are subject to broad interpretations—including, for example, cases of economic exploitation—were restricted by subsequent General Assembly resolutions. Any references to self-determination in the context of economic measures were excluded and references were made to the context of the use of force.[24] Therefore, as Cassese stated, the foreign domination concept is related to interventions involving the use of force and military occupation.[25]

Secondly, external self-determination can also result from recognising the right to self-determination to some groups inside the states according to constitutional laws. In this regard, Article 47 of the Constitution of Ethiopia establishes that 'Nations, Nationalities and Peoples within the States enumerated in sub-Article 1 of this article have the right to establish, at any time, their own States'.[26] In the same vein, Article 74 of the Constitution of Uzbekistan refers to the right of secession of the Republic of Karakalpakstan from the Republic of Uzbekistan 'on the basis of a nation-wide referendum held by the people of Karakalpakstan'. The constitution of Serbia and

[22] At the present the United Nations has 17 Non-Self-Governing Territories listed, which remain on the agenda of the Special Committee on Decolonization. See https://www.un.org/dppa/decolonization/en/nsgt

[23] The ICJ confirmed that this was the situation of the Palestine People in the Occupied Territories. ICJ, *Legal Consequences of the Construction of a Wall in the Occupied Palestinian Territory*, Advisory Opinion of 9 July 2004: ICJ Reports 1975, para 118.

[24] See Cassese (1995), p. 93. Cassese refers to the Charter of Economic rights and Duties of the states, which does no refer to self-determination when condemning economic coercion, or to General Assembly Resolution 38/16 on Universal realization of the right of peoples, which condemns the 'acts of foreign mili-tary intervention, aggression and occupation, since these have resulted in the suppression of the right of peoples to self-determination'.

[25] Ibid. p. 93.

[26] It must be noted that before the 1995 Constitution, the reference to self-determination in the 1987 Constitution was radically different, since it was just included in the preamble, declaring that 'the unity of our country and the equality of nationalities, based in our right of self-determination, is ensured'. The Constitution of the People's Democratic Republic of Ethiopia, Review of Socialist Law, 1988, n° 2, vol. 14. It was under this 1987 constitution when the Transitional Government of Ethiopia, after a long war, recognized the right of self-determination to the people of Eritrea that acquired independence. See Dugard (2013), pp. 178–179.

Montenegro allows member states to 'initiate the proceedings for the change in its state status or for breaking away from the state union of Serbia and Montenegro'. And Article 4.2 of the Constitution of Liechtenstein establishes that 'Individual communes have the right to secede from the State'. The implementation of these rights recognised in constitutions would entail a change in the international status of these peoples and therefore an exercise of external self-determination.

The second component of self-determination, i.e., the internal one, has been the object of different interpretations: linking the principle to the people of a state as a whole,[27] to certain groups within a state,[28] to a right of participation,[29] to the relation of the people with the government,[30] or the relation of the government with other states.[31] A broad definition of internal self-determination was given by Kohen, who established that the concept '*implique la liberté pour le peuple de choisir sa forme de gouvernement, son système économique et social et la façon de pourusivre librement son développement économique, social et culturel.*[32]

This definition can be linked to that included in Resolution 2625 (XXV). Indeed, the Resolution refers to the right to determine the political status, which affects not only the external political status according to external self-determination, but also the internal status: it entails deciding the form of government as well as the economic and social system. In addition, the Resolution refers to the right to 'pursue their economic, social and cultural development'. The right to define the internal political status is understood in Resolution 2625 (XXV) as free from external interference,[33] which means that it is a right of the peoples with respect to other states. This definition is naturally closely linked to the principle of non-intervention in the internal affairs of the states,[34] but it differs from self-determination because the latter is a right held by peoples, while non-intervention is a principle recognised to the states. In any case, if one assumes Kohen's maxim: 'un Etat = un peuple',[35] the holders of these two principles will be both once the state is created. Therefore, the right to determine the internal political status and to pursue one's own economic, social, and cultural development is applicable today to all peoples in a colonial context or—outside the colonial context—to the existing States.

[27] Kohen (2007), p. 969; Higgins (1991), p. 170.

[28] Cassese (1995), p. 108 et seq.

[29] Hofbauer Jane (2016), p. 77; Raic (2002), p. 238; Benchikh (2007), p. 808; Maccorquodale (1994), p. 532.

[30] Weller (2009), p. 23; Thornberry (1994), p. 175; Maccorquodale (1994), p. 532.

[31] Kohen (2007), p. 968.

[32] Ibid, p. 964.

[33] Kohen (2020), p. 145.

[34] Benchikh considers that the right understood in this way may be invoked by authoritarian regimes and opens the door to the confiscation of the principle of self-determination, since the states can declare the exercise of this right and the same time in which the oppress the population. Benchikh (2007), p. 812.

[35] Kohen (2007), p. 968.

A second interpretation of internal self-determination refers to the relationship of the peoples (understood as the State's whole population) and the government. It is inferred from the definition of self-determination in human rights conventions. Article 1 of both the International Covenant on Civil and Political Rights (ICCPR) and the International Covenant on Economic, Social and Cultural Rights (ICESCR) recognises that 'all peoples have the right to self-determination. By virtue of that right, they freely determine their political status and freely pursue their economic, social and cultural development'. The inclusion of this right in the covenants has been regarded as a shift in the evolution of the right to self-determination, from a right aimed at achieving independence, to a right also designed to protect human rights.[36]

The presence of the right to self-determination in human rights covenants has raised the issue of a right of participation,[37] which, according to some scholars,[38] is confirmed by paragraph 7 of Resolution 2625 (XXV) as it refers to a 'government representing the whole people belonging to the territory without distinction as to race, creed or colour'. In this regard, the right to internal self-determination has been understood as the 'right of people to enjoy the freedom of authentic self-government', which would first entail something other than the absence of external control, but the control of people over the governing bodies.[39] Secondly, self-government would entail the right to choose the political and economic regimes as well as the leaders, linking this right again not only to the absence of external intervention, but also to the right to vote and the right of assembly, association, and expression.[40]

Cassese has expressly associated the right to internal self-determination with a democratic process, considering that it entails people's right to 'choose their legislators and political leaders free from any manipulation or undue influence from the domestic authorities themselves'.[41] Therefore, he links a collective right, that of self-determination, to individual rights: vote, assembly, association, and expression.[42] This assumption goes hand in hand with Cassese's conception of democracy since he considers it a fundamental principle of international law.[43]

This link between collective and individual rights seems difficult to uphold, since the Human Rights Committee stated that the right to self-determination 'is expressed to be a right belonging to peoples and is dealt with in a separate part (Part I) of the Covenant. Self-determination is not a right cognizable under the Optional

[36] Hofbauer Jane (2016), p. 83

[37] Raic (2002), pp. 237 et seq.

[38] Maccorquodale (1994), p. 352; Cassese (1995), pp. 109–112.

[39] Hofbauer Jane (2016), p. 77. Dugard (2013), p. 86.

[40] Hofbauer Jane (2016), p. 77.

[41] Cassese (1995), p. 53.

[42] Ibidem.

[43] Cassese (2005), p. 47.

Protocol',[44] differentiating it from the right laid out in Article 27 of the ICCPR, regarded as an individual right that should not be confused with self-determination. Therefore, self-determination has a distinct character from the rest of the rights included in the Covenant, since its holders and implementation are different.

In addition, the right to democratic governance appears to have lost steam over the twenty-first century,[45] despite the impetus it received following Franck's paper on democratic governance in 1992.[46] Finally, if we take parties' intention into account, it must be noted that as Resolution 2625 (XXV) was negotiated, the socialist and developing countries managed to eliminate any reference to governments that were representative of the whole people, excluding therefore any reference to a democratic government.[47]

At present, it is not possible to affirm that any enforcement entitlement to a democratic governance exists, and therefore, it is difficult to assert that internal self-determination means the right of a state's whole population to participate in a decision-making democratic procedure.

A different interpretation of the right to internal self-determination focused on the relation between the people and the government lies in the concept of a representative government of all groups of people inside the state.[48] The main legal argument is again paragraph 7 of Resolution 2625 (XXV), who has led to consider that all racial and religious groups have a right to international self-determination, being this the right of communities with different character to have this character reflected in the government institutions.[49]

The implementation of this internal right to self-determination has also given rise to diverse opinions. Indeed, it can range from the right to have a government that represents and guarantees the right of these groups, to a right of the groups to participate in the decision-making process, or a right to have different political structures that guarantee a special autonomy or federalist status.[50]

Moreover, there are differences among the groups entitled to such a right, since some scholars consider that they should be racial, ethnic, religious or linguistic groups,[51] while others consider only the racial and religious groups according to Resolution 2625 (XXV).[52]

---

[44] Human Rights Committee, General Comment 23, Article 27 (Fiftieth session, 1994), Compilation of General Comments and General Recommendations Adopted by Human Rights Treaty Bodies, U.N. Doc. HRI/GEN/1/Rev.1 at 38 (1994), para. 3.1.

[45] Marks (2011); d'Aspremont (2011); Charlesworth (2017); Charlesworth (2015).

[46] Franck (1992).

[47] Cassese (1995), p. 118.

[48] Hofbauer Jane (2016), p. 77.

[49] Brownlie (1985), p. 108.

[50] Raic (2002), p. 239.

[51] Hofbauer Jane (2016), p. 78; Raic (2002), pp. 251–255.

[52] Cassese, considers that Resolution 2625 only guarantees this right to racial and religious groups. Cassese (1995), p. 114.

On the contrary, Kohen holds a different opinion, as he states that never has a human group inside a state been recognised in the international level as a different peoples from the whole of the state's people.[53] This is also the opinion of Higgins, who asserts that regarding internal self-determination, it 'is to be understood in the sense of all peoples of a given territory'.[54]

4.1.2 The Holders of the Right to Self-Determination and the Secession Dilemma

The controversy regarding the right to internal self-determination leads to the concept of the people—the holders of the right—and secession. In this regard, outside the colonial context, if we consider a state's whole population as the people, any reference to secession as a manifestation of self-determination must be ruled out. On the other hand, if some groups inside the state are regarded as holders of the right to self-determination, the question of secession as a manifestation of external self-determination of these groups arises: either because they are considered holders of the right, or as a consequence of the violation of the internal right to self-determination, thus shaking the principle of territorial integrity.

The ICJ in Namibia recognised the right of all peoples to self-determination,[55] making it necessary to define the concept of people, especially outside the colonial context. As mentioned earlier, according to some scholars, the right to internal self-determination has been acknowledged for ethnic, racial, religious or linguistic groups, entailing the recognition of these groups as a peoples. On some occasions, the people's characteristics given by UNESCO experts have been described and referred:

> A group of individual human beings who enjoy some or all of the following common features: (a) a common historical tradition; (b) racial or ethnic identity; (c) cultural homogeneity; (d) linguistic unity; (e) religious or ideological affinity; (f) territorial connection; (g) common economic life.[56]

These elements can be confused with the definition of minorities,[57] whose rights are recognised by international law but do not include the right to self-determination.

---

[53]Kohen (2007), p. 969.

[54]Higgins (1991), p. 170.

[55]ICJ, *Legal Consequences for States of the Continued Presence of South Africa in Namibia (South West Africa) notwithstanding Security Council Resolution 276 (1970)*, Advisory Opinion of 21 June 1971: I.C.J. Reports 1971, para. 52.

[56]UNESCO, International Meeting of Experts on further study of the concept of the rights of peoples, Paris 27–30 November 1989. Final Report and Recommendations, SHS-89/CONF.602/7, p. 7.

[57]Thornberry (1994), p. 187.

As explained above, Kohen differs from this opinion, asserting that it is the state's whole population that can be considered as people, the concept of people being linked to a territorial dimension: 'It is the territory which defines the 'people' in legal terms rather than the other way around'.[58] Therefore, it is the spatial scope that determines the existence of peoples, and not objective or subjective characteristics. In the same vein, decolonization unfolded according to territorial demarcations and took the whole colony's inhabitants into account. It was not based on cultural, racial, or religious considerations, or according to some groups or segment of the population.[59] Thus, the practice applying to the naissance of the new states should be applicable to the states already in existence. We should also note that when Resolution 2625 (XVV) was drafted, the proposal of referring to 'all distinct people' was ruled out.[60]

However, even assuming that some religious, racial, or ethnic groups within states can be holders of the right to self-determination and therefore be considered as peoples, the secession outcome raises major concerns regarding the territorial integrity principle together with questions about its legal implementation.

The concept of remedial secession has been adopted in order to legally support the right of secession, which is not recognised in international law.[61] In this sense, remedial secession takes place when:

> a minority (or people who have a right to internal self-determination), which is located on an identifiable part of a State's territory, is transformed into a 'people' who have a right to

---

[58] Kohen (2020), p. 160. This position is opposed to that manifested by judge Dillard in its Separated Opinion the Western Sahara: 'It is for the people to determine the destiny of the territory and not the territory the destiny of the people'. ICJ, *Western Sahara*. Separate Opinion of Judge Dillard, Advisory Opinion of 16 October 1975: ICJ Reports 1975, p. 114.

[59] Raic (2002), p. 209. Raic refers also to the exceptions, being those Ruanda-Burundi, Gilbert and Ellice Islands, and British Cameroon.

[60] Thornberry (1994), p. 183.

[61] As Thornberry affirms: 'States have not accepted secession as a principle of international law'. Thornberry (1994), p. 190. In this regard, the Secretary General U Thant stated that 'As an internal organization, the United Nations has never accepted and does not and I do not believe it will ever accepted the principle of secession of a part of its Member State', UN Monthly Chronicle, February 1970, p. 36. In the same vein, the decolonization process has not been considered an act of secession, since Resolution 2625 (XXV) made clear that 'The territory of a colony or other Non-Self-Governing Territory has, under the Charter, a status separate and distinct from the territory of the State administering it'. A position maintained previously by Resolution 1541 (XV) when equated the non-self-governing territories to 'a territory which is geographically separate and is distinct ethnically and/or culturally from the country administering it'. Also Cassese, even though affirming a right of remedial secession, considers that States have always reject the right of secession of nations, groups and minorities. Cassese (1995), p. 122. Finally, the Supreme Court of Canada was clear establishing that: 'It is clear that international law does not specifically grant component parts of sovereign states the legal right to secede unilaterally from their "parent" state'. Supreme Court of Canada, Reference re Secession of Quebec, [1998] 2 S.C.R. 217, 20 August, 1998, para. 111. On the other hand Dugard considers that remedial secession has its roots in the writings of classical international law jurists, Grotius and Vattel, and in the American declaration of independence. Dugard (2013), p. 113.

exercise ('external') self-determination and secede that territory from the State in question as a last resort to address gross violations of human rights perpetrated against them by the government.[62]

Doubts as to the existence of a right to remedial secession were already posed by the ICJ in the Advisory Opinion on the Unilateral Declaration of Independence of Kosovo:

The international law of self-determination confers upon part of the population of an existing State a right to separate from that State is, however, a subject on which radically different views were expressed by those taking part in the proceedings and expressing a position on the question. Similar differences existed regarding whether international law provides for a right of 'remedial secession' and, if so, in what circumstances.[63]

Nevertheless, it seems that this right was accepted by the Supreme Court of Canada in its decision on the Secession of Quebec, when it declared that: 'a right to external self-determination (which in this case potentially takes the form of the assertion of a right to unilateral secession) arises in only the most extreme of cases and, even then, under carefully defined circumstances'.[64]

The right of remedial secession has been also linked to paragraph 7 of Resolution 2625 (XXV) by means of an *a contrario* reading[65] concluding that in the cases in which the government does not represent the peoples of the territory without distinction as to race, colour or creed, the territorial integrity of that sovereign and independent state may be dismembered or impaired.

This *a contrario* reading also needs to be interpreted further, or else a simple violation of the rights of a racial group inside the state would entail the right of secession. It is therefore necessary that those actions entail a gross violation of human rights.

Consequently, the conclusion would be that in cases where the state itself violates the right to internal self-determination of peoples, the remedy would be a right to external self-determination. This position received a fair amount of support from

[62] Del Mar (2013), p. 79.

[63] ICJ, *Accordance with international law of the unilateral declaration of independence in respect of Kosovo*, Advisory Opinion of 22 July 2010: I.C.J. Reports 2010, para. 82.

[64] Supreme Court of Canada, Reference re Secession of Quebec, [1998] 2 S.C.R. 217, 20 August, 1998, para. 126.

[65] Cassese (1995) p. 120; Dugard (2013), p. 115; Crawford (2007), p. 119; Judge Yusuf also supported the *a contrario* interpretation in its Separate Opinion to the Kosovo Advisory Opinion: 'the saving clause in its latter part implies that if a State fails to comport itself in accordance with the principle of equal rights and self-determination of peoples, an exceptional situation may arise whereby, the ethnically or racially distinct group denied internal self-determination may claim a right of external self-determination or separation from the State which could effectively put into question the State's territorial unity and sovereignty'. ICJ, *Accordance with international law of the unilateral declaration of independence in respect of Kosovo*, Separate Opinion of Judge Yusuf, Advisory Opinion of 22 July 2010: I.C.J. Reports 2010, para. 12.

some scholars,[66] who even identified the requirements for its implementation. According to Dugard, the latter would be:

> (i) There must be a people qualifying as a "self" for the purposes of the right of self-determination, that is a people with a separate identity based on ethnicity, race, religion, language or culture. (ii) The people must occupy a distinct part of the territory of the State and constitute a majority in that territory. (iii) The people must have been denied the right of internal self-determination in the sense that they are denied the right to meaningful participation in government and representation in the political structures of the State. (iv) The people must have been subjected to widespread and gross violations of their fundamental human rights. (v) The people must have exhausted all reasonable opportunities to secure respect for their human rights and to exercise the right of internal self-determination.[67]

However, interpreting paragraph 7 of Resolution 2625 (XXV) as a grounds for remedial secession has also attracted a variety of criticisms. The major one is the fact that this provision was included as a 'saving clause' to guarantee the territorial integrity of states, and the said interpretation would be contrary to its object and purpose.[68] In this regard, Thornberry affirms that taken as a whole, the paragraph focuses on 'forbidding secession by affirming territorial integrity'.[69] In addition, paragraph 7 refers to 'foregoing paragraphs' which is considered a reference to the groups holding the right to self-determination according to the declaration, that is: 'peoples to alien subjugation, domination and exploitation', not to other groups claiming such a right.[70]

A second objection raised by the *a contrario* interpretation concerns secession as the ultimate solution in the case of a gross violation of human rights. First, it is difficult to assert that the state's intention was to allow for secession in those circumstances.[71] Territorial integrity is an essential and valuable principle of international law for states: it is today and it was during the decolonization process. This is why the states attempted to separate decolonization from secession, considering non-self-governing territories as separate entities from colonial states.[72] Resolution 2625 (XXV) was adopted a few years later than the human rights covenants and other regional human rights instruments. But still, to assume that states would risk their territorial integrity to protect the human rights of some groups inside the states

[66] Ibid; Tancredi (2009).

[67] Dugard (2013), p. 117. Johnson has also summarised these requirements as: (1) the people 'must be culturally antithetic to those administering the government of the state'; (2) evidences of the denial of basic human rights to this people; (3) 'the people must be situated in an area that is geographically distinguishable from the rest of the State'. Johnson (1973), pp. 161–162.

[68] Kohen (2020), p. 157.

[69] Thornberry (1994), p. 183.

[70] Kohen (2020) p. 158; Del Mar (2013), p. 94.

[71] We previously mentioned that during the drafting process of Resolution 2625 (XVV) the proposal of referring to 'all distinct people' was ruled out. See Thornberry (1994), p. 183.

[72] A referred above Resolution 2625 (XXV) made clear that 'The territory of a colony or other Non-Self-Governing Territory has, under the Charter, a status separate and distinct from the territory of the State administering it'.

seems too far from the States' real interests—especially considering their general opposition to secession.

In the same vein, it does not seem plausible that the violation of the internal self-determination of some groups (assuming that those groups are holders of the right) should result in external self-determination. The violation of internal self-determination raises questions of state responsibility, the solutions being those established for any violation of international law, from reprisals to sanctions, among others. In this regard, to create a right that would lead to ruling out one of the main principles of international law, the territorial integrity, in order to respond to another breach of international law is contrary to any international legal logic. This solution can be as controversial as humanitarian intervention, in which the prohibition of the use of force, the principle of non-intervention, and the sovereignty of the states were set aside to protect a population facing a gross human rights violation. As Del Mar commented: 'a State is a legal entity, not a human rights solution'.[73]

Finally, Kosovo has been considered as a potential case of remedial secession. Of note regarding the *Kosovo* Advisory Opinion is the fact that the ICJ expressed its doubts about the existence of a right to remedial secession.[74] Second, the Kosovars have never been recognised as a people by the United Nations or by any other international organisation.[75] Therefore, they do not hold the right to self-determination, remedial secession being one of its manifestations. Finally, state interventions in the case illustrated the disparity of opinions on the matter, though the majority of interveners opposed the existence of that principle.[76]

This right, as referred to at the beginning of this section, was one of the justifications used by Russia to defend its intervention in Georgia and Ukraine.[77] This brings to light the risks of manipulating the principle of self-determination[78] and making up doctrines that have no legal bases or the support of the main international institutions and the majority of states.

[73] Del Mar (2013), p. 107.

[74] ICJ, *Accordance with international law of the unilateral declaration of independence in respect of Kosovo*, para 82.

[75] Kohen (2007), p. 978.

[76] Christakis (2011), p. 78 footnote 23. Those whose supported the doctrine were: Albania, Estonia, Finland, Germany, Ireland, The Netherlands, Poland, and Switzerland. Against: Azerbaijan, China, the Republic of Cyprus, Iran, Romania, Serbia, Slovakia, Spain. And neither Frances, United Kingdom nor the United States endorsed the doctrine. It must be said that among the permanent members of the Security Council, only Russia implicitly supported the doctrine. Del Mar (2013), pp. 82–83.

[77] See Ingimundarson (2022). https://lseideas.medium.com/the-kosovo-precedent-russia-s-justification-of-military-interventions-and-territorial-revisions-14ad7ff894e6

[78] On the manipulation of the principle of self-determination see also Kohen and the cases in which it has been used to justify a territorial interest, as demagogic instrument, or making a selective used of it according to national interests. Kohen (2007), pp. 970–977.

4.2 Three Advisory Opinions, Three Peoples Under Struggle: Western Sahara, Palestine and Chagos

The International Court of Justice has issued leading advisory opinions on decolonization and on the principle of self-determination. These opinions have helped to shape the content and implementation of the principle, some of them driving towards the achievement of the peoples' exercise of the right to self-determination.[79] Others, on the other hand, while clearly recognising right of the peoples to self-determination and certain states' violation of international law, have not managed to solve some of the oldest and intricate self-determination controversies.

In this chapter, we will refer to the advisory opinions mentioned above, in order to determine the position of the Court, and also to elucidate whether those situations have common elements that may allow to understand the reluctance and difficulties of implementation of the right to self-determination. We will thus refer to the cases of Western Sahara,[80] Palestine[81] and the Chagos archipelago.[82] There are further cases of non-self-governing territories included in the list of the United Nations,[83] but these three cases can be regarded as among the most controversial and an example of the failure of the United Nations and the international community.

The International Court of Justice has recognised the right of these peoples to self-determination in its three advisory opinions. In the case of *Western Sahara*, the Court clearly established that it

> 'has not found legal ties of such nature as might affect the application of resolution 1514 (XV) in the decolonization of Western Sahara and, in particular, of the principles of self-determination through the free and genuine expression of the will of the peoples of the Territory'[84]

In the same vein, in its advisory opinion on the *Legality of the Wall*, the Court stated that 'Israel is bound to comply with its obligation to respect the right of the Palestinian people to self-determination'.[85]

And finally, in *Chagos*, while not recognising the right to self-determination to Chagossians, the Court referred to the right of a lawful self-determination of Mauritius in this way:

---

[79] ICJ, *International Status of South West Africa*, Advisory Opinion of 11 July 1950: I.C.J. Reports 1950; I.C.J, Namibia. It can be also cited a contentious case, ICJ, East Timor, Judgement of 30 June 1995: I.C.J Reports 1995.

[80] ICJ, *Western Sahara*.

[81] ICJ, *Legal Consequences of the Construction of a Wall in the Occupied Palestinian Territory*.

[82] ICJ, *Legal Consequences of the Separation of the Chagos Archipelago from Mauritius in 1965*, Advisory Opinion of 25 February 2019: I.CJ. Reports 2019.

[83] United Nations. Non Self-Governing Territories. https://www.un.org/dppa/decolonization/en/nsgt

[84] ICJ, *Western Sahara*, para 162.

[85] ICJ, *Legal Consequences of the Construction of a Wall in the Occupied Palestinian Territory*, para. 149.

> the United Kingdom is under an obligation to bring an end to its administration of the Chagos Archipelago as rapidly as possible, thereby enabling Mauritius to complete the decolonization of its territory in a manner consistent with the right of peoples to self-determination.[86]

Though the International Court of Justice has recognised this right in such a clear and unequivocal manner, these three peoples continue today to suffer the consequences of illegal occupation and administration, and their rights have not been enforced.

4.2.1 The Facts

The three peoples of Western Sahara, Palestine and Chagos are struggling for their right of self-determination to be enforced. However, the origin, grounds for application and factual situation differ in all three cases.

Western Sahara is the only one of the three territories to be included in the United Nations non-self-governing territories list. It is a former Spanish colony, which never acceded to self-government due to the occupation of the territory by Morocco[87] and Mauritania (the latter withdrew in 1979),[88] after the advisory opinion of the Court, which led to an armed conflict between the POLISARIO Front and Morocco until 1988.[89] The Court came to recognise the right of Western Sahara people to self-determination, contrary to the interests and position manifested by Morocco. For its part, Morocco considered that according to the principle of self-determination, the people of Western Sahara may have the right to separate from Spain, but they should be reintegrated into the mother state.[90] In 1975, Morocco's occupation of Western Sahara through the 'Green March'[91] was condemned by the Security Council, which deplored 'the holding of the march' and called 'upon Morocco immediately to withdraw from the Territory of Western Sahara all the participants in the march'.[92] The Security Council did not in fact explicitly refer to occupation, but it demanded that Morocco withdraw from Western Sahara.

[86] ICJ, *Legal Consequences of the Separation of the Chagos Archipelago from Mauritius in 1965*, para. 178.

[87] The Green March was an unarmed civilian march launched by the King of Morocco to occupy the territory of Sahara. During four days, they penetrated in the territory of Western Sahara, forcing finally Spain to abandon the territory. See Weiner (1979); Saul (2015), pp. 305–307.

[88] On the historical background see: Cassese (1995), pp. 214–217; Soroeta (2016), pp. 187–191; Devia Garzón (2016), pp. 77–94; Saul (2015), pp. 305–307.

[89] The cease fire took place in 1988, together with the negotiation of the Settlement Plan. Soroeta (2016), p. 198.

[90] ICJ, *Western Sahara*, para 49.

[91] On the occupation of Western Sahara see Saul (2015); Soroeta (2016).

[92] UN Security Council Resolution 380 (1975).

In this scenario, the right to self-determination of the people of Western Sahara stems mainly from the decolonization process, one of the aims of the principle of self-determination included in Resolution 2625 (XXV).

Conversely, although reference is made to occupation in the case of the Palestinian people, the right to self-determination, according to the Court's opinion and the facts, is related to the concept of foreign subjugation, domination and exploitation, specifically foreign military occupation, which, according to Resolution 2625 (XXV), is contrary to the principle of self-determination.

Palestine is not included in the list of non-self-governing territories, and it has been recognised as a State by more than 100 countries, with a status of non-member state at the UN General Assembly. It is also a member of several international organizations.[93] The International Court of Justice recognised the occupation of Palestine territory by Israel, though it refrained at the same time from making a declaration on the legality of such an occupation.[94] In this regard, the Court considered that the Fourth Geneva Convention was applicable to any occupied territory in the event of armed conflict and therefore, it was applicable in the 'Palestinian territories which before the conflict lay to the east of the Green Line and which during that conflict were occupied by Israel'.[95] The Court referred to the occupation of the territories in further paragraphs, upholding for example that 'the territories occupied by Israel have for over 37 years been subject to its territorial jurisdiction as the occupying Power'.[96] This position has also been confirmed by the Security Council, which called for the 'withdrawal of Israel armed forces from territories occupied in the recent conflict'.[97]

In contrast, the case of the Chagos archipelago has not led to armed conflict between the people or their representatives and the colonial power. However, as in the case of Western Sahara, the grounds for self-determination can also be found in the decolonization process, which in this case, was not lawfully completed due to the detachment of Chagos archipelago from Mauritius prior to the granting of its independence. The United Kingdom, while still a colonial power, negotiated the Lancaster Agreement with the *Premie*r of Mauritius, which included the detachment of Chagos that became the British Indian Ocean Territory (BIO). This new colony was not included in the list of non-self-governing territories. According to the Court, the 'detachment was not based on free and genuine expression of the will of the people concerned',[98] since the Lancaster Agreement could not be considered an

---

[93] Farsakh (2021), p. 6.

[94] According to Imseis, the presence of Israel in Palestine is illegal based on the *jus ad bellum*, the *jus in bello*, human rights law and the law of self-determination. Imseis (2020), p. 1071. On the legality of occupations, see Cardona Llorens (2007).

[95] ICJ, *Legal Consequences of the Construction of a Wall in the Occupied Palestinian Territory*, para. 101.

[96] Ibid. para. 112.

[97] UN Security Council Resolution 242 (1967).

[98] ICJ, *Legal Consequences of the Separation of the Chagos Archipelago from Mauritius in 1965*, para. 172.

international agreement due to one of the parties, Mauritius, being under the authority of the other party, the United Kingdom.

Therefore, we have before us three cases in which the principle of self-determination is pending implementation and in which, according to the Court, the United Nations has an essential role to play. In Western Sahara, the advisory opinion was given in order to 'assist the General Assembly to determine the future decolonization policy'.[99] However, the obligations of the United Nations became clearer and stronger in the following advisory opinions, since in the case of the *Wall*, the Court declared that 'the United Nations, and especially the General Assembly and the Security Council, should consider what further actions is required to bring an end the illegal situation resulting from the construction of the wall and the associated regime',[100] which was considered a violation of the right to self-determination. And finally, in Chagos, the Court stated that 'the modalities necessary for ensuring the decolonization of Mauritius fall within the remit of the United Nations General Assembly'.[101]

4.2.2 The Failed Role of the United Nations

At this point, it is necessary to question whether the United Nations fulfilled its role, complying with its obligations and competences regarding the process of decolonization and the implementation of the principle of self-determination. The issue arises despite a number of factors: the large amount of resolutions, mainly from the General Assembly, calling for the respect of the principle of self-determination; the deployment of a United Nations Mission in Western Sahara (MINURSO)[102] to assist in the referendum process; or the different plans proposed by organs of the United Nations or by third actors supported by the United Nations.

An element that should be taken into account in this analysis is the United Nations' tendency to put the people suffering from the violation of their right to self-determination and the perpetrators of that violation on an equal footing. Indeed, UN resolutions call for a negotiated solution—mainly regarding Western Sahara and Palestine—without taking the side of those struggling for their rights. This stance differs substantially from other occupation cases in which the United Nations has not referred at all to negotiated solutions, such as in the cases of South Africa and Namibia, the Soviet Union and Afghanistan, or Iraq and Kuwait. Adopting such a neutral position is thus tantamount to giving some kind of legitimacy to the illegal

---

[99] ICJ, *Western Sahara*, para. 161.

[100] ICJ, *Legal Consequences of the Construction of a Wall in the Occupied Palestinian Territory*, para. 159.

[101] ICJ, *Legal Consequences of the Separation of the Chagos Archipelago from Mauritius in 1965*, para. 179.

[102] UN Security Council Resolution 690 (1991).

acts of the states.[103] On the other hand, in the case of Chagos, the General Assembly, after the advisory opinion, adopted a resolution demanding the United Kingdom to withdraw its colonial administration within 6 months.[104] Yet, no further steps were taken passed the deadline.

One of the most shocking situations was that of Western Sahara and the different plans of the United Nations Secretary Generals to settle the controversy between the POLISARIO Front and Morocco. While Pérez de Cuellar's first plan focused on elaborating the census for the referendum that, according to the Court, would allow to express the free and genuine will of the people, the second plan of Boutros Boutros Gali aimed at reducing military presence in the territory in order to dismantle the MINURSO.[105] None of these plans offered a realistic solution since, as is well known, Morocco would not allow a referendum if a possible outcome would be independence, despite its previous acceptance.[106] In addition, military presence is what allows Morocco to control the territory.[107]

However, a side seemed to have been taken when, according to the former United Nations Under-Secretary General, Kofi Annan's intentions were 'to persuade James Baker III to accept an appointment as Special Representative and try to negotiate a deal based on enhanced autonomy for Western Sahara within the Kingdom of Morocco'.[108] Therefore, among the self-governing options offered by Resolution 1541 (XV), the Secretary General had already chosen integration, which according to the Resolution should be the result of the 'freely expressed wishes of the territory's peoples' 'conducted and based on universal adult suffrage'.[109] Both of Baker's plans were rejected by the representatives of the Western Sahara people. The first was a proposal for autonomy inside Morocco, and the second an autonomy regime for 5 years prior to a referendum, in which the settlers since December 1999 were also eligible to vote.[110]

To date, no further plans have been proposed by the United Nations to guarantee the people of Western Sahara the right to self-determination. The United Nations has limited its activity to calls for negotiation between the parties, and to Security Council statements describing Morocco's 2007 proposal based on an 'autonomy statute for the Sahara region',[111] as 'serious and credible Moroccan efforts to move

[103] Imseis (2020), pp. 1068–1069; Soroeta (2016), p. 203.

[104] UN General Assembly, *Advisory opinion of the International Court of Justice on the legal consequences of the separation of the Chagos Archipelago from Mauritius in 1965*, 22 May 2019. A/RES/73/295.

[105] Soroeta (2016), pp. 202–203

[106] Ibid. p. 202.

[107] Saul (2015), p. 308.

[108] Soroeta (2016), p. 201.

[109] Principle IX. Resolution 1541 (XV).

[110] Soroeta (2016), p. 204

[111] Letter dated 11 April 2007 from the Permanent Representative of Morocco to the United Nations addressed to the President of the Security Council. S/2007/206. https://digitallibrary.un.org/record/597424?ln=en

the process forward towards resolution'.[112] Therefore, it seems that the United Nations is siding with one of the parties, in this case, the one that is occupying the territory,[113] preventing the exercise of the right to self-determination, and violating human rights and humanitarian law.[114] It must be noted that when the Security Council adopted such an assessment of Morocco's proposal for the first time, South Africa was the only state to express its concerns stating that:

> We also continue to be amazed by the relentless attempts by some members of this Council to try to describe the Moroccan proposal as being a "serious and credible effort to move the resolution forward". The fact is that the Moroccan proposal for autonomy is a unilateral attempt to prevent the Saharawi people from claiming their right to self-determination, which is enshrined in the Charter of the United Nations. Two plans have been presented to the Council (. . .) So any attempt to place one proposal over the other would undermine the negotiations process (. . .)[115]

In the case of Palestine, the fact of relying on bilateral negations to solve the conflict, one of the parties being dominant, has also been understood as a legitimisation the occupation of the territory by Israel.[116] In addition, this reliance has been regarded as a barrier to a solution that would guarantee the exercise of the right to self-determination by the people of Palestine.

The two-state solution was adopted by the General Assembly Resolution 181 (II) of 1947, and has been embraced by the United Nations ever since. However, instead of calling for the unconditional application of the two-state solution, the United Nations has supported the negotiation of its implementation[117] between two unequal parties: one of them fully recognised as a state that is militarily superior and is occupying part of the other party's territory; and a second one that has not achieved full recognition by the international community, does not control its

[112]The last of this series of resolutions: UN Security Council Resolution 2654 (2022) from 27 October 2022. The same paragraph mentions the Front POLISARIO proposal without making any assessment about its validity to solve the controversy.

[113]See UN General Assembly, Question of Western Sahara, 21 November 1979, A/RES/ 34/37; UN General Assembly, Question of Western Sahara, 11 November 1980, A/RES/35/19; Saul (2015), p. 301; Soroeta (2016), p. 210.

[114]See among others: UN Security Council, Situation concerning Western Sahara. Report of the Secretary-General. 3 October 2022, S/2022/733. Amnesty International, Report 2022/23. The state of the world's human rights, pp. 258–261. https://www.amnesty.org/en/location/middle-east-and-north-africa/morocco-and-western-sahara/report-morocco-and-western-sahara/; Euro-Mediterranean Human Rights Network (2015) The Human Rights Situation in Morocco and the Western Sahara. https://euromedrights.org/wp-content/uploads/2015/03/20150319-RE-Mission-Report-on-Morocco-and-the-Western-Sahara-EN.pdf; European Parliament, Resolution of 25 November 2010 on the situation in Western Sahara, (2012/C 99 E/16).

[115]UN Security Council, The situation concerning Western Sahara. Report of the Secretary-General on the situation concerning Western Sahara, (S/2007/619). 31 October 2007, Meeting Records, S/PV.5773. https://documents-dds-ny.un.org/doc/UNDOC/PRO/N07/572/64/PDF/N0757264.pdf?OpenElement

[116]Imseis (2020), pp. 1057.

[117]Ibid, p. 1065.

whole territory, is a major humanitarian aid recipient, and whose population is partially displaced. In addition, the Security Council's latest proposal resolutions demanding the end of the occupation, condemning *the facto* annexation of lands and declaring the illegality of the wall, was vetoed by the United States,[118] leaving only the General Assembly's non-binding resolutions in support of the withdrawal.[119]

Finally, no change is visible at all in the Advisory Opinion of the Court on Israel about this specific issue, and we cannot today foresee any future changes regarding its occupation policy.

4.2.3 A Defence of the Right to Self-Determination by the International Community of States?

The United Nations seems to have failed to offer a solution for the peoples awaiting to exercise their right to self-determination. In the meantime, the international community of states has not reached a solution either, adopting in most cases a 'neutral' position, which in practice benefits the stronger party in the controversy.

According to the previously cited ICJ advisory opinions, to respect the right to self-determination is an *erga omnes* obligation, therefore, 'all the states have a legal interest in protecting that right'.[120] However, the scope of that obligation[121] is contested: even though the International Court of Justice has inferred some form of state duties when referring to this obligation, it has not properly clarified the specific content of the obligation. In this latter advisory opinion, the Chagos archipelago, the Court referred to Resolution 2625 (XXV), which established the duty to promote the realisation of the principle of self-determination[122] concluding that 'all member states must cooperate with the United Nations to complete the decolonization of Mauritius'.[123]

Nevertheless, the Court had gone further in its previous decision on the Wall, in which it seems to link the *erga omnes* obligations to those of Article 41 of Articles of

[118] Draft resolution S/2003/980. In 1967 the Security Council adopted Resolution 242 (1967), in which affirmed that a lasting peace in the Middle East should be achieved through two principles: the withdrawal of Israel from the occupied territories and 'acknowledgement of the sovereignty, territorial integrity and political independence of every State'.

[119] See Imseis (2020), p. 1060.

[120] ICJ, *Legal Consequences of the Separation of the Chagos Archipelago from Mauritius in 1965*, para. 180.

[121] Scobbie (2006), p. 946.

[122] ICJ, *Legal Consequences of the Separation of the Chagos Archipelago from Mauritius in 1965*, para. 180

[123] Ibid. 182.

the Responsibility of States for Internationally Wrongful Acts (ARSIWA).[124] In this regard, the Court concluded after analysing the *erga onmes* nature of the right of self-determination[125] and some humanitarian law obligations[126] that states are under an obligation not to recognize the illegal situation and not to render aid or assistance. However, the Court decreases the level of demands of the third obligation of Article 41 ARSIWA: 'cooperate to bring to an end through lawful means', simply declaring that 'it is for all states (. . .) to see to it any impediment (. . .) to the exercise by the Palestinian people of its right of self-determination is brought to an end'.[127] This reference has led the right to self-determination to be considered as a *jus cogens* norm, and to be included by the International Law Commission in the list of norms having the status of *jus cogens.*[128] This opinion is also shared by some scholars[129] and by judges Robinson, Sebutinde and Cançado Trindade. The latter stated, in their separate opinions in Chagos, that the right to self-determination had already achieved the status of a *jus cogens norm.*[130]

Nonetheless, the question is whether the states complied with their obligation e*rga omnes*—assuming that it is possible to effectively determine the content of the obligation, or at least whether they had complied with their obligations enshrined in Resolution 2625 (XXV): to promote the realisation of the principle to self-determination.

[124] As Sparks states, although the Court refers to *erga omnes* obligations, it associates the legal consequences of the breach of self-determination with the breach of jus cogens norms. Sparks (2023), pp. 211–212.

[125] ICJ, *Legal Consequences of the Construction of a Wall in the Occupied Palestinian Territory*, paras. 155–156.

[126] Ibid., para. 157.

[127] Ibid., para. 159.

[128] Conclusion 23. Draft conclusions on identification and legal consequences of peremptory norms of general international law (jus cogens). Yearbook of the International Law Commission, 2022, vol. II, Part Two.

[129] Sparks (2023), pp. 215–219; Orakhelashvili (2006), pp. 133–134; Hilpold (2022), p. 204; Kohen (2007), p. 964.

[130] Judge Cançado Trindade considers that 'respect for the right to self-determination of peoples has crystallized as an imperative for the United Nations, in conformity with contemporary international law'. ICJ, *Legal Consequences of the Separation of the Chagos Archipelago from Mauritius in 1965*, Separate Opinion of Judge Cançado Trindade, Advisory Opinon of 25 February 2019: I.CJ. Reports 2019, para. 120. Judge Sebutinde affirms that 'While the inalienable right to self-determination is *jus cogens* (i.e. from which no derogation is permitted), the corresponding obligation incumbent upon the administering Power, is an obligation erga omnes (in which the international community as a whole is interested.)'. ICJ, *Legal Consequences of the Separation of the Chagos Archipelago from Mauritius in 1965*, Separate Opinion of Judge Sebutinde, Advisory Opinon of 25 February 2019: I.CJ. Reports 2019, para. 13. And Judge Robinson, while complaining about the little analysis by the Court to this question, offers and analysed the materials that come to support the jus cogens character of the right of self-determination. ICJ, *Legal Consequences of the Separation of the Chagos Archipelago from Mauritius in 1965*, Separate Opinion of Judge Robinson, Advisory Opinon of 25 February 2019: I.CJ. Reports 2019, paras. 70–82.

Western Sahara can be regarded as an example of support dissolution: as years go by, no solution is achieved, and the states are starting to act as if it were a case of *fait accompli*. The settlement plan endorsed by the Security Council[131] established a referendum to decide the future of Western Sahara, however, since Morocco presented its plan[132] for an autonomy statute for Western Sahara within Morocco in 2007, support for this plan has grown without any explicit reference to the referendum. The last controversial step was taken by Spain, the former colonial power,[133] which sent a letter to the King of Morocco in March 2022 declaring that 'Spain considers the Moroccan proposal for autonomy presented in 2007 as the most serious, credible and realistic basis for the resolution of this difference'.[134] Therefore, Spain took sides, expressly and publicly adopted the mentioned Security Council's position, and, in addition, increased its support for the Morocco's plan. This position had been previously criticised by South Africa, but not by Spain, when it was invited to participate in the first session in which that position was adopted.[135] In addition, Morocco's occupation of the territory and the ban to exercise the right to self-determination was reduced to a mere '*diferendo*': a difference, disagreement or discrepancy, when the controversy actually refers to the violation of fundamental principles, obligations and rights of international law.

In the same line, France adopted the view that 'the Moroccan autonomy plan is a serious, credible basis for discussions',[136] while affirming that the solution should be in accordance with the United Nations resolutions.

Germany has also followed the same position in support of Morocco's plan and abandoning the express recognition of the right to self-determination of the people of Western Sahara. In August 2022, in a joint Declaration, it stated that 'Germany

[131] UN Security Council Resolution 658 (1990).

[132] Letter dated 11 April 2007 from the Permanent Representative of Morocco to the United Nations addressed to the President of the Security Council. S/2007/206. https://digitallibrary.un.org/record/597424?ln=en

[133] In 1976 Spain informed the Secretary General the end of its presence in the territory and the exempt from any responsibility in connection with the administration of Western Sahara, but the Spanish courts and the scholars still consider Spain the administrative power. In this regard, in the list of non-self-governing territories there is no mention to the administrative power, just a reference to the letter sent to the Secretary-General by Spain. Letter dated 26 February 1976 from the Permanent Representative of Spain to the United Nations addressed to the Secretary-General. A/31/56. S/11997. https://digitallibrary.un.org/record/551155. The Audiencia Nacional in 2014 stated that 'the administering Power of Western Sahara remains Spain, although de jure but not de facto'. Audiencia Nacional. Sala de lo Penal, procedimiento ordinario n° 80/2013, Auto 40/2014, para. 4.

[134] González (2022). https://elpais.com/espana/2022-03-23/la-carta-de-pedro-sanchez-a-mohamed-vi-debemos-construir-una-nueva-relacion-que-evite-futuras-crisis.html

[135] Report of the Secretary-General on the situation concerning Western Sahara (S/2007/619). United Nation Security Council, S/PV.5773. 31 October 2007. https://documents-dds-ny.un.org/doc/UNDOC/PRO/N07/572/64/PDF/N0757264.pdf?OpenElement

[136] Ministry for Europe and Foreign Affairs (2022). https://www.diplomatie.gouv.fr/en/country-files/morocco/news/article/western-sahara-q-a-21-mar-2022

considers, in this respect, the autonomy plan presented in 2007 as a serious and credible effort by Morocco and as a good basis for a solution agreed upon between both parties'.[137]

This statement was adopted after the breach of diplomatic relations between Morocco and Germany[138] following the critics of Germany to the recognition of the sovereignty of Morocco over Western Sahara by the United States.[139] This has been so far the clearest example of recognition of a *fait accompli*: the annexation of Western Sahara by Morocco.

While all states mentioned above, except the United States, referred to the United Nations as a framework to solve the controversy, they also referred to a negotiated solution in which Morocco's proposal was considered the optimal solution. In addition, in those declarations, the states did not mention what the United Nations, mainly the General Assembly and the International Court of Justice, actually demanded: the manifestation of the genuine and free will of the people, in this case, through a referendum. According to Resolution 2625 (XXV) and the *erga omnes* nature of the right to self-determination, the states should have focused on demanding and making Morocco comply with its obligation of allowing the referendum in Western Sahara to take place, including the option for independence, based on a census elaborated by the MINURSO.[140] On the contrary, the position taken by the states on this issue was to support Morocco's demands, i.e., that of the party that clearest violates international law.

Of the three cases, Palestine has received the most attention from the international community and is the case in which most efforts have been made. In this regard, the 1978 Camp David Accords,[141] the 1993 Oslo Accords[142] or the Quarter Road Map in 2003[143] were considered major steps in the resolution of the conflict. We must

[137] Federal Foreign Office (2022). https://www.auswaertiges-amt.de/en/newsroom/news/joint-declaration-germany-morocco/2548280

[138] Eljechtimi and Lawson (2021). https://www.reuters.com/world/africa/morocco-recalls-its-ambassador-berlin-over-western-sahara-2021-05-06/

[139] The White House (2020). https://trumpwhitehouse.archives.gov/presidential-actions/proclamation-recognizing-sovereignty-kingdom-morocco-western-sahara/

[140] The MINURSO started its work based on the census elaborated by Spain in 1974, but the lack of agreement between Front POLISARIO and Morocco on the identification process delayed the results until 2000. Morocco did not accept the results, which in practice entailed a vote in favour of independence, and decided to abandon the referendum solution and offered the mentioned proposal of an autonomy Western Sahara inside Morocco. See Theofilopoulou (2006). https://www.usip.org/sites/default/files/sr166.pdf

[141] Camp David Accords: The Framework for Peace in the Middle East. Jimmy Carter Presidential Library and Museum. https://www.jimmycarterlibrary.gov/research/additional-resources/camp-david-accords/framework-for-peace-in-the-middle-east

[142] Declaration of Principles on Interim Self-Government Arrangements. Knesset. https://web.archive.org/web/20021115183950/http://knesset.gov.il/process/docs/oslo_eng.htm

[143] A performance-based road map to a permanent two-State solution to the Israeli-Palestinian conflict. Letter dated 7 May 2003 from the Secretary-General addressed to the President of the Security Council. S/2003/529. https://digitallibrary.un.org/record/493931

highlight, however, that none of these agreements mentioned the right to self-determination of the Palestinian people. Cassese considers, in any case, that a right to internal self-determination can be inferred from the reference to the 'legitimate rights of the Palestinian people' in the Oslo agreement. This statement should be linked to the compromise of withdrawing from the West Bank and Gaza Strip that would lead to the full implementation of the right of self-determination, but without specifying the procedure to follow, which should again be object of negotiation.[144] On the contrary, Farsakh affirmed that the Oslo process undermined the possibility of a viable Palestinian state[145] which was confirmed 'with the failure of the final status negotiations, after the Camp David Summit in 2000, to bring about Palestinian territorial independence'.[146]

All the mentioned initiatives rely on the support of the community of states, all of them focusing on the necessity of negotiations, but without considering what judge Al-Khasawneh would later state in the *Wall* case: 'the negotiations are means to an end and cannot in themselves replace that end'.[147] Therefore, the negotiations cannot remove the final implementation of the right to self-determination of the Palestinian people from the equation. And above all, this right cannot await the outcome of negotiations. In addition, in the case of Palestine, the states have subjected the exercise of the right to self-determination to the success of a negotiation between two unequal parties. This approach to the exercise of the right to self-determination does not appear to be in line with the duty to promote it included in Resolution 2625 (XXV).

Finally, the Chagos case seems to have gone unnoticed outside the United Kingdom. No express positions had been taken by third Western states; no proposals of settlement outside those of the United Nations General Assembly and the African Union have been made.[148] This situation could be surprising given the award of the Arbitral Tribunal constituted under Annex VII of UNCLOS, which rendered that the establishment of a protected area surrounding the Chagos archipelago was a breach of UNCLOS, and the United Kingdom had the obligation to return Chagos archipelago when it was no longer needed for defence purposes.[149] In addition to this award, the International Court of Justice rendered its decision establishing that the

[144] Cassese (1995), pp. 243–245.

[145] Farsakh (2021), p. 1.

[146] Ibid. p. 7.

[147] ICJ, *Legal Consequences of the Construction of a Wall in the Occupied Palestinian Territory*, Separate Opinion of Judge Al-Khasawneh, Advisory Opinion of 9 July 2004: ICJ Reports 1975, para. 13.

[148] African Union, Assembly of Head of States and Governments. Resolution on Diego García. 99 (XVII) (1980); African Union, The Assembly, Decision on the Sovereignty of the Republic of Mauritius Over the Chagos Archipelago, Decision 331 (2010).

[149] Permanent Court of Arbitration, Chagos Marine Protected Area Arbitration (Mauritius v. United Kingdom), 18 March 2015.

continued administration of Chagos by the United Kingdom was illegal,[150] the United Kingdom having the obligation to bring its administration to an end.[151] In fact, the Western states' lack of action and express position on the issue can be observed in the casting of the Resolution 71/292, which requested the advisory opinion, and in which a significant number of states voted against or abstained.[152] The Chagos question is supported by the global south countries which naturally have a more militant position regarding the right to self-determination. Therefore, in not making the full exercise of self-determination of Mauritius a common cause, the community of states is again falling to comply with its obligations, in this case overlooking the violation of an *erga omnes* right by the United Kingdom.

4.3 Self-Determination in a Europe of Integration

While the previous sections addressed the right to self-determination in third countries, the present section centres on the said right alleged by some independent movements within the European Union. The reasons that led us to focus on the internal perspective are the particular effects, developments, and risks that this particular right may entail regarding the Europe Union's integration process. In addition, the EU's stance towards those independent movements has been the object of critical analysis, because the EU has sometimes exceeded its competences and has therefore taken a position on domestic issues. The latter illustrates the major implications of these processes for the European project.

According to the external self-determination concept in international law referred to above, and also inferred from the United Nations resolutions and international practice, this right is recognised to peoples under colonial domination or under alien subjugation, domination and exploitation. Therefore, outside these situations, the appropriate term is secession.[153]

The transfer of these conclusions to the European Union's movements calling for independence and claiming the exercise of self-determination[154] entails that they must be analysed in the framework of secession. In this regard, the only situation remaining from colonialism in the EU is already specifically regulated,[155] and there

[150] ICJ, *Legal Consequences of the Separation of the Chagos Archipelago from Mauritius in 1965*, para. 177.

[151] Ibid. para. 182.

[152] General Assembly, 88th Plenary Meeting, Official records, A/71/PV.88, 22 June 2017.

[153] On secession, see Dugard (2013).

[154] For example, the law approved by the Catalonian Parliament for holding a referendum was called, Law for a self-determination referendum. Ley 19/2017, de 6 de septiembre, del referéndum de autodeterminación.

[155] After the United Kingdom withdrawal, the territories of the member states included in the United Nations list of non self-governing territories are French Polynesia and New Caledonia. These territories have a special regulation in Part Four TFEU.

is no situation of alien domination inside the EU.[156] In addition, most approaches to the study of these movements focus on the legality of the secession, because, despite references to self-determination, the conclusion is that we are in fact facing cases of secession.

As Connolly[157] has remarked, we can consider that the existence of nationalist movements calling for independence within a European integration process is an incongruity in which the features of the nation-state seem to be blurred. However, it is also remarkable that most of these movements consider themselves pro--European,[158] therefore aiming at independence within the European Union. On the other hand, as we will analyse in this section, the seeking of European membership after independence and its complex implementation has also been used as an instrument by parent states to discourage secession aspirations.

Some of these movements in the European Union have also been considered to have economic grounds, in the sense that advanced regions wish to break away from their backward parent states 'in order to retain control of their revenues and avoid subsidizing poorer regions'.[159] This assumption seems to set secessionist movements in contradiction with the principle of solidarity among the member states included in Article 2 of the Treaty of the European Union (TEU).

4.3.1 The European Union and Secessionism

In line with the absence of secession regulation in international law, there is no reference to the legal bases for secession inside the European Union in the treaties. In fact, references to the opposite[160] can be found in European Union treaties, such as in Article 4.2 TEU according to which 'The Union shall respect (. . .) fundamental structures, political and constitutional' of the member states. Therefore, the European Union must respect the regional system established in the States, the distribution of competences among the regions, and the constitutional systems that may allow seeking independence inside the state or not. However, Article 4.2 TEU also refers to the respect of the 'essential State functions, including ensuring the territorial integrity of the State', which embodies the European Union's clear alignment with state policies to protect their territorial integrity—that are obviously considered to be threatened by those secessionist movements. In this regard, as

[156] It is difficult today to point to an external source of domination, since as Delanty refers, citing Foucault: 'domination is multifarious; it is internal as well as external'. Delanty (2022), p. 100.

[157] Connolly (2013), p. 52.

[158] Sedda (2021), p. 128. In any case, the Scottish National Party opposed to integration considering that they were transferring 'the sovereignty over Scotland from one alien government in London to another in Brussels'. Connolly (2013), p. 78.

[159] Ibid., p. 94.

[160] See Walker (2014), p. 23.

commented by Almqvist, European Union support to secessionist movements 'would mean disrespecting the territorial sovereignty and integrity of a member state',[161] as member states have exclusive competence in territorial issues.

The European Union follows the concept of states as primary subjects, despite having altered the nature of sovereignty and statehood[162] by acquiring competences in areas traditionally reserved to states. This position suggests that the European Union also considers states as territorial entities with the primary function of protecting their territory, and it is not easy for a state to relinquish it.[163]

Nonetheless, depending on the territory, the secession of a member state's partial territory may also require changing its status according to EU Law, so it is not an exclusively internal issue. In this regard, Greenland and New Caledonia are included in the list of overseas countries,[164] and due to an agreement between theses territories and their parent states, Denmark and France, they may have the right to secede. In application of that agreement, and after negotiations with France, the indigenous people of New Caledonia reached an agreement to hold a referendum on independence. This referendum was in fact divided into three referendums, since if the results of the first two referendums were negative regarding independence, a third one had to be held. It took place in 2021 and the outcome was also negative.[165] If the result had been in favour of independence, Article 355.6 of the Treaty on the Functioning of the European Union (TFEU) would have had to be enforced. This Article establishes the amendment of the status of overseas countries, which are expressly included in Annex II of the treaties. A European Union decision on remaining out of EU jurisdiction would therefore be necessary.[166] It must be noted that the New Caledonia case was, actually, linked to the exercise of self-determination, since this territory is included in the United Nations list of non-self-governing territories.

The case of Greenland is different since it is not a non-self-governing territory, but it acquired the right to independence in 2008 through the Act on Greenland Self-Government, which was adopted following a referendum.[167] According to Article 8, the people of Greenland can decide on independence, an agreement being necessary between Greenland's executive power and the Danish government. An

[161] Almqvist (2019), p. 137.

[162] Connolly (2013), p. 100. According to Schimmelfenning, the European integration has transformed the 'the relevance of the national borders, the exercise of sovereignty and the notion of self-determination'. Schimmelfenning (2019), p. 23.

[163] Delanty (2022), p. 108.

[164] Annex II. Consolidated version of the Treaty on the Functioning of the European Union, 26 October 2012, OJ L. 326/47–326/390; 26.10.2012.

[165] République Francaçaise. Vie publique. Nouvelle-Calédonie: les résultats du 3e référendum d'autodétermination du 12 décembre 2021. https://www.vie-publique.fr/eclairage/18649-nouvelle-caledonie-3e-referendum-dautodetermination-12-decembre-2021

[166] López Jurado (2013), p. 18

[167] Act no. 473 of 12 June 2009. Act on Greenland Self-Government. https://www.stm.dk/media/11338/10-notifikation-af-7-oktober-2009-til-fn-s-generalsekretaer-om-selvstyreloven.pdf

outcome in favour of independence will also require the application of Article 355.6 TFEU to change its status according to EU treaties.

In the case of New Caledonia, unlike in the case of other independence movements, i.e., Catalonia and Scotland, the European Union adopted a neutral position and did not issue any statements. However, even though the European Union's attitude has been labelled as 'conservative neutrality',[168] some statements of the European Commission presidents may suggest a different conclusion. In this regard, following the results of the Scotland referendum in favour of remaining in the United Kingdom, José Manuel Durão Barroso, the president of the European Commission, welcomed the result, considering that 'this outcome is good for the united, open and stronger Europe that the European Commission stands for'.[169] In addition, before holding the referendum, Barroso declared that the accession of an independent Scotland to the European Union would be 'extremely difficult if not impossible',[170] thus discouraging independence. Together with these declarations, the Presidents Prodi and Barroso also stated that the accession of the new independent states to the European Union would not be automatic, as it was necessary to apply for membership[171] and naturally to achieve the unanimity of all member states—using in this case the process of accession as a deterring tool. In the same line, following the Unilateral Declaration of Independence of Catalonia, the President of the European Council, Donald Tusk,[172] declared that Spain would be the European Union's only interlocutor.[173]

The European Union's attitude can be explained not only based on its commitment to the territorial integrity of the member states, but also because those movements may trigger a 'more complex reconfiguration of Europe' leading to a cascade of new states.[174]

The European Union's veiled anti-secession position does not resemble that maintained towards other secessionist movements outside the organization. In

[168] Walker (2014), pp. 16–25.

[169] Euroactive (2014). https://www.euractiv.com/section/uk-europe/video/eu-says-scotland-s-no-vote-good-for-united-and-stronger-europe/

[170] Walker (2014), p. 17.

[171] Crawford and Boyle (2013), p. 103; Walker (2014), p. 16.

[172] Declaració dels Representants de Catalunya. 10 October 2017. https://static1.ara.cat/ara/public/content/file/original/2017/1010/20/declaracio-d-independe-ncia-signada-per-jxs-i-la-cup-0a28a46.pdf

[173] Almqvist (2019), p. 137. On the other hand, when the European Commission was asked by a member of the European Parliament about the position of the Commission regarding the declaration, Juncker answered that 'It is not for the Commission to express a position on questions of internal organisation related to the constitutional arrangements of a particular Member State'. Parliamentary questions. Question for written answer E-011776-15 to the Commission. https://www.europarl.europa.eu/doceo/document/E-8-2015-011776_EN.html

[174] Sedda (2021), p. 138.

these cases, the EU's position has been called 'pragmatic approach',[175] understood as a position based on the maintenance of peace and security.

In the case of Kosovo, the European Union did not adopt any official position, each member state deciding unilaterally the path to follow regarding the recognition of the state, given the different opinions among them. In this respect, today, only five member states have failed to recognise Kosovo: Spain, Romania, Slovakia, Greece, and Cyprus. In addition, in the Kosovo case, a number of European Union member states intervened in the written statements before the International Court of Justice, endorsing the doctrine of remedial secession.[176]

On the contrary, in the case of the dissolution of the Soviet Union and the dismemberment of Yugoslavia, the member states of European Community embarked at the time on the recognition of new states. This policy has been categorised for example as premature recognition in the cases of Bosnia,[177] Slovenia and Croatia.[178] The European Communities decided that it was time to focus on values, considering that the recognition of those new states would bring stability, and 'Guidelines on the Recognition of New States in Eastern Europe and in the Soviet Union' were adopted for this purpose in 1991. While referring to the principle of self-determination, the Guidelines establish the requirements for states to be recognised,[179] none of them constituting the legal requirements accepted for statehood.[180] According to McWhinney, the most interesting innovation was to create a bridge between the declaratory theory of recognition and a value-oriented test of recognition linked to constitutive theory.[181]

In the case of Yugoslavia, the European Communities also opted to recognise the new states based on the Badinter Commission report. According to this report, the new republics were based on the disintegration or breaking-up of Yugoslavia, the case therefore not being one of secession.[182] According to the Commission,

---

[175] Almqvist (2019), p. 137.

[176] Del Mar (2013), pp. 82–83.

[177] Almqvist (2019), p. 133.

[178] McWhinney (2002), p. 204.

[179] 'Respect for the provisions of the Charter of the United Nations and the commitments subscribed to in the Final Act of Helsinki and in the Charter of Paris, especially with regard to the rule of law, democracy and human rights. Guarantees for the rights of ethnic and national groups and minorities in accordance with the commitments subscribed to in the framework of the CSCE. Respect for the inviolability of all frontiers which can only be changed by peaceful means and by common agreement. Acceptance of all relevant commitments with regard to disarmament and nuclear non-proliferation as well as to security and regional stability. Commitment to settle by agreement, including where appropriate by recourse to arbitration, all questions concerning State succession and regional disputes'. Declaration on 'Guidelines on the Recognition of New States in Eastern Europe and in the Soviet Union'. Extraordinary EPC Ministerial Meeting. Brussels, 16 December 1991.

[180] Convention on Rights and Duties of States adopted by the Seventh International Conference of American States. Montevideo, 26 December 1933.

[181] McWhinney (2002), p. 209.

[182] Arbitration Commission, Conference on Yugoslavia, Opinion No 1, 20 November 1991.

Yugoslavia could no longer meet the criteria to be a federal state as it was undergoing dissolution.[183]

4.3.2 *A Membership for Secessionist Territories?*

One of the most controversial issues regarding secessionist movements inside the European Union has been the EU membership of these potentially new states. In this regard, the analysis runs from automatic membership to the application of the membership procedure included in Article 49 TEU.

It was assumed that after the secession, the parent state would retain international legal personality and therefore European Union membership. Even though there is no regulation for this specific situation in international law and EU law, this has been the practice of other international organizations. In this regard, references have been made to Article 4 of the Vienna Convention on Succession of States in respect of Treaties,[184] which entails the application of the said Convention to the constitutive treaties of international organizations, but without specifying the requirements that the successor state needs to consider in order to remain a member of the organization.

When observing the practice of other international organizations, it seems necessary to refer to the United Nations, since this organization has faced this situation in different contexts. We can mention in this regard the cases of India and Pakistan in which the latter had to apply for membership,[185] and the cases of Malaysia and Singapore, in which the new state applied for membership to the United Nations.[186] The same process was followed by Montenegro after gaining independence from Serbia,[187] as well as by South Sudan, which was quickly admitted to the United

[183] Ibid.

[184] Walker (2014), p. 15.

[185] UN General Assembly, *Admission of Yemen and Pakistan to membership in the United Nations*. 30 September 1947, A/RES/108(II). In the case of Pakistan a legal opinion by the Assistant Secretary-General for Legal Affairs was approved of 8 August 1947, stating that: 'On this analysis, there is no change in the international status of India; it continues as a State with all the treaty rights and obligations, and consequently, with all the rights and obligations of membership in the United Nations. The territory which breaks off, Pakistan, will be a new State; it will not have the treaty rights and obligations of the old State, and it will not, of course, have membership in the United Nations'. A/CN.4/149 and Add.1 The Succession of States in relation to Membership in the United Nations—Memorandum prepared by the Secretariat. Yearbook of the International Law Commission:- 1962,vol. II.

[186] UN General Assembly, *Admission of Singapore to membership in the United Nations*. 21 September 1965, A/RES/2010(XX).

[187] UN General Assembly, *Admission of the Republic of Montenegro to membership in the United Nations*, 28 June 2006, A/RES/60/264,

Nations after acquiring independence from Sudan.[188] In all these cases, the parent states maintained their membership, applying the principle of state continuity according to which changes in the territory, population or constitutional structures do not affect the nature of the state.[189] In fact, the Sixth Committee established that a 'State that is a Member of the Organization of the United Nations does not cease to be a member simply because its constitution of its frontiers have been subject to changes'.[190]

Another element to consider when deciding on membership of the parent state is whether the state retained the majority of the territory, institutions and government, and therefore embodies the continuator state and retains membership.[191]

In the case of the European Union, since there is no specific regulation in the treaties, these would be the solutions applicable to Spain and Catalonia, the United Kingdom and Scotland, or to any other possible cases of secession, for example that of Corsica from France.[192] The case of Belgium and Flanders has been regarded as a singular issue, since they have two different communities, with separate languages, religion, institutions, and even political parties.[193] In addition, Flanders would retain most of the territory, population and economic resources,[194] which would make it difficult for Wallonia to be considered the continuator state and to keep its membership. Given this situation, a 'velvet divorce' has been considered to be the most appropriate solution,[195] which was also the one adopted in the case of Czechoslovakia when it was split into two new states.

Finally, keeping the membership would also entail changes in the treaties, since the parent states would see its population, territory or income reduced, thus affecting membership conditions,[196] e.g., the number of seats at the European Parliament.

However, the most controversial issue has been the new state's membership, since as mentioned previously, the two stronger independent movements have been characterised by a pro-European position, even using Europeanism as an element of differentiation with respect to a Eurosceptic United Kingdom in the case of Scotland.

---

[188] UN General Assembly, *Admission of the Republic of South Sudan to membership in the United Nations*, 14 July 2011, A/RES/65/308

[189] Epiney and Egbuna-Joss (2015), p. 83.

[190] First Committee: admission of new Members: letter, dated 47/10/08, addressed to the Chairman of the first Committee / from the Chairman of the sixth Committee. A/C.1/212. https://digitallibrary.un.org/record/697903?ln=es

[191] Walker (2014), pp. 15–16.

[192] In these case it seems that the Corsican have opted for demanding more autonomy instead of secession, but still a division inside the movement between these two options. See Delanty (2022), p. 103.

[193] See Connolly (2013), pp. 62–66.

[194] Walker (2014) p. 24.

[195] Ibid., p. 24; Connolly (2013), p. 90.

[196] Crawford and Boyle (2013), p. 100.

A new state's automatic membership of an international organisation was rejected by the International Law Commission when drafting the Vienna Convention on Succession of States, affirming that:

> practice appears now to have established the principle that a new State is not entitled automatically to become a party to the constituent treaty and a member of the organization as a successor State, simply by reason of the fact that at the date of the succession its territory was subject to the treaty and within the ambit of the organization.[197]

This was also the opinion expressed by former Presidents of the Commission when asked about the membership of the potential new states in the context of the Scotland and Catalonia referendum, affirming that they should apply for membership. In 2012, President Barroso declared in a letter to Lord Tugendhat that 'a new independent state would, by the fact of its independence, become a third country with respect to the EU and the Treaties would no longer apply on its territory',[198] adding a reference to Article 49 TEU. This was the same position that Prodi had adopted 10 years earlier.[199] Later, in 2014, Barroso went further, affirming that accession would be 'extremely difficult if not impossible'.[200] Juncker qualified this declaration some months later and opened the door to a special treatment for Scotland since it already met the 'core-EU requirements'.[201] In the same line, in 2013, when asked about the pro-independence protests in Catalonia, the European Commission's spokesperson stated that 'an independent state, because of its independence, would become a third country *vis a vis* the EU and as of the day of the independence the EU treaties will no longer apply'.[202]

Therefore, automatic membership has been dismissed in international practice as well as by European Union institution representatives. According to Epiney,[203] this practice can be explained by the fact that, to be a member of an international organization it is necessary to comply with a number of requirements that cannot be verified in cases of automatic membership. In addition, automatic membership would entail the imposition of a new member to the other members of the organization.

As a result, new states should apply for membership as regulated in Article 49 TEU. Nevertheless, Scotland also referred to the application of Article 48 TEU

197 Draft articles on Succession of States in respect of Treaties with commentaries 1974. Yearbook of the International Law Commission, 1974, vol. II, Part One.

198 Letter from José Manuel Barroso, President of the European Commission, to Lord Lord Tugendhat (SC/12–13/EA68). https://www.parliament.uk/globalassets/documents/lords-committees/economic-affairs/ScottishIndependence/EA68_Scotland_and_the_EU_Barrosos_reply_to_Lord_Tugendhat_101212.pdf

199 Crawford and Boyle (2013), p. 103.

200 BBC (2014). https://www.bbc.com/news/uk-scotland-scotland-politics-26215963

201 Connolly (2013), pp. 16–17.

202 Euractive (2013). https://www.euractiv.com/section/eu-elections-2014/video/brussels-says-an-independent-catalonia-would-need-to-leave-eu/

203 Epiney and Egbuna-Joss (2015), p. 89.

instead of Article 49 TEU, which would imply amending the treaties to adapt them to the new state membership. This system would avoid the Article 49 TEU process but would not solve the main problem that these new states may encounter when applying for membership: the requirement of unanimity.

Despite the Scottish proposal, it is widely accepted that the process to be followed will be that of Article 49 TEU, and in this regard, Article 50 TEU has been used as a legal basis. Indeed, paragraph 5 establishes that if the state that has withdrawn from the European Union wishes to re-join, it shall follow the procedure set out in Article 49 TEU. Therefore, if a former state that seeks to re-join the European Union must be subjected to this procedure, so should a former region of a European Union state that wishes to re-join as a state. Nevertheless, Crawford and Boyle left the door open to a variation in the accession process provided it has been negotiated. In this case, it is necessary to remember that it will also be necessary to amend the treaties.[204] For example, Article 52 TEU among many others will need to be amended, as it includes the list of member states.

Finally, regarding the amendment of the treaties and the accession process, as Barroso clearly and polemically stated, both of them would require obtaining unanimity among the member states, Spain's agreement being especially difficult to obtain. Barroso referred to Spain regarding the non-recognition of Kosovo and concluded that the state would maintain the same approach to Scotland or any new state arising from secession,[205] advancing in this way the position of a member state on such a sensitive issue.[206]

To conclude, the European Union has maintained a pragmatic approach to secessionist movements. It recognises these new states emerging out of the European Union on different grounds, but is reluctant to give any chance of success or encourage secessionist movements within the European Union. This approach may be based on the idea that secessionist movements could threaten the region's integration policy and stability.

References

Almqvist J (2019) EU and the recognition of states. In: Jordana J, Keating M, Marx A, Wouters J (eds) Changing borders in Europe: exploring the dynamics of integration, differentiation, and self-determination in the European Union. Routledge, New York

BBC (2014) Scottish independence: Barroso says joining EU would be 'difficult'

Benchikh M (2007) La confiscation du droit des peuples à l'autodétermination interne. In: Droit du pouvoir, pouvoir du droit. Mélanges offerts à Jean Salmon. Bruylant, Bruxelles

[204] Crawford and Boyle (2013), p. 101.

[205] BBC (2014). https://www.bbc.com/news/uk-scotland-scotland-politics-26215963

[206] In this regard, Spain removed its consul in Edinburg for saying that an independent Scotland would be member of the European Union. De Miguel (2019). https://elpais.com/internacional/2019/06/08/actualidad/1559989319_702022.html

Brownlie I (1985) The rights of peoples in modern International Law. Bull Aust Soc Legal Philos 104:108
Cardona Llorens J (2007) Le principe du droit des peuples à disposer d'eux-mêmes et l'occupation Étrangère. In: Droit du pouvoir, pouvoir du droit. Mélanges offerts à Jean Salmon. Bruylant, Bruxelles
Cassese A (1995) Self-determination of Peoples. Cambridge University Press, Cambridge
Cassese A (2005) International Law. Oxford University Press, Oxford
Charlesworth H (2015) Democracy and International Law. In: Recueil des Cours. Collected courses of the Hague Academy of International Law, vol 371
Charlesworth H (2017) International legal encounters with democracy. Global Pol 8(1):34
Christakis T (2011) The ICJ Advisory Opinion on Kosovo: has International Law something to say about secession? Leiden J Int Law 24(1):73
Connolly CK (2013) Independence in Europe: secession, sovereignty, and the European Union. Duke J Comp Int Law 51:52
Craven M, Parfitt R (2018) Statehood self-determination, and recognition. In: Evans M (ed) International Law. Oxford University Press, Oxford
Crawford JR (2007) The creation of states in International Law. Oxford University Press, Oxford
Crawford J, Boyle A (2013) Annex A opinion: referendum on the independence of Scotland – International Law aspects. Scotland Analysis: Devolution and the Implications of Scottish Independence, UK Government
d'Aspremont J (2011) The rise and fall of democracy governance in International Law: a replay to Susan marks. Eur J Int Law 22(2):549
De Miguel R (2019) Exteriores destituye al cónsul en Edimburgo por decir que una Escocia independiente entraría en la UE. El País
Del Mar K (2013) The myth of remedial secession. In: French D (ed) Statehood and self-determination: reconciling tradition and modernity in International Law. Cambridge University Press, Cambridge
Delanty G (2022) What does self-determination mean today? The resurgence of nationalism and European integration in question. In: Foster R, Grzymski J (eds) The limits of Europe. Identities, spaces, values. Cambridge University Press, Cambridge
Devia Garzón DA (2016) Problemáticas de autodeterminación en Timor Oriental y Sahara Occidental: los contextos que propiciaron la intervención internacional. Estudios Internacionales 184:77
Dugard J (2013) The secession of states and their recognition in the wake of Kosovo. In: Recueil des Cours. Collected courses of the Hague Academy of International Law, vol 357
Eljechtimi A, Lawson H (2021) Morocco recalls its ambassador to Berlin over Western Sahara. Reuters
Epiney A, Egbuna-Joss A (2015) Separatist demands in EU member states: selected legal problems. In: Belser EM, Fang-Bär A, Massüger N, Oleschak Pillai RO (eds) States falling apart?. Secessionist and autonomy movements in Europe. Staempfli, Bern
Euractive (2013) Brussels says an independent Catalonia would need to leave EU
Euroactive (2014) EU says Scotland's NO vote good for "united and stronger" Europe
Farsakh L (2021) Introduction: the struggle for self-determination and the Palestinian Quest for Statehood. In: Farsakh L (ed) Rethinking statehood in Palestine. Self-determination and decolonization beyond partition. University of California Press, Oakland
Federal Foreign Office (2022) German-Moroccan Joint Declaration, 25.08.2022
Franck TM (1992) The emerging right to democratic governance. Am J Int Law 86(1):46
González M (2022) La carta de Pedro Sánchez a Mohamed VI: "Debemos construir una nueva relación que evite futuras crisis". El País
Higgins R (1991) International Law and the avoidance, containment and resolution of disputes. In: Recueil des Cours. Collected courses of the Hague Academy of International Law, vol 230
Hilpold P (2022) 'Humanizing' the Law of self-determination –the Chagos Island case. Nordic J Int Law 91:204

Hofbauer Jane A (2016) Sovereignty in the exercise of the right to self-determination. Brill, Leiden
Imseis A (2020) Negotiating the illegal: on the United Nations and the illegal occupation of Palestine, 1967–2020. Eur J Int Law 31(3):1071
Ingimundarson V (2022) The 'Kosovo Precedent': Russia's justification of military interventions and territorial revisions in Georgia and Ukraine. Strategic Update, LSE Ideas
Johnson D (1973) Toward self-determination - a reappraisal as reflected in the declaration of friendly relations. GA J Int Comp Law 3(1):161–162
Kohen M (2007) Sur quelques vicissitudes du droit des peuples à disposer d'eux-mêmes. In: Droit du pouvoir, pouvoir du droit. Mélanges offerts à Jean Salmon. Bruylant, Bruxelles
Kohen M (2020) Self-Determination. In: Viñuales J (ed) The UN Friendly Relations Declaration at 50: an assessment of the fundamental principles of International Law. Cambridge University Press, Cambridge
López Jurado C (2013) La secesión de territorios no coloniales y el soberanismo catalán. Revista Electrónica de Estudios Internacionales 26:18
Maccorquodale R (1994) Self-determination: a human rights approach. Int Comp Law Q 43(4):532
Marks S (2011) What has become of the emerging right to democratic governance? Eur J Int Law 22(2):507
McWhinney (2002) Self-determination of peoples and plural-ethnic states secession and state succession and the alternative, Federal option. In: Recueil des Cours. Collected courses of the Hague Academy of International Law, vol 294
Ministry for Europe and Foreign Affairs (2022) France Diplomacy. Western Sahara Q&A
Orakhelashvili A (2006) Legal consequences of the construction of a wall in the occupied Palestinian Territory: opinion and reaction. J Conflict Sec Law 11(1):119
Raic D (2002) Statehood and the law of self-determination. Brill, Leiden
Saul B (2015) The status of Western Sahara as occupied territory under international humanitarian law and the exploitation of natural resources. Glob Change Peace Sec 27(3):305
Schimmelfenning F (2019) Differentiation and self-determination in European integration. In: Jordana J, Keating M, Marx A, Wouters J (eds) Changing borders in Europe: exploring the dynamics of integration, differentiation, and self-determination in the European Union. Routledge, New York
Scobbie I (2006) Unchart(er)ed waters?: consequences of the advisory opinion on the legal consequences of the construction of a wall in the occupied Palestinian territory for the responsibility of the UN for Palestine. Eur J Int Law 16(5):946
Sedda F (2021) National self-determination and the limits of Europe. In: Mangiapane F, Migliore T (eds) Images of Europe. Law and visual jurisprudence. Springer, Cham
Soroeta J (2016) The conflict in Western Sahara after forty years of occupation: International Law versus Realpolitikpp. Ger Yearb Int Law 59:187–191
Sparks T (2023) Self-determination in the International Legal System. In: Whose claim, to what right? Hart Publishing, London
Tancredi A (2009) A normative 'due process' in the creation of states through secession. In: Kohen M (ed) Secession: International Law perspectives. Cambridge University Press, Cambridge
The White House (2020) Proclamation on recognizing the sovereignty of the Kingdom of Morocco over the Western Sahara
Theofilopoulou A (2006) The United Nations and Western Sahara. A never-ending affair. Special Report 166. United States Institute for Peace
Thornberry P (1994) The principle of self-determination. In: Lowe V, Warbrick C (eds) The United Nations and the principles of International Law: essays in memory of Michael Akehurst. Routledge, London, New York
Walker N (2014) Beyond secession? Law in the framing of the national polity. Edinburgh School of Law Research Paper Series. Research Paper Series No 2014/51
Weiner JB (1979) The Green March in historical perspective. Middle East J 33(1):20–33
Weller M (2009) Escaping the self-determination trap. Brill, Leiden

Chapter 5
An 'Optional' Principle of Non-Intervention?

In 1793, the French Constitution proclaimed that the French Republic '*ne s'immisce point dans le gouvernement des autres nations; il ne souffre pas que les autres nations s'immiscent dans le sien*'.[1] Yet at that very time, France had already initiated a practice of intervention to support those peoples with the intent of overthrowing the monarchy.[2] This can summarise state practices throughout the centuries regarding the principle of non-intervention. As Potter stated many years later in 1930, '*des hommes d'Etat français, britanniques, américains et autres ont défini l'intervention et l'ont tour à tour approuvée ou condamnée, selon les besoins de la politique du moment, d'une façon quelque peu cynique et changeante*'.[3]

The principle of non-intervention is an old principle in international law, as demonstrated by the proclamation of the French Constitution. However, this principle is, actually, even older since it reflects the Grotian model[4] and Westphalian system[5] based on state prerogatives and independence—which have contributed to a particular state practice.

Observing the history of this principle, a new official proclamation can be found in the nineteenth century with the Monroe Doctrine. This doctrine had similar results to that of the French Constitution: on the one hand, it asserted the non-intervention of the European powers in the affairs of the American states, and on the other, the United States later initiated a sort of hegemony on the American continent.[6] In this regard, it is not possible to affirm the existence of a common practice of the principle

[1] Constitution du 24 juin 1793. https://www.conseil-constitutionnel.fr/les-constitutions-dans-l-histoire/constitution-du-24-juin-1793

[2] Grewe (2000), p. 419.

[3] Potter (1930), p. 613.

[4] Cassese (2005), p. 56.

[5] Jamnejad and Woods (2009), p. 349; Wright (1960), p. 536.

[6] Ouchakov made reference to the opinions of Martens and Oppeheim on this issue. See Ouchakov (1974), p. 9.

G. Fernández Arribas, *Contemporary Challenges to the Fundamental Principles of International Law and EU Interaction*, European Union and its Neighbours in a Globalized World 19, https://doi.org/10.1007/978-3-031-75453-1_5

of non-intervention in the nineteenth century. Indeed, states engaged in two different practices at the same time: a practice relating to the principle of non-intervention in certain domains and a practice relating to the right to intervene in others. Examples of the latter include those based on contractual titles, self-help, or humanitarian interventions.[7]

The principle of non-intervention underwent its greatest shift in the twentieth century with the adoption of the United Nations Charter, but the situation continues to be highly uncertain. In this regard, state practice has been to justify interventions—even those involving the use of force—while making great efforts to establish exceptions,[8] and affirming at the same time the existence of the principle of non-intervention, honouring it by its recognition in international treaties. The scenario has led to a schizophrenic practice: states and scholars recognise the fundamental and compulsory nature of the principle but consider its violation necessary in some cases,[9] setting aside any legal grounds and affecting the coherence of international law.[10]

This situation shows a gap between the broad concept of the principle of non-intervention and state practice.[11] It could lead one to believe that the principle is of minor importance in the international system, or even that the principle is 'dead and buried'.[12] However, its main role in the maintenance of peaceful coexistence[13] could suggest rather that it constitutes a fundamental principle of international law, not only in 1970 with the adoption of the General Assembly Resolution 2625 (XXV), but also in the twenty-first century.

5.1 The 'Nebulous' Concept of Intervention

These erratic state practices regarding this principle also result from the fact that international society has turned over time into an international community. In this regard, Westphalian society based on the sovereign and absolute independence of states has gradually shifted towards a community system that aims to accomplish common goals. In this community, international law is regulating an increasing number of domains, having a special impact on human rights,[14] and broadening the role of international organisations. In this new community, the states face a dilemma between their old and well-internalised concept of independence, and the

[7] Grewe (2000), pp. 489–490.

[8] Ibid, p. 654; Ouchakov (1974), p. 12.

[9] Cassese (1999), pp. 792–796. The main example is the doctrine of humanitarian intervention.

[10] Roberts (2009), p. 179.

[11] Jamnejad and Woods (2009), p. 353.

[12] Kohen analyses those statements. See Kohen (2012), p. 158.

[13] Ouchakov (1974), p. 73; Wright (1960), p. 527.

[14] Cassese (2005), p. 54; Tomuschat (1999), p. 237.

need to limit their prerogatives to achieve shared interests, including the intervention of a third party.

Nevertheless, added to the underlying reasons for erratic state practices mentioned above is the ambiguous and 'elastic'[15] definition of the concept of non-intervention or, as Wright defined it, 'a nebulous area of action'.[16] A first common approach to the concept of non-intervention after and before Resolution 2625 (XXV) corresponds to the first reference to the principle of non-intervention in the said Resolution: 'No State or group of States has the right to intervene directly or indirectly, for any reason whatever, in the internal or external affairs of any other State'. However, one of the most cited definitions of the principle by scholars is that of Oppenheim at the beginning of the twentieth century: 'intervention is a dictatorial interference by a State in the affairs of another State for the purpose of maintaining or altering the actual conditions of things'.[17] In any event, though the definition helps to clarify the concept, it is not precise enough, leaving the door open to many interpretations. For example, What does 'dictatorial' mean exactly, and what are the 'affairs of another state'? Even though these topics were later studied and developed, it is not possible today to find an accurate definition of the principle that allows to clearly identify the cases of intervention, and the reason may lie in the nature of the principle.

In addition, due to its lack of express reference and definition in the United Nations Charter, the principle of non-intervention differs, for example, from that of the non-use of force. Therefore, it is necessary to infer it from different articles. Thus, the principle of non-intervention can be inferred from the following elements: Article 1.2 that refers to the equality among nations; the principle of sovereignty included in Article 2.1; and the prohibition of the use of force included in Article 2.4.[18] All these references can also serve to shape the principle of non-intervention. In the same vein, some scholars have also considered Article 2.7, which establishes the principle of non-intervention by the United Nations as a provision applicable to states. In this regard, it would be nonsensical to forbid an intervention by the United Nations and not to apply that same prohibition to its member states,[19] or to allow states to do what the Organization is forbidden to do.[20] However, this opinion is still a minority one.[21] In any case, despite the express reference in Article 2.7, the Charter does not offer any definition that helps to identify and qualify state actions.

This lack of express reference to the principle of non-intervention in the Charter has not prevented the General Assembly from adopting a large number of resolutions

[15] Buchan and Tsagourias (2017), p. 173.

[16] Jiménez de Aréchaga (1978), p. 114, footnote 201.

[17] Opemheim (1905), p. 341.

[18] Damrosch (1989), pp. 7–8; Jiménez de Aréchaga (1978), p. 112; Kunig (2008), p. 3.

[19] Ouchakov (1974), p. 37.

[20] Jiménez de Aréchaga (1978), p. 112.

[21] Tomuschat (1999), p. 232; Kunig (2008), p. 3; Damrosch (1989), p. 7.

on the principle.[22] These resolutions, together with the international treaties that proclaim the principle[23] and state practice have led to establishing the existence of a customary principle of non-intervention, recognised by the ICJ in the *Nicaragua* case[24] and confirmed in the *Armed Activities* case.[25] In *Nicaragua,* the Court referred to two essential General Assembly resolutions: Resolution 2131 (XX)[26] and 2625 (XXV), the former a political declaration and the latter a reflection of international law.[27] But again, the definition given by Resolution 2625 (XXV), which has a legal nature, has not been considered appropriate to identify the precise content of the principle: Jiménez de Aréchaga[28] upheld that it was too broad, and Tomuschat and Damrosch[29] stated that it was not clear.

The drawbacks of this definition owe perhaps to initial drafting difficulties, as Western European states and the United States were in confrontation with Soviet states[30] and non-aligned countries.[31] This face-off continued for years and reached a decisive point in 1981 when the General Assembly adopted the Declaration on the Inadmissibility of Intervention and Interference in the Internal Affairs of States,[32] which was passed against the will of many (mostly Western) states[33] due to the 'broad range of acts'[34] that constituted an interference in internal affairs.

These different positions regarding the content of the principle of non-intervention reveal the existence of different blocks in the international community that still alive today. In this regard, despite possible common principles and ends suggesting the existence of a community, this community still presents features that also characterise international society: heterogeneity and fragmentation.

---

[22] According to Jamnejad and Woods there are more than 35 resolutions that make reference to the principle of non-intervention. Mainly Resolutions 36/103 (1981), Resolution 21/31 XX (1965) and 2625 (xxv). Jamnejad and Woods (2009), p. 350.

[23] Jamnejad and Woods (2009). pp. 362–367.

[24] ICJ, *Military and Paramilitary Activities in and against Nicaragua* (Nicaragua v. United States of America), Judgment of 27 June 1986: I.C.J. Reports 1986, para 209.

[25] ICJ, *Armed Activities on the Territory of the Congo* (Democratic Republic of the Congo v. Uganda), Judgment of 19 December 2005: I.C.J. Reports 2005, para 162.

[26] UN General Assembly, D*eclaration on the Inadmissibility of Intervention and Interference in the Internal Affairs of States*, 9 December 1981, A/RES/36/103.

[27] Jamnejad and Woods (2009), p. 353.

[28] Jiménez de Aréchaga (1978), p. 115.

[29] Tomuschat (1999), p. 231; Damrosch (1989), p. 8.

[30] Russia was favor of a broad concept of non-intervention in order to defend its system and its influence over the soviet states. See Rosenstock (1971).

[31] Ibidem.

[32] UN General Assembly, A/RES/36/103.

[33] See Tomuschat (1999), p. 237; Rosenstock (1971), p. 727; Kunig (2008), p. 5; Nasu (2013), p. 30; On the contrary Ouchakov, defending the soviet thesis, considers that the Resolution represents a universal legal opinion. Ouchakov (1974), p. 71.

[34] Nasu (2013), p. 30.

Given the fact that the definitions of the General Assembly resolutions are insufficient to clearly determine the content of the principle of non-intervention, scholars have considered the International Court of Justice's definition in the *Nicaragua* case as highly authoritative, establishing the decisive elements of any act of intervention. In any case, the Court took the General Assembly resolutions into consideration to develop the content of the principle. According to the Court:

> the principle forbids all States or groups of States to intervene directly or indirectly in internal or external affairs of other States. A prohibited intervention must accordingly be one bearing on matters in which each State is permitted, by the principle of State sovereignty to decide freely. One of these is the choice of a political, economic, social and cultural system, and the formulation of foreign policy. Intervention is wrongful when it uses methods of coercion in regard to such choices, which must remain free ones. The element of coercion, which defines, and indeed forms the very essence of, prohibited intervention, is particularly obvious in the case of an intervention which uses force, either in the direct form of military action, or in the indirect form of support for subversive or terrorist armed activities within another State.[35]

Coercion is, therefore, the element that can help to identify an intervention. This is clear in the case of the use of force but it can also have other manifestations—as set out in Resolution 2625 (XXV) in its reference to the use of economic, political or other measures to coerce a state. Nevertheless, does this definition really offer a clear and precise definition of the principle of non-intervention? One that clarifies which actions can be considered to constitute an intervention?

Examining Potter's (1930) elements of the principle of non-intervention, we can observe both a lack of accuracy and the presence of multiple options that are still present today. In other words, despite the large number of General Assembly resolutions and International Court of Justice judgements, elusive features of the principle of non-intervention dating back to 1930 still characterise the principle in the twenty-first century:

> L'intervention peut porter sur les affaires intérieures ou extérieures (. . .). Elle peut être le fait d'un ou plusieurs Etats à l'encontre d'un ou de plusieurs autres. Elle peut viser un Etat ou son territoire ou ses nationaux ou les biens (. . .) et comporter ou non le recours ou la menace de recourrir à la force militaire. Elle peut s'exercer par la guerre ou par toutes autres mesures (. . .) avec ou sans le consentement de l'Etat intéressé.[36]

However, even if the concept of coercion can help to identify acts of intervention, coercion can also be the object of various interpretations in cases other than those involving the use of force: What does economic coercion mean? What does political coercion mean?[37] In addition, the interpretation and content of what the Court calls 'matters in which each State is permitted (. . .) decide freely'—also named the '*domain reserve*'—may also vary depending on the epoch.[38] As the Permanent

---

[35] ICJ, *Military and Paramilitary Activities in and against Nicaragua*, para. 205.

[36] Potter (1930), p. 623.

[37] Cassese (2005), p. 55; Jiménez de Aréchaga (1978), p. 115, Tomuschat (1999), pp. 234–236; Jamnejad and Woods (2009), pp. 348 and 370; Buchan and Tsagourias (2017), p. 171.

[38] Kunig (2008), p. 1; Kohen (2012), p. 160; Ouchakov (1974), pp. 45–55.

Court of International Justice established in 1923, what constitutes domestic jurisdiction is a relative question that depends on the development of international relations.[39]

This fluctuating and uncertain content of the principle of non-intervention has led to maintaining the same controversial practice of exceptions throughout the centuries, producing the illusion of a principle that states decide to apply or respect according to their interests in any given situation. Today's humanitarian interventions and interventions by invitation have received a new impetus because of the rise of internal armed conflicts, proxy wars and the growing role of human rights. In addition, technological developments have led to new forms of interventions, i.e., cyber ones, which make it harder to identify acts of intervention as well as to attribute them. In the sections that follow, we will attempt to determine an evolution of the principle based on the concepts mentioned above. We shall also explore whether the established existence of an international community has led to limiting the number of exceptions made to the principle of non-intervention or has contributed to framing them.

5.2 How Human Rights Created a 'Right' to Intervene

The principle of non-intervention is understood as a shield: one that guarantees that vital and delicate domestic interests are not affected by international relations.[40] In other words, the principle of non-intervention is designed to preserve the sovereign will.[41] However, the growing role played by human rights, a major feature in the evolution of the international community, has weakened this shield. As Tomuschat stated, 'the international community is progressively moving from sovereignty-centred to a value-oriented or individual-oriented system'.[42] Therefore, in this section, we will attempt to elucidate whether human rights have eroded the principle of non-intervention—acknowledging, for example, the doctrine of humanitarian intervention—or, on the contrary, whether the international community has preserved the fundamental principle of non-intervention while simultaneously pursuing common solutions to gross human rights violations.

---

[39] PCIJ, *Nationality Decrees Issued in Tunis and Morocco*, Advisory Opinion, 1923 P.C.I.J. Series B-No. 4, p. 24. In 1949 the Institute of International Law asked its members if it was possible to identify in advance the domain reserve of the states. The majority of them considered that it was not possible, but Kaekenbeck also considered that its content was not only indeterminate but legally indeterminable. See Ouchakov (1974), p. 49. In the same line, Koskenniemi affirms that domestic jurisdiction has not inherent or natural content, which could be 'determinable only by taking a legal approach; by looking at present regulation and what areas it leaves open for States to regulate municipal law'. Koskenniemi (2005), p. 250.

[40] Cassese (2005), p. 54.

[41] Tomuschat (1999), p. 234; Jamnejad and Woods (2009), p. 371.

[42] Tomuschat (1999), p. 236.

5.2.1 The Background of Humanitarian Intervention

Humanitarian intervention can be regarded as one of the deepest forms of intervention. It became the focus of many international law analyses at the end of the 1990s and in the early 2000s due to the North Atlantic Treaty Organization (NATO) intervention in Kosovo,[43] even though NATO did not rely on humanitarian intervention as a legal justification.[44]

Humanitarian intervention has been used to justify foreign interventions for many centuries. Along with invitation, it is the main justification, continually used in state practice. Significant illustrations of this doctrine[45] can be found in the nineteenth century when states used it to intervene in order to protect the population. In most cases however, such interventions concealed other purposes, e.g., the intervention of the European powers in Greece or the United States intervention in Cuba.[46] It was also in the nineteenth century that scholars began to justify these interventions based on a mantra that would be repeated a century later: it is not legal, but it is legitimate.[47]

There are, however, earlier references to this practice. As early as in the sixteenth century, Vitoria stated:

> (T)he prince has the authority not only over his own people but also over foreigners to force them to abstain from harming others; this is his right by the law of nations and the authority of the whole world.[48]

The fact that humanitarian intervention has a long history does not alter most scholars' opinion that such a right of humanitarian intervention does not exist.[49] They do, however, leave the door open to other types of interventions that do not entail the use of force. At first sight, this position may contradict today's fresh human rights impetus and the international community's new purpose of guaranteeing their respect. Indeed, the international community is sometimes obliged to contemplate terrible massacres after having unsuccessfully resorted to all available legal methods of prevention. As Secretary General Kofi Annan stated:

---

[43] This has been the most cited intervention in the twentieth Century, but many others took place. India in Pakistan, Vietnam in Cambodia, Tanzania in Uganda, United Kingdom and United States in Iraq for safe haven corridors, ECOWAS IN Liberia and ECOWAS in Sierra Leone. See Henderson (2018), pp. 387–392.

[44] Ibid, p. 394.

[45] Grewe (2000), pp. 491–493.

[46] Ibid, p. 490.

[47] See Ibid, pp. 494–595; Roberts (2009); Cassese (1999).

[48] Pagden and Lawrance (1991), p. 305.

[49] Among others: Shaw (2017); Kohen (2012), p. 162; Kunig (2008), p. 9; Prandler (2008. Koskenniemi refers to cases in which the General Assembly has condemned interventions in Kampuchea, Nicaragua, Afghanistan and Greneda without referring to the justifications or motivations of the interveners. Koskenniemi (2005), p. 237.

> In the context of Rwanda: if in those dark days and hours leading up to the genocide a collation of states had been prepared to act in defence of the Tutsi population, but did not receive prompt Security Council authorization, should such a coalition have stood aside and allowed the horror to unfold?[50]

The humanitarian intervention doctrine is based on the use of force against a third state to prevent or to put an end to gross human rights violations.[51] This use of force is one of the main obstacles to establishing its legality. Indeed, the prohibition of the use of force is a *jus cogens* norm, and it would therefore be difficult to reconcile this doctrine with the said norm. In addition, in the *Nicaragua* case, the International Court of Justice affirmed that the use of force is an obvious violation of the principle of non-intervention.[52] Humanitarian intervention thus clearly entails, *prima facie*, the violation of the principle of non-intervention.

5.2.2 Legalising Intervention

Human rights have undoubtedly come to limit the domestic jurisdiction of the states[53] which, according to Tomuschat, has produced 'an incisive amputation *ratione materiae*'[54] of the principle of non-intervention. In this regard, during the third quarter of the century, a certain number of states were reluctant to acknowledge an international role in the protection of human rights, especially the URSS, Asian

---

[50] Address by Kofi Annan to the Fifty-fourth session of the UN General Assembly, 20 September 1999.

[51] In any case, to give an appearance of legality some requirements have been established, as for example a previous declaration by the Security Council of a breach of peace or threat to the peace. In the same line, the UK Foreign Secretary Robin Cook in a speech in 2000 stated that: 'a set of ideas to help the international community decide when it is right to act. First, any intervention is by definition a failure of prevention. Force should always be the last resort; second, the immediate responsibility for halting violence rests with the state in which it occurs; but, third, when faced with an overwhelming humanitarian catastrophe and a government that has demonstrated itself unwilling or unable to halt or prevent it, the international community should act; and finally, any use of force in this context should be collective, proportionate, likely to achieve its objective, and carried out in accordance with international law'. Diplomacy for Democracy. Robin Cook's full speech, part II. 28 January 2000. The Guardian. https://www.theguardian.com/politics/2000/jan/28/ethicalforeignpolicy.foreignpolicy

[52] ICJ, *Military and Paramilitary Activities in and against Nicaragua*, para. 205. On the difference between these two principles see Buchan and Tsagourias (2017), pp. 173–174.

[53] Remiro Brotons (1996), p. 29.

[54] Tomuschat (1999), p. 236.

states[55] and developing countries.[56] Nevertheless, it is widely admitted today not only that international human rights institutions have a role in their protection, but so does the international community as a whole. Therefore, since criticisms regarding human rights violations cannot be considered as an intervention in internal affairs, pressures to comply with human rights obligations that constitute acts of intervention are today widely accepted.[57] An example would be the European Union's recent sanctions against Russia or China.[58]

We can interpret this outcome in three different ways. The first would be to consider that human rights are no longer part of a state's domestic affairs,[59] and, therefore, states are not intervening in the internal affairs of another state when they decide to take on actions to protect human rights. The second option is to consider that an exception to the principle of non-intervention has been established: coercion to make a state comply with its human rights obligations is allowed. And the third option would be applying the circumstances precluding wrongfulness, though this latter case requires further analysis.

The principle of non-intervention is not a *jus cogens* norm,[60] so the circumstances precluding wrongfulness would be applicable, specifically distress and necessity.

According to the Articles on Responsibility of States for Internationally Wrongful Acts (ARSIWA),[61] distress is applicable if the author of the act has no other way 'of saving the author's life or the lives of other persons entrusted to the author's care'.[62] In this case, it requires considering that the lives of the nationals of the intervened state are entrusted to the person or persons taking the decision to intervene, that is, the high authorities of the foreign state. In this regard, in today's international

[55] Nasu (2013), pp. 33–44; Tomuschat (1999), p. 237. Recently ASEAN changed its statement on the situation in Myanmar after the coup d'état, in order to eliminate references to 'political prisoners'. Allard (2021), https://www.reuters.com/world/asia-pacific/asean-changed-myanmar-statement-release-political-detainees-sources-2021-04-25/; Strangio (2021), https://thediplomat.com/2021/04/assessing-the-outcome-of-aseans-special-meeting-on-myanmar/

[56] Jamnejad and Woods (2009), p. 37; In the Jakarta Conference in 1992, the Heads of State or government of the non-aligned countries recognized that 'No country, however, should use its power to dictate its concept of democracy and human rights or to impose conditionalities on others'. Tenth Summit Conference of Heads of State or Government of the Non-Aligned Movement, Jakarta, Indonesia, 1 6 September 1992. http://cns.miis.edu/nam/documents/Official_Document/10th_Summit_FD_Jakarta_Declaration_1992_Whole.pdf

[57] Jiménez de Aréchaga (1978), p. 114; Damrosch (1989), pp. 38, 42. In any case, Damrosch goes further trying to establish a link between democratic governments, the right of the people to choose freely and human rights, in order to justify interventions.

[58] Council Implementing Regulation (EU) 2021/478 of 22 March 2021 implementing Regulation (EU) 2020/1998 concerning restrictive measures against serious human rights violations and abuses, OJ L 99, 22.03.2021.

[59] Jiménez de Aréchaga (1978), p. 114.

[60] Jamnejad and Woods (2009), p. 380.

[61] UN General Assembly, *Responsibility of States for internationally wrongful acts: resolution*, 8 January 2008, A/RES/62/61.

[62] Article 24. Ibid.

community, the emergence of *erga omnes* norms, among which human rights are included, entails the existence of norms that concern all states, all of them having a legal interest in their protection.[63] However, the fiction of entrusting the life of nationals to foreign authorities would go much further than the real purpose of distress. Therefore, it would be difficult to use distress to legally justify intervention in third states to protect human rights.

For its part, according to Article 25.1 ARSIWA, necessity can only be invoked when it 'is the only way for the state to safeguard an essential interest against a grave and imminent peril'. In this case, we should consider that the protection of human rights and the prevention of international crimes constitute essential interests of the states and international community. Indeed, as established in the ARSIWA commentaries: 'Unlike distress (Article 24), necessity consists not in danger to the lives of individuals in the charge of a State official but in a grave danger either to the essential interests of the State or of the international community as a whole'.[64] Nevertheless, to invoke necessity, the effects of the actions taken—in this case, the effects of the intervention—must be balanced against the intervened state's interests at stake. In other words, the protection of human rights must be balanced in regard to the consequences of the violation of the principle of non-intervention and the acts of coercion exercised by a state or organisation. However, can we apply the same solution in the case of humanitarian intervention and use of force?

When analysing humanitarian intervention, we cannot overlook how the intervention is conducted, i.e., by means of the use of force: the most extreme form of intervention which should probably be considered as a qualified form of intervention. When applying necessity, we need to consider the consequences of that intervention regarding the interests and rights of the intervened state. In this regard, the ICJ established in the *Nicaragua* judgement that:

> the use of force could not be the appropriate method to monitor and ensure such respect (human rights) (. . .) the protection of human rights, a strictly humanitarian objective, cannot be compatible with the mining of ports, the destruction of oil installations, or again with the training, arming and equipping of the *contras*.[65]

In the case of humanitarian intervention, we must recognise that the violation of state sovereignty, the bombing of a state's territory, the partial occupation of the country, the consequences of armed intervention on the population, or the loss of lives, which could be included as the consequences of a humanitarian intervention, would clearly affect the states' essential interests. Consequently, it seems difficult to balance the mentioned consequences of intervention with the equally terrible consequences of the gross and grave violation of human rights, e.g., genocide. It is thus necessary to tilt the scales on one side, not only from a legal perspective but also from a moral

---

[63] ICJ, *Barcelona Traction, Light and Power Company, Limited*, (Baelgium v. Spain), Judgment of 5 February 1970: I.CJ. Reports, 1970, para. 33.

[64] Draft articles on Responsibility of States for Internationally Wrongful Acts, with commentaries 2001, Yearbook of the International Law Commission, 2001, vol. II, Part Two, p. 80

[65] ICJ, *Military and Paramilitary Activities in and against Nicaragua*, para. 268.

viewpoint. In this regard, it has been stated that the use of armed force in the service of assistance sometimes produces effects that are at least as regrettable as those caused by the situation it seeks to resolve because of its disproportionality and lack of opportunity.[66]

Therefore, based on Article 25.1 ARSIWA, an intervention to protect human rights could be considered legal when it does not entail the use of force. In this case, the 'values take precedence over the rule of non-intervention'.[67] This position has also been confirmed by the Institute of International Law, which stated that measures taken by the states towards another state due to the violation of Article 1 of the Charter cannot be considered unlawful interference provided they do not entail the use of force.[68]

However, in the case of humanitarian intervention, this not only raises the question of the violation of the principle of non-intervention but also of the violation of the prohibition of the use of force. Such a situation has led to justifying humanitarian intervention based on the legitimacy and pursuit of alternative options that may allow intervention, using force, to guarantee the respect for human rights.[69] The latter indeed remains a hallmark of the international community.

The latest solution put forward in the twenty-first century is the concept of Responsibility to Protect, coined by the United Nations in the 2005 UN World Summit outcome document.[70] According to this document, every state has the primary responsibility to protect its population from genocide, war crimes, ethnic cleansing, and crimes against humanity, but it also entrusts this responsibility to the international community through the United Nations, entailing collective actions. This protection can be exercised through peaceful means, but when those measures are considered insufficient, they can also be implemented through actions according to Chapter VII of the United Nations Charter.

This concept of Responsibility to Protect should also be analysed in the context of Article 2.7 of the Charter which forbids the organisation to intervene in other states' internal affairs.[71] In this regard, the same arguments applying to a state intervention could also apply to the United Nations. Therefore, we can consider that since human rights are no longer an internal affair of the states, the United Nations can adopt those

---

[66] Remiro Brotons (1996), p. 31.

[67] Tomuschat (1999), p. 238. See also Damrosch (1989), p. 42.

[68] IDI 1989 Resolution 'The protection of human rights and the principle of non-intervention in the internal affairs of the states', p. 2, Article 2.

[69] The Constitutive Act of the African Union has been considered an example of international treaty allowing humanitarian intervention, therefore giving some kind of legal support to this doctrine, since its article 4 establishes "the right of the Union to intervene in a Member State pursuant to a decision of the Assembly in respect of grave circumstances, namely: war crimes, genocide and crimes against humanity". In any case, it has also been argued that humanitarian intervention based on this article and using force equally represents a violation of international law if not authorised by the Security Council. Kleczkowska (2020), p. 16.

[70] UN General Assembly, 2005 World Summit Outcome: Resolution, 24 October 2005, A/RES/60/1.

[71] See Watson (1997); Gilmour (1967).

measures without violating Article 2.7. Regarding the application of necessity, and according to the Draft Articles on the Responsibility of International Organizations (DARIO), this requires that the organisation have the 'function to protect the interest in question',[72] which does not pose any problem in the case of the United Nations. Article 1.3 of the Charter sets out that one of the purposes of the United Nations is to promote and encourage the respect for human rights. Together with the organisation's practice and the large number of resolutions adopted by the different institutions—mainly the General Assembly[73]—the protection of human rights is visibly one of the organisation's main functions. This system, therefore, would not breach the non-intervention principle, nor the prohibition of the use of force, because the Security Council's authorisation is required to intervene.[74]

The Responsibility to Protect was first tested in the Libyan conflict in which the Security Council affirmed that the Libyan authorities had the responsibility of protecting their population and adopted Resolution 1973 (2011).[75] This Resolution referred to the gross violation of human rights committed by the parties in the conflict and authorised the use of force to protect the population.[76] The intervention was carried out by NATO and has been the object of much criticism, especially from China, Germany, and Russia,[77] since the outcome was a change of government following the support given to the rebels. This intervention also raised the issue of an *ultra vires* action since it went beyond the protection of the civilian population.[78] Later, the United Kingdom and Denmark[79] attempted to base a decision to intervene in Syria on the Responsibility to Protect. However, following the damaging intervention in Libya, this option was rejected by the Security Council. Eight draft resolutions to intervene in Syria were vetoed, most of them because of Libya's shadow.[80] In addition, a feeling of mistrust has taken hold among BRICS regarding the Responsibility to Protect considering: "(1) suspicions about the West's real motives behind R2P advocacy and (2) their perceptions of the West's attack on postcolonial states and thus destabilize states in the Global South in the name of R2P".[81] Therefore, there seem to be few signs that this system will be used in the future.

---

72 Report of the International Law Commission, Draft Articles on the Responsibility of International Organizations, Doc. A/66/10 (2011). Article 25. 1 a).

73 Tomuschat (1999), p. 233.

74 See Kohen (2012), p. 163; Remiro Brotons (1996), p. 33.

75 UN Security Council Resolution1973 (2011).

76 The authorization excludes foreign occupation force of any form on any part of Libyan territory. Resolution 1973 (2011), para 4.

77 Kohen (2012), p. 164.

78 Ibidem.

79 Henderson (2018), p. 403.

80 See Akbarzadeh and Saba (2019).

81 Nuruzzaman (2022), p. 5

In any event, the Libya case sanctioned the major human rights step accomplished, since the Security Council confirmed that gross violations of human rights entailed a breach of peace and authorised the use of force in order to enforce them.

Yet can the Responsibility to Protect be considered effective? The International Commission's previous reports on Intervention and State Sovereignty[82] and of the High-Level Panel on Threats, Challenges and Change[83] recognised the existence of a state responsibility to protect even in the absence of a Security Council's authorising decision—though applying some precautionary principles.[84] However, this position was not accepted in the World Summit outcome document,[85] which did not establish any procedure in cases where the Security Council failed to take any decision. Therefore, in the case of a veto in the Security Council, we may again be in that situation described above by the Secretary General: having to decide whether to intervene in breach of fundamental principles of international law or to stand aside and allow the most horrendous international crimes to be committed.

5.3 Intervention by Request: The Muddy Justification

Intervention by request continues to be one of the most controversial subjects of international law, generating a diversity of scholarly opinions.[86] The issue has also been controversial among states, which have adopted different interpretations and positions regarding activities—mainly military ones—undertaken in third state territories.[87] Suffice it to mention two recent cases: the Russian intervention in Ukraine in 2014 as well as in 2022,[88] and the intervention of several countries in Syria's armed conflict.[89]

The concept of intervention by request can be analysed from a broad perspective linked to the principle of non-intervention, or from a more particular and specific viewpoint, focusing only on armed intervention. The latter entails the entry of foreign troops into the territory of the intervened State and it would affect the prohibition of the use of force.

[82] The Responsibility to Protect: Report of the International Commission on Intervention and State Sovereignty. International Development Research Centre. December 2001.

[83] A more secure world: our shared responsibility. Report of the High-level Panel on Threats, Challenges and Change. General Assembly, 2 December 2004, A/59/565.

[84] See Prandler (2008), pp. 713–719.

[85] UN General Assembly, *World Summit Outcome*, 16 September 2005, A/RES/60/1.

[86] The work developed by the Institute of International Law includes the different positions. Institut de Droit International (2009).

[87] See Ruys and Corten (2018); Díaz Barrado (1989).

[88] See Vermeer (2014); Green et al. (2002); O'Connell (2018); Gill (2022), p. 122.

[89] See Bannelier-Christakis (2016); Pozo Serrano (2016).

In this case, as in the previous section, we will focus on the principle of non-intervention, but considering its close relation to the prohibition of the use of force. Therefore, we will analyse different kinds of interventions in internal armed conflicts.[90] This has recently become a major issue because of growing internal armed conflicts and the practice of proxy wars.

5.3.1 Consent: The Cornerstone of Intervention by Request

Intervention by request in an internal armed conflict does not entail solely the use of force directly against the state. In this regard, Article 2 of the 1974 Resolution on the principle of non-intervention in civil wars,[91] adopted by the Institute of International Law, indicates that the acts of providing assistance to any party in a conflict can be considered as intervention, for example: the sending of volunteers, instructors or military technicians; the training of regular or irregular forces; the supply of arms; or the provision of financial or economic aid to the parties, whenever it could have a decisive effect on the conflict. These acts were also taken into consideration by the Institute of International Law in its subsequent 2009 Report on intervention by invitation[92] to analyse the concept of military aid. In the same vein, regarding the aforementioned activities, in the *Nicaragua* case, the Court also pointed out that financial assistance, supply of arms, logistical assistance, as well as the training of the *contras* did not constitute an armed attack; they could be considered, however, as a threat or use of force in addition to constituting an intervention in the internal and external affairs of another state.[93]

Having determined the acts that constitute *a prima facie* violation of the principle of non-intervention when linked to an internal armed conflict, we need to focus on the justification, which in this case is the invitation to intervene. Most abuses take place regarding this invitation and its interpretation, turning the doctrine of intervention by request into a blurred concept employed by the states to justify the most blatant violations of the principle of non-intervention.

Regarding the invitation, the issue to address here is that of the validity of the invitation: that is, the validity of the consent to intervene. Article 20 ARSIWA establishes that the consent must be valid, although it does not include the validity requirements, which makes it necessary to resort to the comments of the articles as well as to the preparatory works of the International Law Commission. In this regard, the comments[94] of Article 20 state that consent must be prior to or at the time the act

[90] See Institut de Droit International (2011).

[91] Institut de Droit International (1975).

[92] Institut de Droit International (2009), p. 311.

[93] ICJ, *Military and Paramilitary Activities in and against Nicaragua*, paras. 195, 228, 242.

[94] Report of the International Law Commission, Draft Articles on the Responsibility of International Organizations, Doc. A/66/10 (2011).

occurs. *A posteriori* consent would be invalid and would only have effects on the right to invoke state responsibility.[95]

Secondly, consent must be validly given, which affects the body responsible for providing it. This leads towards the issue of determining which authority within the state has the power to give consent, a question that has not only been raised regarding the capacity of state authorities but also regarding regional authorities.[96] In any case, the most controversial question would be whether consent should be granted by *de jure* or *de facto*[97] governments, or, in cases where this is not clear, who is in power. These situations also pose the problem of premature recognition,[98] which has been regarded as a violation of the principle of non-intervention Therefore, we could be facing a situation in which, in order to justify an intervention based on the government's request, a previous violation of the principle of non-intervention could have taken place through a premature recognition by the government whose consent is sought. An example of this premature recognition can be observed in Russia's recognition of the Donbas secessionist territories.[99]

Although the International Law Commission did not resolve this issue, the Institute of International Law conducted a more in-depth analysis in its 2009 Report focusing on three aspects: effectiveness, recognition, and democratic legitimacy.[100] On the other hand, state practice has shown that these principles are not applied jointly, and on some occasions, they have been declared incompatible. Illustrations include the recognition of a legitimate government in exile in connection with the principle of effectiveness, or the same principle in connection with the authorisation given by an overthrown government that controls a small part of the territory.

In any event, none of the elements appear to serve the sole justification of an intervention by invitation. And practices vary. Thus, while the Transitory Federal Government was recognised as a government by the international community in Somalia, its request for intervention was not considered sufficient due to the absence of effective power over the territory, thereby requiring authorisation from the Security Council.[101] Conversely, Russia justified its intervention in Crimea by stating that it was executed at the request of the deposed President Yanukovych whom Russia considered Ukraine's legitimate president, even though he had fled to Moscow and did not have effective control over the territory.[102]

Yanukovych's situation also seems to bring up the question of democratic legitimacy. Indeed, according to ARSIWA commentaries, 'sometimes the validity

---

[95] UN General Assembly, *Responsibility of States for internationally wrongful acts*, 8 January 2008, A/RES/62/61; Crawford (2002), p. 163.

[96] See Kolb (2018).

[97] International Law Association (2018), p. 73; Byrne (2016), pp. 107–110.

[98] Tomuschat (1999), p. 236, Jamnejad and Woods (2009), p. 373.

[99] Kilibarda (2022).

[100] Institut de Droit International (2009), p. 321.

[101] Corten (2010), p. 281; Institut de Droit International (2009), p. 34.

[102] See Vermeer (2014); Byrne (2016), p. 109; Buchan and Tsagourias (2017), p. 183.

of consent has been questioned because the consent was expressed in violation of relevant provisions of the State's internal law'.[103] In this case, accusations were made: Yanukovych's removal was against Ukraine's Constitution[104] and, therefore, questions about the effective application of this requirement were raised.[105] The reason was that despite the possible violation of a fundamental national law, the new government was recognised by the majority of states and international organisations.[106] In any case, the question of democratic legitimacy can be understood as a manifestation of today's international community. Indeed, in past times, this issue was not on the table when determining the validity of consent. The rise of new values has led to the introduction of a new requirement—democracy—which first, entails setting aside the requirement of effective control in favour of political views,[107] and second, affects the core of the principle of non-intervention, that is, the freedom to choose the political system.

Another requirement for valid consent is that it be clearly established. This requirement does not prevent implicit or tacit consent; however, this type of consent should not be confused with presumed consent, which consists of a consideration that the state would have given its consent had it been possible to request consent.[108] Therefore, consent must actually be expressed.[109] This issue has been analysed in connection with the US-led coalition air strikes carried out against the Islamic State in Syria because unlike Russia, the coalition did not have the invitation of the Syrian government.[110] In this sense, the possible existence of passive consent was analysed given that during the first year of intervention, Syria did not oppose the coalition's strikes against the Islamic State. We would, therefore, be facing a type of implicit or tacit consent since, as Corten pointed out, based on the Court's opinion in the case of *Armed Activities*, 'a simple tolerance may suffice to demonstrate its existence'.[111]

---

[103] Report of the International Law Commission, Draft Articles on the Responsibility of International Organizations, Doc. A/66/10 (2011), p. 73. Russia has intervened in Ukraine not only with direct use of force but also adopting economic measures against Ukraine, the threat of the use of force given the approval in the Russian parliament and the by supplying arms to rebels. Buchan and Tsagourias (2017), p. 177.

[104] Buchan and Tsagourias (2017), p. 183; The vote in the Parliament felt short of the majority required by the constitution. See Deeks (2014), https://www.lawfareblog.com/russia-ukraine-reader-responds

[105] See De Wet (2016), pp. 983–990.

[106] Buchan and Tsagourias (2017), p. 184.

[107] Roth (2017), p. 215.

[108] Report of the International Law Commission, Draft Articles on the Responsibility of International Organizations, Doc. A/66/10 (2011), pp. 112–113.

[109] Crawford (2002), p. 164; Cassese (2005), p. 370.

[110] Bannelier-Christakis (2016), pp. 766–773; Pozo Serrano (2016), pp. 176–179.

[111] Corten (2010), p. 273. In any case it must be notice that previously the Permanent Court of International Justice stated in the Danube case, the toleration does not give rise to a legal right or the acceptance of a right. PCJI, Jurisdiction of European Commission of Danube Between Galatz and Braila, Advisory Opinion, 1927 P.C.I.J. Series B-No. 14, paras. 93–95.

Finally, the consent must be freely given and must not have been vitiated by error, fraud, corruption, and coercion.[112] Among these elements, coercion could be the most appropriate method to obtain consent to authorise an intervention in a third state, and according to Corten, it has been evoked in certain situations.[113] The example given is the Russian military intervention in Czechoslovakia in which President Slovoda was considered to have been coerced to request the intervention.[114] Recently, doubts have been cast regarding Yanukovych's consent, since it was given once he was in Russia, the intervening state.[115]

5.3.2 *On the Legality of the Intervention in Non-International Armed Conflicts*

Having analysed the elements of consent, we will now move on to the controversial issue of the prohibition of intervention in non-international armed conflicts. From a theoretical viewpoint, it could be relatively easy to confirm the validity of this principle given the existence of several United Nations General Assembly resolutions that include the mentioned prohibition, such as Resolution 2625 (XXV). The latter is at the heart of our study and states that 'every State has the duty to refrain from organizing, instigating, assisting or participating in acts of civil war or acts of terrorism in another State'. In addition, Resolution 2131 (XX) clearly sets out that 'All States must also refrain from (...) intervening in a civil war of another State'.[116] Added to this, as mentioned, is the 1975 Institute of International Law Resolution on the principle of non-intervention in civil wars,[117] which, in Article 2, establishes the prohibition of aid to the parties in an armed conflict.

Despite the above, scholars are not unanimous.[118] In some cases, they consider that the elements indicated must be connected to other resolutions, state practice, or ICJ jurisprudence. Thus, Doswald-Beck considered that together with the

---

[112] Report of the International Law Commission, Draft Articles on the Responsibility of International Organizations, Doc. A/66/10 (2011), nota 28, p. 73; Institut de Droit International (2009), p. 402; Crawford (2002), p. 163; Corten (2010), pp. 269–272; Díaz Barrado (1989), pp. 284 y ss.

[113] Corten (2010), p. 270.

[114] Hafner (2018), p. 145.

[115] Buchan and Tsagourias (2017), p. 184.

[116] UN General Assembly, Declaration on the Inadmissibility of Intervention in the Domestic Affairs of States and the Protection of their Independence and Sovereignty, 21 December 1965, A/RES/2131 (XX).

[117] Institut de Droit International (1975), p. 12.

[118] See Bennouna (1974); De Wet (2020); De Wet (2016); Fox (2015), pp. 816–840; Schachter (1984); Christakis and Mollard-Bannelier (2005); Byrne (2016); Doswald-Beck (1985); Gray (2014); Díaz Barrado (1989); Shaw (2017), pp. 800–801.

aforementioned resolutions, Resolution 36/103[119] did not decisively clarify whether a government can receive support during a non-international armed conflict, but could be of interest in order to analyse the evolution of this principle. Indeed, when the Resolution declares an intervention's inadmissibility or interference in a state's internal affairs, it focuses on the prohibition of providing aid to rebels or secessionist movements, not to the state government.[120] Likewise, it has been noted[121] that in the Nicaragua case, the International Court of Justice established that intervention at the request of the state was allowed,[122] while analysing the legality of the United States' intervention based on "financial support, training, supply of weapons, intelligence and logistic support"[123]Finally, intervention by government request has also been considered unlawful when its purpose is 'to shift the balance of power in the internal conflict'[124] or when the movement against the government has popular support and is not a mere *coup d'état.*[125]

In any case, the most controversial issue lies in the realm of state practice, which has led some scholars, such as De Wet, to conclude that the practice confirms the right of states to request military assistance from third states during an internal armed conflict.[126] There are genuinely plentiful cases in practice in which states have intervened in such conflicts. However, it is necessary to point out that in none of them has a state claimed the existence of a right to intervene in a non-international armed conflict. In fact, in all the cases in which said interventions have been questioned, the states have justified the intervention based on other principles or rights, or they have simply denied that it was a case of intervention in an internal conflict.[127] Therefore, considering the elements of custom, although there may be evidence in practice (understood as participation in situations of internal armed conflict), there is no *opinio iuris.* It is therefore not possible to refer to a state's recognition of a right to intervene in internal armed conflicts. In this regard, taking various examples,[128] Russia's intervention in Syria has been justified as a case of self-defence and fighting against terrorism.[129] Saudi Arabia's intervention in Yemen was justified as a case of counter-intervention, with President Hadi pointing out in

---

[119] UN General Assembly, Declaration on the Inadmissibility of Intervention and Interference in the Internal Affairs of States, 9 December 1981, A/RES/36/103.

[120] Doswald-Beck (1985), pp. 211–212.

[121] Gray (2014), p. 627.

[122] ICJ, *Military and Paramilitary Activities in and against Nicaragua*, para. 246.

[123] Ibid, para. 242.

[124] Buchan and Tsagourias (2017), p. 184.

[125] Fitzmaurice (1957), pp. 178–179.

[126] De Wet (2020), p. 9.

[127] Bennouna (1974), p. 59; Christakis and Mollard-Bannelier (2005), p. 128.

[128] As Millán Moro states, the spiritual element of customary norms can be inferred from the practice of the states by explaining practice, defending positions with legal arguments, protesting against conduct of third states. Millán Moro (1990), p. 159.

[129] Bannelier-Christakis (2016), pp. 761–766.

his request letter that the Houthi militias received support from 'regional powers'.[130] The Vietnamese intervention in Cambodia was justified based on the principle of self-defence and the right of self-determination of the Cambodian people.[131] The Belgian intervention in the Congo was justified on the basis of the right of nationals abroad to be protected.[132] And in several French interventions in Chad, France always denied that it was a foreign intervention or that it was fighting the rebels.[133]

In sum, intervention seems accepted among scholars in the case of minor incidents, such as helping to resolve internal disorders, but it is more controversial in scenarios of intervention in non-international armed conflicts.[134]

5.4 Twenty-First Century Cyber-Interventionism

In 2016, after Russia's interference in the United States elections,[135] Brian Egan, the US Department Legal Adviser, affirmed that 'States need to do more work to clarify how the international law on non-intervention applies to States' activities in cyberspace'[136].

Russia's practice regarding that interference in the US elections campaign was part of a policy dating back to Soviet Union times. That practice was called "active measures" and it included disinformation. The difference this time was the greater success of those measures since they produced a response by the United States government,[137] reports from official institutions,[138] and multiples analyses by scholars.

In the past, Western countries perceived that these activities would have little success in Western democracies because of the strength of the media.[139] In this regard, Wright considered in 1960 that 'if a state is so inefficient, corrupt or naïve in

[130] Ferro and Ruys (2018), p. 901.

[131] Fox (2018), p. 244.

[132] Kolb (2018), p. 78.

[133] Doswald-Beck (1985), p. 219.

[134] Shaw (2017), p. 801.

[135] According to Tsagourias the Russian operations included 'hacking into the Democratic National Committee emails and the release of confidential information as well as disinformation operations'. Tsagourias (2020), p. 49.

[136] Brian (2016). https://2009-2017.state.gov/s/l/releases/remarks/264303.htm

[137] The President Obama decided to expel Russian diplomats in response for the interference of Russia. Statement by the President on Actions in Response to Russian Malicious Cyber Activity and Harassment, 2016. https://obamawhitehouse.archives.gov/the-press-office/2016/12/29/statement-president-actions-response-russian-malicious-cyber-activity

[138] Committee of Foreign Relations United States Senate, Putin's Asymmetric Assault on Democracy in Russia and Europe: Implications for U.S. National Security, 2018; European Parliament, Kremlin trolls in the US presidential election, February 2018.

[139] Torres Soriano (2022), p. 6.

its administration that outside influences of this kind, unsupported by military threats or invasions, can destroy its independence, it ought not to claim the prerogatives of a sovereign state'.[140]

According to President Obama, Russia's intentions were to interfere with or undermine the election process and institutions.[141] The latter was confirmed by the Director of National Intelligence who considered that the purpose was to 'undermine public faith in the US democratic process'.[142] In fact, this fit some of the definitions used in the past by the Soviet Union when referring to active measures, since they referred to undermining the trust in the state leaders and institutions or discrediting and weakening key opponents.[143]

Today, we can consider that the objective of disinformation activities goes beyond changing people's opinions. Indeed, they aim at weakening the state itself, and at exerting a corrosive effect on society. The intention is to undermine interpersonal cohesion and trust in order to make the society vulnerable, deeply hindering its ability to coordinate a unified response in case of future coercion.[144] The European Parliament also affirmed that disinformation can destabilise European democracy. It considered that foreign intervention, like Russia's in the US elections, 'aims to introduce doubt, uncertainty and mistrust, not just to alter the result of elections but to delegitimise the entire electoral process'.[145]

5.4.1 *The Link with International Law*

An ongoing question regarding these operations is whether they can amount to a violation of international law, regarding either the principle of sovereignty, the principle of non-intervention, the use of force through subversive propaganda,[146] or the principle of self-determination.

The former analysis on propaganda can also be linked to these kinds of activities, though the international obligations breached by propaganda are not clear. In this

[140] Wright (1960), p. 530

[141] Statement by the President on Actions in Response to Russian Malicious Cyber Activity and Harassment, 2016.

[142] According to the Director the activities were also focused on 'denigrate Secretary Clinton and harm her electability and potential presidency'. Office of the Director of National Intelligence (2017). https://www.dni.gov/files/documents/ICA_2017_01.pdf

[143] Torres Soriano (2022), p. 5

[144] Torres Soriano (2022), p. 3. At the same time, Khrushev in 1959 declared that 'the principle of peaceful coexistence signifies a renunciation of interference in the internal affairs of other countries with the object of altering their system of government or mode of life or for any other motives'. Wright (1960), p. 526.

[145] European Parliament resolution of 9 March 2022 on foreign interference in all democratic processes in the European Union, including disinformation.

[146] Wright (1960), p. 529.

regard, Whitton affirmed in 1948 that in cases of defamatory attacks against state's constitutions, governmental institutions, or forms of government,

> the injured state would certainly be justified in entering a protest and demanding appropriate reparation. For governments and state officials are enjoined not only to scrupulous abstention from active interference in the affairs of other states, but also from criticism of foreign laws and institutions.[147]

This statement allows us to infer the violation of the principle of non-intervention. Later, in 1971, he considered that a duty to refrain from defamation of foreign leaders existed based on the 'traditional right of a sovereign to the respect of other sovereigns',[148] thereby linking it this time with the principle of sovereignty of the states.

This issue has become more pressing today given the opportunities offered in this regard by cyberspace. In cyberspace, it is easier to disseminate information. Access is easier and therefore the audience is amplified[149] due to 'increasing global connectivity and the growing reliance of states on information technology'.[150] Therefore, while such kinds of activities were common in the past,[151] cyberspace has increased their effect and quantity.

Nevertheless, despite adopting retortions due to Russia's interference, President Obama was not able to determine the exact breach of the international obligation, referring to Russia's activities as a 'violation of established international norms of behaviour' and 'aggressive activities'.[152] Neither the European Parliament's resolution nor the US Senate's report clarified the violation of a specific obligation of international law.

In its description of the principle of non-intervention, Resolution 2625 (XXV) refers to 'interferences or attempted threats against the personality of the State or against the political, economic and cultural elements, are in violation of international law'. In this section, we will therefore focus on the violation of this principle through cyber-activities, mainly through interventions in electoral processes or referendums. In this regard, not only can we refer to the 2016 US elections interference, but also to the reported interferences in France's 2016 presidential elections, in Catalonia's

[147] Whitton (1948), p. 376

[148] Whitton (1971), p. 19.

[149] Tsagourias (2020), p. 16.

[150] Schmitt (2017), Rule 66 p. 312.

[151] Regarding for example interventions of Russia and the United States in electoral processes, Levin estimates up to 117 electoral meddling from 1947 to 2000. Levin (2016), p. 94. And according to the recent study from Princeton, Russia has launched at least 76 disinformation campaigns against third states in between 2011–2020. Torres Soriano (2022), p. 7. The international Court of Justice in Nicaragua stated the trespass of the principle of non intervention was not infrequent. ICJ, *Military and Paramilitary Activities in and against Nicaragua*, para 202.

[152] Statement by the President on Actions in Response to Russian Malicious Cyber Activity and Harassment, 2016.

2017 independence referendum, in Macedonia's 2018 referendum, in the elections to the European Parliament in 2019, or in the US elections in 2020.[153]

5.4.2 *Cyber-Intervention in Electoral Processes and the Principle of Non-Intervention: Not an Easy Answer*

As mentioned at the beginning of this chapter, no clear definition of intervention exists that would allow us to perfectly identify each case of intervention. And it becomes even more difficult in cyberspace given its particularity and the absence of a physical territory, which has always been linked to state sovereignty.

The definition given by the International Court of Justice in *Nicaragua* was considered the basis to identify intervention though stressing that the Court definition could be interpreted differently regarding the main elements: *domain reserve* and coercion. In any case, based on that definition, we shall now proceed to analyse whether cyber-interference in electoral processes can amount to a violation of the principle of non-intervention.

5.4.2.1 Domaine Réservé

According to the Court's definition and that of Resolution 2625 (XXV), the principle of non-intervention refers to non-intervention in a state's internal and external affairs. The areas in which intervention is not allowed are those considered *domaine réservé*, which according to Court, refers to domains in which states have to decide freely, i.e., have to choose their own political, economic, social, and cultural system.[154]

Although what can be understood as *domaine réservé* may change according to the evolution of international society, the election process inside the state is undoubtedly included in *domaine réservé* matters. Resolution 2625 (XXV) refers to the freedom to choose the political system, which includes holding elections in the way the state has chosen.

Most recent interferences in electoral processes have taken place in democratic countries, which means that their system is 'based on the freely expressed will of the people to determine their own political, economic, social and cultural systems and their full participation in all aspects of their lives'.[155] To express their will, which in

---

[153] Cervell Hortal (2023), p. 3. Metodieva (2018). https://www.gmfus.org/news/how-disinformation-harmed-referendum-macedonia; Rotondo and Salvati (2018), p. 209.

[154] ICJ, *Military and Paramilitary Activities in and against Nicaragua*, para 205.

[155] UN Commission on Human Rights, Commission on Human Rights resolution 2000/47 Promoting and consolidating democracy, 25 April 2000, E/CN.4/RES/2000/47.

these democracies is conducted through voting, 'voters should be able to form opinions independently, free of violence or threat of violence, compulsion, inducement or manipulative interference of any kind'.[156]

Taking this concept of democracy into account and its relation to the right to freely choose its political system, actions aiming at manipulating voter opinions affect the people's free will. Therefore, they have an impact on their capacity to choose the political system, complying with the first element of the concept of intervention: intervention in a *domaine réservé*.

Cyberspace facilitates the manipulation of voter opinions, since online platforms are easily accessible and can greatly influence voting preferences.[157] According to Tsagurias, two main cyber operations were used in the 2016 US election interference. The first, called doxing, consists of exposing, disgracing or undermining 'a particular individual, campaign, or organisation in order to influence public opinion',[158] in this case candidate Clinton.[159] The second consisted of disinformation, that is, 'the fabrication or deliberate distortion of news content aimed at deceiving an audience, polluting the information space to obscure fact-based reality, and manufacturing misleading narratives about key events or issues to manipulate public opinion',[160] which was implemented mainly through social media.[161] According to a report of the European External Action Service's East StratCom Task Force project, 'EUvs Disinfo', this disinformation can be disseminated over social media via fake identities, purchasing online sites to propagate it, or using trolls, fake accounts or bots that spread the messages.[162]

Since these cyber activities clearly affect the states' *domaine réservé*, it is necessary to analyse coercion, the second element, which has led to a shift in the way we regard these kinds of interferences as violations of the principle of non-intervention.

---

156 UN Human Rights Committee (HRC), CCPR General Comment No. 25: Article 25 (Participation in Public Affairs and the Right to Vote), The Right to Participate in Public Affairs, Voting Rights and the Right of Equal Access to Public Service, 12 July 1996, CCPR/C/21/Rev.1/Add.7, para 19.

157 European Parliament (2022), Foreign interference in all democratic processes in the European Union. European Parliament resolution of 9 March 2022 on foreign interference in all democratic processes in the European Union, including disinformation (2020/2268(INI)).

158 Tsagourias (2020), p. 8.

159 The operation consisted in the exfiltration of documents from the Democratic National Committee and the feed and seed the material to media sources that presented it in a damaging way for Clinton. Barela (2017).

160 EU vs Disinformation. Methods of foreing electoral interventions, https://euvsdisinfo.eu/methods-of-foreign-electoral-interference/

161 Rotondo and Salvati (2018), p. 210. On Russian trolls in social media see European Parliament (2018) Kremlin trolls in the US presidential election. At a glance.

162 EU vs Disinformation. Methods of foreign electoral interventions, https://euvsdisinfo.eu/methods-of-foreign-electoral-interference/

5.4.2.2 Coercion

As mentioned earlier, the concept of coercion has also raised interpretation problems regarding its different qualifications: economic coercion or political coercion. A broad definition of coercion could be that coercion takes place when 'one or more States seek to compel—rather than persuade—another to act in a certain way by applying various kinds of pressure'.[163] For Buchan and Tsagurias, coercion is an 'imperative pressure',[164] and the Tallinn Manual refers to forcing the state.[165] Therefore, coercion must present some kind of intensity that allows differentiating it from persuasion.

In this regard, it is worth noting that the European Union's regulation on the protection of the Union and its Member States from economic coercion by third countries uses a more extensive definition of coercion. It establishes that coercion exists when a third country 'interferes in the legitimate sovereign choices of the Union or a Member State by seeking to prevent or to obtain the cessation, modification or adoption of a particular act by the Union or a Member State'.[166] However, to make such an assessment, it is necessary to consider the 'intensity, severity, frequency, duration, breadth and magnitude of the third country's measure and the pressure arising from it',[167] i.e., aligning its definition with the approach based on the scale and effects described below.

The existence of coercion in cyber interventions seem to be widely recognised when the cyber activities affect physical elements.[168] These activities would consist in accessing the cyber infrastructure of the electoral process, for example when disrupting 'the systems which control electoral counts to change the outcome of an election; or operations to disrupt another State's ability to hold an election at all, for example by causing systems to malfunction with the effect of preventing voter registration'.[169] These situations comply with the definition included in the Tallinn Manual, which requires that the coercive act have the potential for compelling the target State to engage in an action that it would otherwise not take.[170] Indeed, once the system is controlled by the third state, the targeted state could not act in a different way.

---

[163] Sender (2012).

[164] Buchan and Tsagourias (2017), p. 171.

[165] Schmitt (2017), Rule 66, para 18.

[166] Article Regulation (EU) 2023/2675 of the European Parliament and of the Council of 22 November 2023 on the protection of the Union and its Member States from economic coercion by third countries. OJ L 2023/2675, 7.12.2023. On this Regulation see Ruys and Rodríguez Silvestre (2021).

[167] Ibid. Article 2.2, a).

[168] Cervell Hortal (2023), p. 9.

[169] Attorney General Suella Braverman: International Law in Future Frontiers, 19 May 2022. https://www.gov.uk/government/speeches/international-law-in-future-frontiers

[170] Schmitt (2017), para 21.

In any case, the Tallinn Manual has also recognised that for coercion to exist, the acts do not need to be physical,[171] as in the case of the cyber interferences in electoral processes mentioned above. They centred on doxing and mainly disinformation, bringing them closer to the concept of persuasion. A way to differentiate these activities from persuasion is to link them with the definition of democratic elections referred to above, in which free exercise must be done without inducement or manipulation. If we take the concept of disinformation and its effects into account, it is easy to conclude that it restricts freedom of election since they are manipulating, inducing, and compelling citizens to act in a specific way, and the latter to not have the necessary tools or means to follow an opposite course. This situation deprives the state of the freedom of choice, as it is forced to act in an involuntary manner.[172] In addition, according to Tsagurias, the intervening state is taking control and this is the clearest manifestation of coercion: the state authority and will have been manipulated, so the foreign state can control the will of the people and that of the emerging government.[173]

For some commentators,[174] the scale and effects of the cyber activities need to be considered to assess the existence of coercion and the violation of the principle of non-intervention. Therefore, the spread of fake news or 'alternative truths' would not be enough: it is necessary to check whether the influence has really changed the results of the elections.[175] This would seem difficult to demonstrate, since it requires knowing the results of the elections in advance. Others consider that the number of people and values affected must be computed, together with the extent to which they are affected[176]—which could be substantial in the case of cyber disinformation. In this regard, interferences in the electoral process not only aim at altering the election results but also at harming the whole electoral and democratic system. In the same vein, as mentioned earlier, cyberspace exponentially increases the number of citizens who can be reached.

This latter interpretation of coercion is also linked to a holistic analysis[177] in which it will be necessary to determine coercion case by case, analysing all the facts linked to the intervention. In this regard, not all disinformation acts would be regarded as intervention acts. It would be necessary to analyse the act in a broader context, in connection with other acts or the specific goal of the responsible state,

[171] Ibid., para 20.

[172] Ibid., para 18.

[173] Tsagourias (2020), pp. 15–17.

[174] Barela (2017); Cervell Hortal (2023), p. 16; Rotondo and Salvati (2018), p. 212.

[175] Cervell Hortal (2023), p. 16. This approach is that can be in contradiction with the opinion of Tallin Manual which establishes that is the operation fails to produce the outcome has no bearing on whether this Rule has been violated. Schmitt (2017), Rule 66, para 29. Also Rotonda and Salvati consider that the intervention must not be necessary succeful. Rotondo and Salvati (2018), p. 212.

[176] Rotondo and Salvati (2018), p. 212; Barela (2017).

[177] Rotondo and Salvati (2018), p. 213; Ohlin (2017), p. 1593.

together with the effects of that act and others with the same purpose. In a nutshell, it will be necessary to analyse the whole campaign against the targeted state.

These approaches could lead to a broader concept of coercion, considered as a conduct that interrupts, compromises or weakens the state's authority.[178]

Added to these interpretations of coercion, others consider that the concept of coercion is outdated and not useful, especially in the case of cyber interventions.[179] According to this stance, it is necessary to eliminate coercion from the cyber activity assessment in order to determine the existence of an intervention. The new standard proposed by Kilovaty considers that the wrongfulness of the intervention should be based on 'whether the cyber intervention prevented the state from freely exercising functions associated with its internal and external affairs', therefore, whether it should 'focus on the deprivation of the free choice'.[180]

This position is in line with that which considers that the existence of intervention without coercion is possible when a foreign state usurps essential governmental functions.[181]

By avoiding the concept of coercion, it is easier to consider that a cyber intervention amounts to a violation of the principle of non-intervention in an electoral process. Those scholars however focus on the usurpation of vote tallying, since counting votes can be clearly regarded as a governmental function. This approach requires a physical act, and it would exclude the most common interferences such as doxing and disinformation, which according to Ohlin can give the impression of an illegal act—though such a conclusion is unclear.[182] To solve the issue, it is necessary to focus again on the democratic process, which implies that the state guarantees free voting, giving voters the opportunity to form their opinions without intervention, manipulation or inducement. For that purpose, states regulate the media system through national law, giving citizens access to the information needed to form an opinion. Therefore, when a state loses control over that essential function in a democracy, it is possible to infer the usurpation of governmental functions.

5.4.2.3 Intent and Knowledge

Finally, intent and knowledge[183] have also been used to determine the existence of an act of intervention. According to the intent requirement, it is necessary to demonstrate that the foreign state's intention was to intervene in another state's internal or external affairs. In the case of cyber intervention in elections, it would be

[178] Cortés Martín (2019), p. 58. In any case Cortes Martin considers that is difficult to conclude that the recent interventions in electoral campaign may amount to a coercive intervention.

[179] Kilovaty (2019), p. 89.

[180] Kilovaty (2019), p. 90.

[181] Kilovaty (2019), p. 88; Efrony and Shany (2018), p. 642; Ohlin (2017), pp. 1594–1595.

[182] Ohlin (2017), p. 1595.

[183] Schmitt (2017), Rule 66, paras 25 and 27.

easy to elucidate the intention in the cases of physical acts, for example when manipulating the results. It would not be difficult to demonstrate the intention either in cases of doxing or disinformation taking the content of the messages and the addresses into account, all of them at a particular moment in time and in connection with an electoral process. Furthermore, intent may allow differentiating these activities from general propaganda.[184]

The question of knowledge of the targeted state has given rise to different approaches. In the Tallinn Manual,[185] the majority adopted the view that knowledge is not a precondition for the violation of this principle. On the other hand, a minority considered that it was necessary for the state to be aware of the coercive act, which finally leads the state to act in a different way. The Manual uses the example of the altering of electronic ballots, which, according to the majority, constitutes an act of coercion because the state is unknowingly forced to seat a candidate by the actions of another state. For a minority, coercion means pressure on the state, compelling it to act in a particular way, which can only be done if the state knows it. Finally, according to Tsagurias, knowledge is not a constitutive element of intervention and it would only be useful to claim responsibility for intervention.[186]

5.5 The European Union as a Paradigm of Intervention to Promote the Respect of Human Rights: A Practice-Based Approach

Human rights have modified the limits and the conception of non-intervention. Indeed, not only is the use of force sometimes taken into consideration today to implement the respect for human rights, but areas that were considered at the beginning of the twentieth century a *domaine réservé* have now become domains of international concern. In this regard, expressing opinions on the extent to which third states comply with international human rights standards is no longer considered as an intervention in internal affairs. Moreover, the actions taken by states and international organisations to push third states to comply with those mentioned standards are largely accepted.

On this specific subject, the European Union has played an important role as part of its mandate. Indeed, according to Article 2.5 TFEU, the European Union shall promote its values in its relations with the world and contribute to the protection of human rights.[187] In addition, the European Union went a step further in November

[184] Tsagourias (2020), p. 198.

[185] Schmitt (2017), Rule 66, para 25.

[186] Tsagourias (2020), p. 20.

[187] A further analysis on this activity and the principle of non-intervention in Fernández Arribas and Wessel (2023).

2020 with the adoption of the EU Action Plan on Human Rights and Democracy 2020–2024.[188]

The Action Plan establishes a new global European Union sanctions regime regarding human rights violations and includes a list of instruments to promote human rights and democracy. It should be noted that this Plan is designed for the EU's external actions, as the EU has other mechanisms at its disposal to ensure compliance with human rights and democracy among its member states.

Regarding the promotion of human rights and the guarantee of their respect, two main lines of actions have been adopted that could cross the red line of intervention: restrictive measures and conditionality in international agreements.

5.5.1 Conditionality to Promote Respect for Human Rights

In the 1990s, the European Union launched a policy that consisted of introducing a provision in its international agreements, whether trade or development agreements, which allowed suspending the agreement or adopting other negative actions in the case of violations of human rights by the parties. Even though these provisions have been included in multiple agreements, one of the most significant was the Cotonu Agreement[189] and its replacement, the Partnership Agreement between the European Union and members of the Organisation of African, Caribbean and Pacific States. Article 101 establishes a consultation procedure followed by a process based on the adoption of 'appropriate measures' in cases in which one of the parties has failed to fulfil its obligations regarding human rights, democracy, and the rule of law.[190] This provision has led the European Union to adopt 'appropriate measures' against several African countries. One such case is that of Burundi: in 2016, the European Union decided to suspend its financial support or disbursements of funds directly benefiting the Burundian administration or institutions.[191] Another case is that of the Central African Republic in which the European Union decided in 2003 to partially

[188] General Secretariat of the Council, EU Action Plan on Human Rights and Democracy 2020–2024, Brussels, 18 November 2020, https://www.consilium.europa.eu/media/46838/st12848-en20.pdf. Since 2012, when the EU adopted the Strategic Framework on Human Rights and Democracy, there has been two plans (2012–2014 y 2015–2019).

[189] 2000/483/EC: Partnership agreement between the members of the African, Caribbean and Pacific Group of States of the one part, and the European Community and its Member States, of the other part, signed in Cotonou on 23 June 2000, OJ L 317, 15.12.2000.

[190] Partnership Agreement Between the European Union and its member States, of the one part, and the members of the Organisation of African, Caribbean and Pacific States, other part (not in force yet). https://ec.europa.eu/international-partnerships/system/files/negotiated-agreement-text-initialled-by-eu-oacps-chief-negotiators-20210415_en.pdf

[191] Council Decision (EU) 2016/394 of 14 March 2016 concerning the conclusion of consultations with the Republic of Burundi under Article 96 of the Partnership Agreement between the members of the African, Caribbean and Pacific Group of States, of the one part, and the European Community and its Member States, of the other part. OJ L 73, 18.3.2016.

suspend its cooperation applicable to the operations concerning roads and macroeconomic support.[192] All these actions were designed to force the state to comply with human rights or democratic demands.[193] Taking into consideration the definition of non-intervention included in Resolution 2625 (XXV), we must acknowledge its link to the above-mentioned measures, since it expressly refers to the prohibition of using economic measures to coerce another state. On the other hand, in the *Nicaragua* case, the International Court of Justice did not consider the economic measures adopted by the United States, including the cessation of economic aid as a violation of the principle of non-intervention.[194] It has been considered that the legality of these kinds of actions must be linked to effects on the country and on citizens. In addition, the legitimacy of coercion measures to make states comply with the protection of human rights is internationally accepted and recognised.[195] This again illustrates how the international community's interests and values prevail over the individual interests and rights of the states.

5.5.2 Restrictive Measures: The Contentious Method

The European Union has also adopted restrictive measures against third states and individuals because of human rights violations, and some recent controversies

---

[192] 2003/837/EC: Council Decision of 24 November 2003 concluding the consultation procedure opened with the Central African Republic and adopting appropriate measures under Article 96 of the Cotonou Agreement. OJ L 319, 4.12.2003.

[193] In any case, the EU has been accused of double standards regarding the application of human rights clauses in trade agreements, not only because of the absence of human rights clauses in certain trade agreements such as those with Japan or Canada, but also because as stated by Bartel: 'it appears that with some countries at least (to date, Canada, Japan, Australia, New Zealand and the UK, and to a lesser degree Malaysia and Thailand), the standard for adopting appropriate measures is higher than usual. Rather than any violation of essential elements triggered such measures, it is only serious, or very serious violations that can have this effect (leading one to wonder what is 'essential' about norms that are not violated to this extent)'. Bartels (2023), p. 29. In the same vein, the suspension of the EU-Israel Association agreement has been unsuccessfully requested by different intuitions, such as by the European Parliament in 2002, the Parliamentary Assembly of the Council of Europe also in 2002, or the Committee of the UK House of Commons in 2004. Bartels (2004), p. 370. In fact, in 2014, certain EP members addressed a question to the European Commission concerning the suspension of the EU-Israel Association Agreement, and the Commission responded as follows: "The EU has consistently called on the government of Israel to allow for the full respect of international law and international human rights in the occupied territories. The EU has put on hold in June 2009 the upgrading of EU-Israel relations pending progress in the Peace Process and implementation of shared values. However, the EU is not considering the suspension of existing agreements or sanctions, which would require the unanimous decision of the Council". European Parliament. Parliamentary Question - E-008366/2014. https://www.europarl.europa.eu/doceo/document//E-8-2014-008366_EN.html

[194] ICJ, *Military and Paramilitary Activities in and against Nicaragua*, para. 244.

[195] Damrosch (1989), pp. 42 et seq.

involve Russia and China. In March 2021, the European Union adopted sanctions against Chinese officials because of human rights violations against the Uyghur Muslim minority in the Xinjiang region.[196] The Chinese government's answer was to consider these sanctions as a gross interference in China's internal affairs.[197] In the same vein, the European Union adopted targeted sanctions against Russian senior officials because of their participation in the persecution of Navalny, the opposition leader, and because of human rights violations.[198] Russia has already declared that previous restrictive measures adopted against Russian nationals accused of participating in Navalny's poisoning to be a violation of the Helsinki principles of non-intervention in internal affairs.[199]

These latter measures against Russia were adopted in the framework of an escalation of the confrontation between the European Union and Russia, in which Russia had previously accused the European Union of intervening in Ukraine's internal affairs during the events leading to President Yanukovych's flight:

> Why did that problem need to result in street demonstrations? Why do those street demonstrations need to be encouraged from abroad by members of the European Union? Why did the representatives of several countries of the European Union need to appear at those meetings, which were ignited by protests against a decision taken by the Ukrainian leadership? Why did some officials need to talk about stirring up the public and opposition leaders? Why did there have to be such crude interventions in the internal affairs of a sovereign State?[200]

These European Union actions took place after Russia exerted pressure on Ukraine to prevent it from signing the Association Agreement with the European Union,[201] which was also considered an intervention in Ukraine's external affairs.

---

[196] Council Implementing Regulation (EU) 2021/478 of 22 March 2021 implementing Regulation (EU) 2020/1998 concerning restrictive measures against serious human rights violations and abuses. OJ L 99I, 22.3.2021.

[197] Foreign Ministry Spokesperson Announces Sanctions on Relevant EU Entities and Personnel 2021/03/22. https://www.fmprc.gov.cn/mfa_eng/xwfw_665399/s2510_665401/t1863106.shtmly. It must be noted the reluctance position of the ASEAN states to analyse human rights violations among its member states. See Nasu (2013).

[198] Council Decision (CFSP) 2021/372 of 2 March 2021 amending Decision (CFSP) 2020/1999 concerning restrictive measures against serious human rights violations and abuses. OJ L 71 I, 2.3.2021. Previously the EU had adopted sanctions against six official suspected of been participated in the poisoning of Navalny. These restrictive measures were adopted on the framework of the actions of the EU against the proliferation of chemical weapons. Council Implementing Regulation (EU) 2020/1480 of 14 October 2020 implementing Regulation (EU) 2018/1542 concerning restrictive measures against the proliferation and use of chemical weapons. OJ L 341, 15.10.2020.

[199] Statement by the Ministry of Foreign Affairs of the Russian Federation in response to EU sanctions. 22 December 20202. https://www.mid.ru/en/evropejskij-souz-es/-/asset_publisher/6OiYovt2s4Yc/content/id/4510703

[200] UN Security Council, Letter dated 28 February 2014 from the Permanent Representative of Ukraine to the United Nations addressed to the President of the Security Council (S/2014/136), Meeting Records S/PV.7124. This position was also shared by some experts. See Müllerson (2014); Huseynov (2017).

[201] Buchan and Tsagourias (2017), p. 117; Claudín (2013).

In any event, the Russian aggression against Ukraine has led the Union to adopt further restrictive measures, focusing on the violation of humanitarian law. The European Union had, in fact, already adopted numerous sanctions against Russia and its nationals for aggressing Ukraine, but it was the Bucha massacre that led to the inclusion of a new element in its sanctions.

In this regard, when Russian troops passed through Bucha, they left a trail of killings, torture, and rape, as the Union points out in the sanction regulation.[202] Similarly, the Organisation for Security and Cooperation in Europe included photographs and videos of civilians killed in the streets together with accounts of mass graves in its report. This evidence would point to the fact that war crimes and crimes against humanity were committed by Russian forces.[203]

While the latter were not the only war crimes committed in Ukraine,[204] their magnitude led the European Union to adopt restrictive measures against 44 Russian military personnel, most of them commanders, for their involvement in the crimes, considering that they directed the actions from their military unit and thus holding them responsible for them.[205] These sanctions consisted of the freezing of funds and economic resources (deposits in financial institutions or others, balances on accounts, stocks and shares, interest, dividends or other income earned or generated by assets) together with travel restrictions. The Council adopted another implementing regulation a month later that included a new list of individuals accused of being in charge of the troops who committed the Bucha massacre.[206]

However, the situation becomes confusing with regard to the sanctions adopted against another group of Russian military personnel via an implementing regulation of 21st July. Indeed, the new list of sanctioned individuals again included Russian

---

[202] Council Implementing Regulation (EU) 2022/353 of 2 March 2022 implementing Regulation (EU) No 269/2014 concerning restrictive measures in respect of actions undermining or threatening the territorial integrity, sovereignty and independence of Ukraine, OJ L 66, 2.3.2022.

[203] OSCE, Report of the OSCE Moscow Mechanism's mission of experts entitled 'Report on Violations of International Humanitarian and Human Rights Law, War Crimes and Crimes Against Humanity Committed in Ukraine (1 April–25 June 2022)', p. 2. https://www.osce.org/odihr/522616

[204] See United Nations Human Rights, Office of the High Commisisoner (2022), Situation of Human Rights in Ukraine in the Context of the Armed Attack by the Russian Federation (24 February–15 May 2022). https://www.ohchr.org/en/documents/country-reports/situation-human-rights-ukraine-context-armed-attack-russian-federation. The Prosecutor of the International Criminal Court had already pointed out in her preliminary examination in 2020, the commission of war crimes by both parties, specifically she states: 'My Office furthermore found that these crimes, committed by the different parties to the conflict, were also sufficiently grave to warrant investigation by my Office, both in quantitative and qualitative terms'. Corte Penal International, Statement of the Prosecutor, Fatou Bensouda, on the conclusion of the preliminary examination in the situation in Ukraine.

[205] Council Implementing Regulation (EU) 2022/878 of 3 June 2022 implementing Regulation (EU) No 269/2014 concerning restrictive measures in respect of actions undermining or threatening the territorial integrity, sovereignty and independence of Ukraine, OJ L 153, 3.6.2022.

[206] Council Implementing Regulation (EU) 2022/1270 of 21 July 2022 implementing Regulation (EU) No 269/2014 concerning restrictive measures in respect of actions undermining or threatening the territorial integrity, sovereignty and independence of Ukraine, OJ L 193, 21.7.2022.

commanders in charge of troops accused of carrying out killings, rape, and torture in Bucha. However, in this case, there was no mention of war crimes being committed nor, therefore, human rights violations. The regulation states that these persons are responsible for 'supporting or implementing actions or policies which undermine or threaten the territorial integrity, sovereignty and independence of Ukraine, or stability or security in Ukraine'.[207]

In this regard, it is worth noting that to hold a person responsible for committing war crimes is an issue of legal nature, which the European Union addresses it in this case in the Regulation by means of an act of a markedly political nature, i.e., the adoption of sanctions, affecting therefore the right to a fair trial and the presumption of innocence. On the other hand, the well-known Kadi[208] case highlighted the need to properly substantiate the inclusion of these individuals on the sanctions list, which in the Bucha case, with respect to the committing of war crimes, seems difficult to reconcile without a prior judicial or investigative process.

This EU policy on promoting human rights based on restrictive sanctions is undergoing rejection in the Global South, with the thrust of a Russia cornered by Western state sanctions. In this regard, in the tenth BRICS Summit Johannesburg Declaration, the states rejected "the imposition of unilateral coercive measures outside the framework of the UN Charter".[209] This position was made even clearest in the Declaration of the Second Russia–Africa Summit held in Saint-Petersburg in 2023. In a context of adoption of massive restrictive measures against Russia, the Heads of State and Government of the attending states declared that they

> Stand in solidarity to eradicate the practice of confrontation in international affairs, and resist discrediting certain States for political reasons, introducing political or economic restrictive measures under the pretext of human rights advocacy, oppose attempts by certain States to use unfounded accusations of human rights violations as an excuse for interfering in internal affairs and disrupting activities of international organizations.[210]

This declaration follows the path of the Joint Statement of the Russian Federation and the People's Republic of China on the International Relations Entering a New Era and the Global Sustainable Development, which stated that

> the sides believe that the advocacy of democracy and human rights must not be used to put pressure on other countries. They oppose the abuse of democratic values and interference in

[207] Council Implementing Regulation (EU) 2022/1270 of 21 July 2022 implementing Regulation (EU) No 269/2014 concerning restrictive measures in respect of actions undermining or threatening the territorial integrity, sovereignty and independence of Ukraine, OJ L 193, 21.7.2022.

[208] See Lenaerts (2014); Shirlow (2014).

[209] X BRICS Summit Johannesburg Declaration. Johannesburg, South Africa, 25–27 July 2018. http://brics2022.mfa.gov.cn/eng/hywj/ODS/202203/t20220308_10649503.html

[210] Declaration Second Russia–Africa Summit, https://russianembassyza.mid.ru/home/-/asset_publisher/UduihNpxCk6b/content/declaration-of-the-second-russia-africa-summit?inheritRedirect=true

> the internal affairs of sovereign states under the pretext of protecting democracy and human rights, and any attempts to incite divisions and confrontation in the world[211]

Therefore, it is possible to infer that they may be establishing the bases for delegitimatizing and dismantling the system of international protection of human rights.

Finally, within the European Union, this position as defender and promoter of human rights and democratic values led to a striking episode when sanctions were adopted against Austria in 1999 by the fourteen EU members. After Austria's national elections were held that year, the People's Party decided to form a coalition government with the far-right Freedom Party, which led some countries to express their concern and Belgium to requesting a European Council meeting.[212] Following the meeting, the Portuguese presidency released a statement on behalf of the fourteen members of the European Union saying that they had decided to freeze their diplomatic relations with Austria. According to the document:

> Governments of XIV Member States will not promote or accept any bilateral official at political level with an Austrian Government integrating the FPÖ; There will be no support in favour of Austrian candidates seeking positions in international organizations; Austrian Ambassadors in EU capitals will only be received at a technical level.[213]

These actions were interpreted in different ways by the member states, including the suspension of military exercises, school trips or cultural exchanges.[214]

The 'sanctions' were considered by the far-right leader as an intervention in Austria's internal affairs.[215] This question was also posed by some scholars: the actions to implement the EU's commitment towards the protection of human rights, democratic values and to combat racism and xenophobia may contradict the right of states to freely decide about their government and the obligation to respect the results of democratic elections. Here again, we are witnessing a conflict between the implementation of EU values—which, in this case, are deeply rooted in this close community—and the respect of the principle of non-intervention, which would lead to allowing those values to be violated.

Even though the sanctions were lifted some months later,[216] the necessity to protect those values over national interests led to an amendment of Article 7 TEU,

---

[211] Joint Statement of the Russian Federation and the People's Republic of China on the International Relations Entering a New Era and the Global Sustainable Development. February 2022. http://www.en.kremlin.ru/supplement/5770. In this regard, human rights were nor mentioned in the Declaration of the Russian Federation and the People's Republic of China on the Promotion of International Law, 2016. https://www.fmprc.gov.cn/eng/wjdt_665385/2649_665393/201608/t20160801_679466.html

[212] Happold (2000), p. 955.

[213] Statement by the Portuguese Presidency of the EU on behalf of XIV Member States (31 January 2000). See Schermers and Blokker (2011), p. 915.

[214] Freeman (2002), p. 120.

[215] Happold (2000), p. 959.

[216] Ibid. p. 957.

including the possibility of determining not only the existence of a violation of EU principles but also a risk of violation. The latter would allow taking actions to prevent the occurrence of such violations. This is a further step with respect to previous regulations, as it was necessary to wait until the violation has taken place to take action, a limitation that led member states to adopt those 'sanctions' against Austria. The new article focuses on the preservation of EU values and allows preventive actions. This represents, however, a more intrusive position regarding the principle of non-intervention in internal affairs.

References

Akbarzadeh S, Saba A (2019) UN paralysis over Syria: the responsibility to protect or regime change? Int Politics 56(4):536

Allard T (2021) ASEAN changed Myanmar statement on release of political detainees – sources. Reuters

Bannelier-Christakis K (2016) Military interventions against ISIL in Iraq, Syria and Lybia, and the legal basis of consent. Leiden J Int Law 29(3):743–775

Barela SJ (2017) Cross-border cyber ops to erode legitimacy: an act of coercion. Just Security

Bartels L (2004) A legal analysis of human rights clauses in the European Union's Euro-Mediterranean Association Agreements. Mediterr Politics 9(3):370

Bartels L (2023) Assessment of the implementation of the human rights clause in international and sectoral agreements. European Parliament, Directorate General for External Policies of the Union

Bennouna M (1974) Le Consentement a L'Ingérence militaire dans les conflits internes. Libraire Generale de Droit et de la Jurisprudence

Brian JE (2016) Remarks on International Law and Stability in Cyberspace

Buchan R, Tsagourias N (2017) The crisis in Crimea and the principle of non-intervention. Int Comm Law Rev 19(2–3):173

Byrne M (2016) Consent and the use of force: an examination of 'intervention by invitation' as a basis for US drone strikes in Pakistan, Somalia and Yemen. J Use Force Int Law 97(1):107–110

Cassese A (1999) A follow-up: forcible humanitarian countermeasures and opinio necessitatis. Eur J Int Law 10(4):792–796

Cassese A (2005) International law. Oxford University Press, Oxford

Cervell Hortal MJ (2023) Ciberinjerencias en procesos electorales y principio de no intervención (una perspectiva internacional y europea). Revista Electrónica de Estudios Internacionales 45:2

Christakis T, Mollard-Bannelier K (2005) Volenti non fit injuria? Les effects du consentement à l'ntervention militaire. Annuaire Français de droit international 50:102–137

Claudín C (2013) Operation Ukraine. Notes Int CIDOB 79

Corten O (2010) The law against war. The prohibition on the use of force in Contemporary International Law. Hart Publishing, London

Cortés Martín JM (2019) Ciberataques y responsabilidad: sobre las asimétricas incertidumbres del derecho internacional vigente. In: Millán Moro L, and Fernández Arribas (ed.), Ciberataques y ciberseguridad en la escena internacional. Thomson Reuters Aranzadi, Cizur Menor

Crawford J (2002) The International Law Commission's articles on state responsibility. Cambridge University Press, Cambridge

Damrosch LF (1989) Politics across borders: nonintervention and nonforcible influence over domestic affairs. Am J Int Law 83(1):1–50

De Wet E (2016) The modern practice of intervention by invitation in Africa and its implications for the prohibition of the use of force. Eur J Int Law 26(4):983–990

De Wet E (2020) The (im)permissility of military assistance on request during a civil war. J Use Force Int Law 7(1):26–34
Deeks A (2014) Russia in Ukraine: a reader responds. Lawfare Blog
Díaz Barrado CM (1989) Consentimiento, causa de exclusión de la ilicitud del uso de la fuerza en Derecho Internacional. Universidad de Zaragoza, Zaragoza
Doswald-Beck L (1985) The legal validity of military intervention by invitation of the government. Br Yearb Int Law 56(1):189–252
Efrony D, Shany Y (2018) A rule book on the shelf? Tallinn Manual 2.0 on cyberoperations and subsequent state practice. Am J Int Law 112(4):642
Fernández Arribas G, Wessel RA (2023) Promoting the rule of law through EU external relations and the principle of non-intervention under international law. In: Hinojosa-Martínez LM, Pérez-Bernardez C (eds) Enhancing the rule of law in the European Union's external action. Edward Elgar Publishing, Cheltenham
Ferro L, Ruys T (2018) The Saudi-led Military intervention in Yemen's Civil War-2015. In: Ruys T, Corten O (eds) The use of force in International Law. A case-based Approach. Oxford University Press, Oxford
Fitzmaurice G (1957) The general principles of International Law considered from the standpoint of the rule of law. In: Recueil des Cours Collected Courses of The Hague Academy of International Law, vol 92
Fox GH (2015) Intervention by invitation. In: Weller M (ed) The Oxford handbook of the use of force in International Law. Oxford University Press, Oxford
Fox GH (2018) The Vietnamese Intervention in Cambodia-1978. In: Ruys T, Corten O (eds) The use of force in International Law. A case-based Approach. Oxford University Press, Oxford
Freeman B (2002) Austria: The 1999 Parliament elections and the European Union Members' sanctions. Boston College International and Comparative Law Review 25(1):120
Gill FD (2022) The Jus ad bellum and Russia's "special military operation" in Ukraine. J Int Peacekeep 25:122
Gilmour DR (1967) The meaning of "intervene" within Article 2 (7) of the United Nations Charter. An historical perspective. Int Comp Law Q 16(2):330–352
Gray C (2014) The use of force and the International Legal Order. In: Evans MD (ed) International Law. Oxford University Press, Oxford
Green JA, Henderson C, Ruys T (2002) Russia's attack on Ukraine and the Jus ad Bellum. J Use Force Int Law 9(1):4–30
Grewe WG (2000) The Epochs of International Law. Walter de Gruyter, Berlin
Hafner G (2018) The intervention in Czechoslovakia-1968. In: Ruys T, Corten O, Hofer A (eds) The use of force in International Law. A case-based approach. Oxford University Press, Oxford
Happold M (2000) Fourteen against one: the EU Member States' response to freedom party participation in the Austrian Government. Int Comp Law Q 49(4):955
Henderson C (2018) The use of force and International Law. Cambridge University Press, Cambridge
Huseynov V (2017) Revisiting the Ukraine crisis: realist reflections on causes and consequences. CES Work Pap IX(4):582
Institut de Droit International (1975) The principle of non-intervention in civil wars. Mr Dietrich Schindler Rapporteur, Session of Wiesbaden
Institut de Droit International (2009) Present problems of the use of force in International Law. Sub-group: Intervention by Invitation, Gerhard Hafner Rapporteur, Session Naples
Institut de Droit International (2011) Present problems of the use of force in International Law. Sub-Group C – Military assistance on request. Gerhard Hafner Rapporteur, Session Rodhes
International Law Association (2018) Final report on aggression and the use of force, Sidney Conference
Jamnejad M, Woods M (2009) The principle of non-intervention. Leiden J Int Law 22(2):349
Jiménez de Aréchaga E (1978) International Law in the past third of a century. In: Recueil des Cours. Collected courses of the Hague Academy of International Law, vol 159

Kilibarda P (2022) Was Russia's recognition of the separatist Republics in Ukraine 'Manifestly' Unlawful? EJIL Talk!
Kilovaty I (2019) The Elephant in the room. AJIL Unbound 113:89
Kleczkowska A (2020) The meaning of treaty authorisation and ad hoc consent for the legality of military assistance on request. J Use Force Int Law 7(2):16
Kohen M (2012) The principle of non-intervention 25 years after the Nicaragua Judgment. Leiden J Int Law 25(1):158
Kolb R (2018) The Belgian Intervention in the Congo-1960 and 1964. In: Ruys T, Corten O (eds) The use of force in International Law. A case-based Approach. Oxford University Press, Oxford
Koskenniemi M (2005) From apology to Utopia. The structure of International Legal Argument. Cambridge University Press, Cambridge
Kunig P (2008) Intervention, prohibition of. In: Wolfrum R (ed) Max Planck Encyclopedia of Public International Law
Lenaerts K (2014) The Kadi Saga and the rule of law within the EU. SMU Law Rev 76(4):707
Levin DH (2016) Partisan electoral interventions by the great powers: Introducing the PEIG Dataset. Confl Manag Peace Sci 36(1):94
Metodieva A (2018) How disinformation harmed the referendum in Macedonia. Ger Marshal Fund US
Millán Moro L (1990) La Opinio Iuris en el Derecho Internacional Contemporáneo. Editorial Centro de Estudios Ramón Areces, Madrid
Müllerson R (2014) Ukraine: victim of geopolitics. Chin J Int Law 13(1):133–145
Nasu H (2013) Revisiting the principle of non-intervention: a structural principle of International Law or a political obstacle to regional security in Asia? Asian J Int Law 3(1):30
Nuruzzaman M (2022) "Responsibility to protect" and the BRICS: a decade after the intervention in Libya. Glob Stud Q 2(4):5
O'Connell ME (2018) The crisis in Ukraine – 2104. In: Ruys T, Corten O, Hofer A (eds) The use of force in International Law. A case-based approach. Oxford University Press, Oxford
Office of the Director of National Intelligence (2017) Background to "assessing Russian activities and intentions in Recent US elections": the analytic process and cyber incident attribution
Ohlin JD (2017) Did Russian cyber interference in the 2016 election violate International Law? Texas Law Rev 85:1593
Opemheim L (1905) International Law. A tratise, vol I. Logman, Green and Co., London
Ouchakov NA (1974) La compétence interne des états et la non-intervention dans le droit international contemporain. In: Recueil des Cours. Collected courses of the Hague Academy of International Law, vol 141
Pagden A, Lawrance J (eds) (1991) Francisco Vitoria, political writings. Cambridge University Press, Cambridge
Potter PB (1930) L'intervention en droit international modern. In: Recueil des Cours. Collected courses of the Hague Academy of International Law, vol 32
Pozo Serrano P (2016) El uso de la fuerza contra el Estado Islámico en Irak y Siria: problemas de fundamentación jurídica. Anuario Español de Derecho Internacional 32:141–182
Prandler A (2008) The concept of 'responsibility to protect' as an emerging norm versus 'humanitarian intervention. In: International Law between universalism and fragmentation. Festschrift in Honour of Gerhard Hafner. Brill/Nijhoff, Leiden
Remiro Brotons A (1996) Civilizados, bárbaros y salvajes en el nuevo orden internacional. McGraw-Hill, Madrid
Roberts A (2009) Legality vs legitimacy: can uses of force be illegal but justified? In: Alston P, Macdonalds E (eds) Human rights, intervention and the use of force. Oxford University Press, Oxford
Rosenstock R (1971) The declaration of principles of international law concerning friendly relations: a survey. Am J Int Law 65(5):713–735
Roth BR (2017) Whither democratic legitimism? Contextualizing recent developments in the recognition and non-recognition of governments. AJIL Unbound 108:215

Rotondo A, Salvati P (2018) Fake news, (Dis) information and the principle of non-intervention. Cyber Defense Rev 14-15:209
Ruys T, Corten O, Hofer A (2018) The use of force in International Law. A case-based approach. Oxford University Press, Oxford
Ruys T, Rodríguez Silvestre F (2021) L'Union contre-attaque : la proposition d'Instrument Anti-Coercition (IAC) de l'UE vue sous l'angle du droit international. Annuaire Français de Droit International 67:143–171
Schachter O (1984) The right of states to use armed force. Mich Law Rev 82(5):1620
Schermers HG, Blokker NM (2011) International Institutional Law. Martinus-Nijhoff/Brill Publishers, Leiden
Schmitt MN (2017) Tallinn manual 2.0 on the International Law applicable to cyber operations. Cambridge University Press, Cambridge
Sender O (2012) Coercion. In: Wolfrum R (ed) The Max Planck Encyclopedia of Public International Law. Oxford University Press, Oxford
Shaw M (2017) International Law. Cambridge University Press, Cambridge
Shirlow E (2014) Taking Stock: assessing the implications of the Kadi Saga for International Law and the Law of the European Union. Melb J Int Law 18(2):534
Strangio S (2021) Assessing the outcome of ASEAN's special meeting on Myanmar. The Diplomat
Tomuschat C (1999) International Law: ensuring the survival of mankind on the eve of a new century. In: Recueil des Cours. Collected courses of the Hague Academy of International Law, vol 281
Torres Soriano MR (2022) Operaciones de influencia vs. desinformación: diferencias y puntos de conexión. Instituto Español de Estudios Estratégicos. Documento de Opinión 64:6
Tsagourias N (2020) Electoral cyber interference, self-determination and the principle of non intervention y cyberspace. In: Broeders D, Van den Berg B (eds) Governing cyberspace: behavior, power and diplomacy. Rowman & Littlefield, London
Vermeer Z (2014) Intervention with the consent of a deposed (but legitimate) government? Playing the Sierra Leone card. EJIL: Talk!
Watson JS (1997) Autointerpretation, competence, and the continuing validity of Article 2(7) of the UN Charter. Am J Int Law 71(1):60–83
Whitton BJ (1948) Propaganda and International Law. In: Recueil des Cours. Collected courses of the Hague Academy of International Law, vol 72
Whitton JB (1971) Hostile international propaganda and International Law. Annals Am Acad Pol Soc Sci 398:19
Wright Q (1960) Subversive intervention. Am J Int Law 54(3):536

Chapter 6
The Prohibition of the Use of Force Under Attack

The prohibition of the use of force is a fundamental modern principle of international law proclaimed in the United Nations Charter in 1945.[1] Despite its recent history, the principle is arguably one of the most contested, some commentators even claiming that it fell into desuetude[2] within a short space of time. Just as Franck asked, 'Who killed art. 2.4?',[3] some scholars are questioning whether given the frequent violation of rule, we can in fact consider that states have given their consent to it. They are also raising the question as to whether it is necessary to adapt the rule to the new security context to avoid it being ignored altogether by the states.[4]

On the other hand, contrary to these negative positions, Crawford and Nicholson clearly regard that the Charter, together with the application of the principle of the prohibition of the use of force have been successful. They support their argument referring to the decline in the number of wars since World War II.[5] Russia's aggression against Ukraine has nevertheless called for an in-depth analysis of the fragility of the principle as well as its future, as it is among the most flagrant violations of the principle since the mentioned World War. Despite its clear condemnation by the international community[6] however, actions directed towards stopping it have differed among Western countries and their allies, and the Global South.[7]

---

[1] Cassese (2005), p. 55; Schmidt (2003), p. 521.

[2] Remiro Brotons refers to the problems faced today by this principle. Remiro Brotons et al. (2007), p. 1056.

[3] See Simpson (2008), p. 198.

[4] Schmidt (2003), p. 546.

[5] Crawford and Nicholson (2015), p. 101.

[6] UN General Assembly, *Aggression against Ukraine*, 2 March 2022, A/RES/ES-11/1.

[7] Ghilès (2023).

G. Fernández Arribas, *Contemporary Challenges to the Fundamental Principles of International Law and EU Interaction*, European Union and its Neighbours in a Globalized World 19, https://doi.org/10.1007/978-3-031-75453-1_6

This recent attack on the principle of the prohibition of the use of force and the different positions referred to above, suggest perhaps an erosion of the principle rather than its disappearance.

Despite Grotious' statement '*sed quia bellum pacis caufa fufcipitur*',[8] the principle of the prohibition of use of force is essential to ensure peaceful relations between states and the existence of the international community. Therefore, attempts to diminish its value, erode it, or deny its existence can have grave consequences for the international system and for the survival of the international community. By examining new interpretations of the principle as well as state practice, we will be able to determine the strength of the principle and its role in the international community.

Contemporary problems regarding the principle of the prohibition of the use of force stem essentially from the practices of states that are contrary to this principle.[9] They also derive from attempts to legalise these practices through new interpretations of the principle or the elaboration of new legal theories. We may, nonetheless, encounter issues or contradictions with respect to other fundamental principles, typically the respect for human rights and the well-known theories of humanitarian intervention analysed in the previous chapter.

Regarding the link between the principle of the prohibition of the use of force and other fundamental principles, the violation of the former automatically entails the violation of other major principles, such as peaceful settlement, non-intervention, and sovereign equality. As Toumuschat stated, 'non-use of force was a determination of tremendous legal consequences'.[10] Turning the principle into the cornerstone of international peaceful relations[11] makes it an interesting basis for an analysis of the international community. In this regard, we could focus on the adherence of the members of the international community; the evolution of the members of that international community; the rise of new subjects or actors; the role of this principle in the continuity of the international community; as well as the value, adoption, and interpretation of international norms.

The principle of the prohibition of the use of force illustrates the various main sources of international law because, as stated by the International Court of Justice in the *Nicaragua*[12] case, the prohibition of the use of force is customary law as well as treaty law. However, the prohibition of the use of force has also been regarded as a *jus cogens* norm,[13] and the first attempts to modulate this principle were made taking

[8]"War, however, is undertaken in order to secure peace". Grotious (1625).

[9]Abellán Honrubia (2005), p. 67

[10]Tomuschat (1999), p. 206.

[11]Jiménez de Aréchaga (1978), p. 87.

[12]ICJ, *Military and Paramilitary Activities in and against Nicaragua*, para. 34.

[13]Remiro Brotons et al. (2007), p. 1057; Henderson (2018), p. 24; Orakhelashvili (2015), p. 165. The ICJ referred jus cogens status of the prohibition of the use of force in these terms: 'The International Law Commission, in the course of its work on the codification of the law of treaties, expressed the view that "the law of the Charter concerning the prohibition of the use of force in itself constitutes a conspicuous example of a rule in international law having the character of jus cogens"'. ICJ, Military and Paramilitary Activities in and against Nicaragua, para. 190. Contrary

this status into account. Therefore, the subject of the prohibition of the use of force as a *jus cogens* norm will call for an analysis of the value and complexities that emerge when exploring this type of norm. Of note again is the fact that *jus cogens* norms are among the drivers that propelled international society into an international community. Indeed, they led to identifying common principles and norms that had to be respected by all states because they represented common community interests and values.

6.1 *Jus cogens* and the Prohibition of the Use of Force

According to the definition of *jus cogens* established in Article 53 of the Vienna Convention on the Law of Treaties,[14] a *jus cogens* norm 'is a norm accepted and recognized by the international community of States as a whole as a norm from which no derogation is permitted and which can be modified only by a subsequent norm of general international law having the same character'. This definition does not permit any derogation and has served as a basis to determine the existence of a core element in the prohibition of the use of force: one that is peremptory by nature and is, therefore, not subject to derogation.

6.1.1 *The Core Element of the Prohibition of the Use of Force*

To determine the peremptory content of the principle, we need to turn towards Article 2.4 of the United Nations Charter, which establishes that '(a)ll Members shall refrain in their international relations from the threat or use of force against the territorial integrity or political independence of any state, or in any other manner inconsistent with the Purposes of the United Nations'. Despite the clear content of the article, the Charter system contains exceptions to this principle: Article 51 that regulates self-defence, and Chapter VII that allows the use of force authorised by the Security Council.[15] These two exceptions suggest a narrow concept of the prohibition of the use of force that would have a peremptory character: acts of aggression.[16]

to this position Green highlights the problems of given the status of jus cogens to the prohibition of the use of force. Green (2015), p. 2.

[14] United Nations, Vienna Convention on the Law of Treaties, 23 May 1969, United Nations, Treaty Series, vol. 1155.

[15] Remiro Brotons considers that chap. VII is not an exception but a complement to the prohibition of the use of force. Remiro Brotons et al. (2007), p. 1063.

[16] See Ronzitti (1986), p. 150.

According to this theory, the acts included in the General Assembly Resolution 3314 (XXIX) on the definition of aggression[17] would be those of a *jus cogens* nature, which would, in fact, concur with the system established in the Charter. In this regard, Article 6 of Resolution 3314 (XXIX) establishes that 'nothing in this Definition shall be construed as in any way enlarging or diminishing the scope of the Charter, including its provisions concerning cases in which the use of force is lawful'. Therefore, the Resolution allows the use of force in the cases established in the Charter. In the same vein, the fourth report of Special Rapporteur Dire Tladi on peremptory norms of general international law refers to the prohibition of aggression as a *jus cogens* norm. He considers, however, that other alternative terms exist, such as 'prohibition of the use of force, prohibition of aggressive force and the law of the Charter on the prohibition of force'.[18] In this case, the report is not clear about the proper content of the *jus cogens* norm, since the evidence analysed refers sometimes to use of force and at other times to aggression.

For his part, Orakhelashvili prefers to focus on the Charter provisions to shape the *jus cogens* nature of the prohibition of the use of force. He considers that Article 2.4 and Article 51 'command the status of *jus cogens'*.[19] The result is an extensive concept of the prohibition. Indeed, not only will acts of aggression have a *jus cogens* character, but also other less serious forms of the use of force, as long as they are not used in the course of an action of self-defence.

Moving on to the content of Resolution 2625 (XXV), the principle is defined in general terms, without including express exceptions and as an umbrella term encompassing various actions. The said actions include aggression, which is considered a crime against peace, but also others such as 'encouraging the organisation of irregular forces'. The latter is not considered an act of aggression according to Resolution 3314 because it requires the 'sending by or on behalf of a state'[20] of those groups. Therefore, Resolution 2625 (XXV) builds a broad understanding of the use of force, not just that of act of aggression. In addition, the Resolution also contains the exceptions established in the Charter as it states that '(n)othing in the foregoing paragraphs shall be construed as enlarging or diminishing in any way the scope of the provisions of the Charter concerning cases in which the use of force is lawful'.

For its part, the International Court of Justice has not expressly recognised the prohibition of the use of force as a *jus cogens* norm. However, the reference to the International Law Commission in the *Nicaragua* case and its assertion about its *jus cogens* nature[21] has been interpreted as a recognition of the norm's *jus cogens*

---

[17] UN General Assembly, Definition of Aggression, 14 December 1974, A/RES/3314.

[18] UN General Assembly, Fourth Report on Jus cogens by Dire Tladi, 31 January 2019, A/CN.4/727, para. 62.

[19] Orakhelashvili (2015), p. 165.

[20] Article 3 (g). UN General Assembly, Definition of Aggression, 14 December 1974, A/RES/3314.

[21] ICJ, *Military and Paramilitary Activities in and against Nicaragua*, para. 190.

status.[22] In this regard, the Court established a difference between grave uses of force and less grave uses of force, which has led some scholars to consider that the Court was giving the status of peremptory norm to the former.[23]

To summarise, the status of the prohibition of the use of force as a *jus cogens* norm is without doubt, but the core content of the principle that would have that *jus cogens* status is contested. Regarding this content, we could state that the prohibition of the use of force with a peremptory status would be that outlined by the United Nations system, consisting of the prohibition of the use *of any kind* of force when it is not permitted by Article 51 or authorised by the Security Council. This interpretation would suggest that actions, such as hot pursuit, which are normally justified by necessity, would be regarded as a violation of a *jus cogens* norm.[24] In addition, this interpretation would also conflict with the theory of intervention by request analysed in the previous chapter and which uses consent as justification.[25] This controversial situation has led Henderson to refer to the *sui generis* character of the prohibition of the use of force as a *jus cogens* norm.[26]

The International Law Commission's Second Report on *jus cogens* establishes that the acceptance of a norm as *jus cogens* does not require unanimity and that 'it would be sufficient if a very large majority did so'.[27] Focusing on state practice regarding acceptance, a contradiction can be observed between state practice and the broad concept of prohibition of the use of force. Conversely, it is possible to affirm that the prohibition of aggression, i.e., the narrow concept, is widely accepted in practice. Therefore, considering uses of force other than aggression as a violation of a *jus cogens* norm may raise concerns.

6.1.2 The Risks of the Extensive Interpretations

The *jus cogens* status of the prohibition of the use of force, which does not allow derogations, has led states and commentators to make extensive interpretations of the exceptions to the prohibition of the use of force or narrow interpretations of Article 2.4. Their objective is to accommodate actions that could easily be considered as

---

[22] Orakhelashvili (2015), p. 165; Green (2015), p. 223; UN General Assembly, Fourth Report on Jus cogens by Dire Tladi, paras. 63–64.

[23] Abass (2004), p. 200.

[24] Article 25, UN General Assembly, *Responsibility of States for internationally wrongful acts*, 8 January 2008, A/RES/62/61. See Henderson (2018), p. 67. Corten considers that not all the uses of force constitute a violation of Article 2.4, according to him there is a threshold of gravity. Corten (2010), pp. 67 et seq.

[25] Article 20, UN General Assembly, Responsibility of States for internationally wrongful acts 8 January 2008, A/RES/62/61.

[26] Henderson (2018), pp. 24–25.

[27] UN General Assembly, Second Report on Jus cogens by Dire Tladi, 16 March 2017, A/CN.4/706, para. 67.

violations of this principle. In this regard, we can mention the following: the rescuing of nationals (sometimes justified as an act of self-defence);[28] individual humanitarian intervention (justified as an action to achieve the purposes of the Charter, that is, the promotion of human rights);[29] anticipatory or pre-emptive self-defence; and the theory of unwilling or unable which entails a broad interpretation of Article 51 of the Charter. In this regard, O'Connell warns against the extensive interpretations of peremptory norms and specifically the prohibition of the use of force, affirming that the interpretation may not result in a weaker norm, but that on the contrary an "accurate interpretation may permissibly lead to greater restrictions, not lesser".[30]

Can all these actions and theories be considered an attack on the well-founded principle of the prohibition of the use of force? Crawford and Nicholson established that 'there is no evidence that even a single state considers the prohibition of the use of force not to be binding'.[31] Therefore, we must ask whether attempts to dismantle this principle have taken place, not through its rejection, but through erosion, shaping the principle according to the needs of some major international powers, rather than to the needs of the international community. In this regard, the declarations and positions of some states appear to indicate that the principle is weakening, including in the case of Russia's aggression against Ukraine.

The narrow or broad interpretations of Article 2.4 or Article 51of the Charter mentioned above are not recent: we can trace this kind of practice back to when the Charter was first adopted.[32] However, the 9/11 terrorist attacks led certain states—upported by legal advisors and some scholars—to passionately engage in justifying the use of force against the so-called 'rogue states' or non-state actors in scenarios where the use of force did not appear to comply with the requirements established in the Charter. This behaviour was followed by major international powers such as the United Sates supported by Australia, the United Kingdom, and Israel.[33] Nevertheless, the practice was rejected by other international powers such as China or Russia, who reaffirmed in their cynical 2016 Declaration on the Promotion of International Law 'the principle that States shall refrain from the threat or use of force in violation

[28] See Cassese (2005), p. 367; Bowet (1986), p. 40; Forteau (2015), pp. 954–956; Henderson (2018), pp. 247 *et seq.*

[29] See the statement by the UK Permanent Representative to the United Nations, Sir Jeremy Greenstock, on 24 March 1999 regarding the intervention in Kosovo: 'We have taken this action with regret, in order to save lives'. UN Security Council, Letter dated 24 March 1999 from the Permanent Representative of the Russian Federation to the United Nations addressed to the President of the Security Council (S/1999/320). 24 March 1999, Meeting Records, S/PV.3988. See also Gray (2014), p. 624.

[30] O'Connell (2018), p. 861.

[31] Crawford and Nicholson (2015), p. 112.

[32] See Jiménez de Aréchaga (1978), pp. 86–111; Cheng (1953), pp. 69–99.

[33] UN Security Council Arria-formula meeting: 'Upholding the collective security system of the Charter of the United Nations: the use of force in international law, non-State actors and legitimate self-defence', held on 24 February 2021. S/2021/247, 16 March 2021.

of the United Nations Charter and therefore condemn unilateral military interventions'.[34]

In this chapter, we will focus on two of the uses of force mentioned above: anticipatory as well as pre-emptive self-defence; and the theory of unwilling or unable, which have altered the traditional concept of self-defence, that is, self-defence against states and against an armed attack that has already been launched.[35] These two theories also serve as a basis to analyse some of the major challenges faced by the international community, the evolution and interaction of norms, as well as the recognition of new subjects. These latter elements play an essential role in today's system of international law and its analysis.

6.2 Anticipatory and Pre-Emptive Self-defence as an Expansionist Use of Force in Self-Defence

A state's recourse to self-defence before suffering an armed attack has been extensively studied. There is also much confusion surrounding the terms used to refer to different types of self-defence: preventative, anticipatory, preventive, pre-emptive or interceptive. This section, however, will focus on two concepts that correspond to the most widespread options adopted by states. The first is anticipatory self-defence, meaning 'immediately preceding the launching of an armed attack'.[36] And the second is pre-emptive self-defence, adopted in order 'to prevent more temporally remote threats of an armed attack from coming to fruition at some point in the future'.[37] The former is more widely accepted than the latter.[38]

The intense recent legal development of these two kinds of self-defence owes to a major challenge that the international community is facing today: international terrorism.[39] The menace has led some states and scholars to consider the need to alter a state's approach to international threats. For example, in 2004, Blair stated: 'the risk of this new global terrorism and its interaction with states or organizations or individuals proliferating WMD, is one I simply am not prepared to run'.[40] This fresh approach to international threats required a legal basis and the concepts of

[34] The Declaration of the Russian Federation and the People's Republic of China on the Promotion of International Law, 2016. https://www.fmprc.gov.cn/eng/wjdt_665385/2649_665393/201608/t20160801_679466.html

[35] Kammerhofer (2015), p. 629.

[36] Henderson (2018), p. 277. See also Glennon (2015), p. 86.

[37] Henderson (2018), p. 281.

[38] Bowett (1994); Higgins (1994); Deeks (2015); Sands (2012), p. 351; Simpson (2008), p. 204.

[39] See Security Council 1373 (2001) 28 September 2001; Security Council Resolution 1540 (2004), 28 April 2004; UN General Assembly, In larger freedom: towards development, security and human rights for all: report of the Secretary-General, 21 March 2005, A/59/2005.

[40] 'Prime Minister warns of continuing global terror threat', Sedgefield 2004, Tony Blair (Labour). http://www.britishpoliticalspeech.org/speech-archive.htm?speech=282

anticipatory self-defence and pre-emptive self-defence found their place here. However, the problem was how to frame these new interpretations of self-defence in Article 51 of the UN Charter.

To analyse self-defence, we must interpret Article 51 bearing Dire's requirements in mind: this article must be interpreted in good faith; taking into account the content and purpose of the Charter; as an exception to the general rule of the prohibition of the use of force; and taking into account other principles of international law, such as territorial integrity or equal sovereignty.[41]

Considering those requirements, the first problem to address when analysing anticipatory and pre-emptive self-defence in relation to Article 51 is the provision content, which establishes that '(n)othing in the present Charter shall impair the inherent right of individual or collective self-defence if an *armed attack occurs* against a Member of the United Nations'.[42] According to the above definition of anticipatory or pre-emptive self-defence, states do not need to be actually subjected to an armed attack, only to the threat of an armed attack. The latter was included in the concept of prohibition of the use of force but was not expressly included in Article 51 as an action that may entitle the use of force in self-defence. In this regard, the definition of self-defence drafted by the Leiden Policy Recommendations on Counter-Terrorism and International Law[43] is surprising since it accepts 'the use of force in self-defence in response to an armed attack, *or an imminent threat thereof*, in accordance with Article 51 of the Charter', introducing the word 'threat' as if it were part of Article 51.

6.2.1 Can Customary Law Be a Basis for Anticipatory and Pre-Emptive Self-Defence?

One of the main legal arguments to resolve the lack of reference to a threat of an armed attack in Article 51 is based on the word 'inherent' included at the beginning of the said article, and on its relation to customary law. As mentioned above, in the *Nicaragua* case, the International Court of Justice identified the dual nature of the prohibition of the use of force as both customary law and treaty law obligation, while also considering that their content could differ.[44] In the same vein, the Court confirmed the customary law character of Article 51, stating that: 'The Court therefore finds that Article 51 of the Charter is only meaningful on the basis that there is a "natural" or "inherent" right of self-defence, and it is hard to see how this can be other than of a customary nature'.[45]

[41] Tladi (2017), p. 4.

[42] Emphasis added.

[43] Schrijver and Van Den Herik (2010).

[44] ICJ, *Military and Paramilitary Activities in and against Nicaragua*, para. 175.

[45] *Ibid.*, para. 176.

These Court statements have been regarded as essential to examine the relationship between customary law and treaty law. Certain scholars and states, however, have also used them to reinterpret the clear wording of Article 51, in most cases referring to the Caroline incident. In this latter case, Daniel Webster, the US Secretary of State, addressed a letter in 1841 to the British Ambassador establishing that in order to claim self-defence, the government had 'to show a necessity of self-defence, instant, overwhelming, leaving no choice of means, and no moment for deliberation',[46] making no reference to the requirement of a prior armed attack. This formula was also referred to in the Nuremberg Tribunal,[47] which according to some commentators confirmed its value.[48]

However, a number of lacunae can be found in this interpretation. First, the Caroline incident—where the Caroline ship was captured and destroyed by British forces on United States territory—took place after previous military actions by rebels on Canadian territory.[49] It was therefore possible to consider this action as a response to a previous attack.[50]

Second, we should deem that it is anachronistic to base the existence of a custom in the twenty-first century on a single incident that took place in 1837.[51] Indeed, in the nineteenth century, the recent prohibition of the use of force to which the rule of self-defence is an exception did not exist. More than a single piece of nineteenth century evidence should be taken into account to determine the content of the right to self-defence as a custom. We should also examine how the practice has evolved, and mainly after 1945.[52] In this regard, in *Nicaragua,* when analysing the value of the customary character of the prohibition of the use of force, the International Court of Justice considered that issues such as necessity, proportionality, or the concept of armed attack were not included in Article 51,[53] considering customary law essential to interpret those concepts, but not to change the content of Article 51.

---

[46] British-American Diplomacy. The Caroline case https://avalon.law.yale.edu/19th_century/br-1842d.asp

[47] 'It must be remembered that preventive action in a foreign territory is justified only in case of an 'instant, overwhelming, and leaving no choice of means, and no moment for deliberation'', International Military Tribunal, Judgment of 1 October 1946, p.41.

[48] Cheng (1953), p. 87.

[49] Corten (2010), p. 409; Cheng (1953), p. 85; British-American Diplomacy. The Caroline case https://avalon.law.yale.edu/19th_century/br-1842d.asp

[50] Corten (2010), p. 409.

[51] In addition, the incident took place between two states, being difficult to refer to a custom of general character. It is therefore necessary address more cases or evidences in order to talk about a custom. In the same line, and regarding the *opinion juris*, the International Court of Justice in the Gulf of Maine case established that 'a set of customary rules whose presence in the opinion juris of States can be tested by induction based on the analysis of a sufficiently extensive and convincing practice'. ICJ, Delimitation of the Maritime Boundary in the Gulf of Maine Area, Judgment, of 12 October 184: I.C.J. Reports 1984, para. 111.

[52] Tladi (2017), p. 4.

[53] ICJ, *Military and Paramilitary Activities in and against Nicaragua*, para. 176.

In addition, we must remember that the Nuremberg Tribunal was a criminal tribunal and that the judges were experts in criminal law.[54] Therefore, their conclusions cannot be considered authoritative regarding such theoretical issues strongly linked to international law.

With respect to the elements of customary law, practice and *opinio juris*, to base the existence of a custom on a single letter sent by the US Secretary of State would not pass, for example, the US Supreme Court's test in the *Paquete Habana* case that unfolded almost 60 years later. In this latter case, in order to establish the existence of a custom, the Supreme Court considered orders from the fifteenth century onwards, as well as treaties, judgements of local courts, state practices during wars and scholarly opinions.

Finally, even though the existence of that custom can be traced back to the nineteenth century, interpreting the word 'inherent' based on a nineteenth century custom would leave the clear requirement laid out in Article51 without effect: an 'armed attack occurs'. As Millán Moro stated in his analysis of the International Court of Justice case law, a treaty interpretation cannot contradict its letter and spirit.[55] Moreover, the Court established that the

> first duty of a tribunal which is called upon to interpret and apply the provisions of a treaty, is to endeavour to give effect to them in their natural and ordinary meaning in the context in which they occur. If the relevant words in their natural and ordinary meaning make sense in their context, that is an end of the matter.[56]

Even though this reasoning may clearly support the need for an armed attack to occur, it must also be acknowledged that Article 31.1 of the Vienna Convention refers to the object and purpose.[57] In this case, the purpose is to save state integrity and to allow the state to protect itself from an armed attack. Therefore, to oblige states to wait until the armed attack has taken place, despite having the possibility of avoiding it or confronting it beforehand, would not be in line with the object and purpose of Article 51 of the Charter. It could also produce an outcome that would be 'manifestly absurd or unreasonable' according to Article 32 of the Vienna Convention. This situation may serve to give some validity to the theory of anticipatory self-defence, but we must remember that the definition of anticipatory is vague and that it is impossible to clearly establish the precise moment in which it can be exercised. Therefore, the theory creates the risk that powerful states use it to justify any use of force.

---

[54] See Corten (2010), p. 417.

[55] Millán Moro (2007-2008), p. 487.

[56] ICJ, *Competence of Assembly regarding admission to the United Nations*, Advisory Opinion: I.C. J. Reports 1950.

[57] Millán Moro (2007-2008), pp. 500–502.

6.2.2 *Instrumentalising International Organizations to Expand the Concept of Self-Defence*

The legality and acceptance of anticipatory self-defence has also been justified based on the position of international organisations. Indeed, due to their growing activity and role in the international community, they have become an instance of legitimation.[58] Therefore, as long as we can trace back and identify the acceptance of a specific action of use of force by an international organisation, it could have the appearance of legality. This is also a reason why some decisions of international organisations are instrumentalised, misused and misinterpreted—and not only in the domain of the use of force.

Regarding the United Nations and anticipatory self-defence, one of the most commonly cited documents is the report of the High Level Panel on Threats, Challenges and Change established by the Secretary General to discuss the United Nations reform on its 60th anniversary.[59] In this document, the panel members concluded that a 'threatened Sate, according to long established international law, can take military action as long as the threatened attack is imminent', and rejected pre-emptive self-defence when the threat 'is not imminent but still claimed to be real: for example the acquisition with allegedly hostile intent, of nuclear weapons-making capability'.[60] In any case, owing to the opposition of the majority of states, this statement, which was also confirmed by the Secretary General,[61] was not included in the final document adopted by the United Nations members as a whole.[62] Therefore, the former document cannot be considered authoritative on the issue. It highlights that the consent-based system is still at the heart of international law and confirms the narrow interpretation of Article 51, ensuring protection against the abuses of the use of force.

The endorsement of uses of force by the United Nations that could be qualified as pre-emptive self-defence has also been used to confirm their legality. In this regard, in the 2003 Operation Iraqi Freedom, the United States justified the use of force against Iraq considering an extensive interpretation of the Security Council Resolution 1441. According to the United States, Resolution 1441 activated the previous Resolution 678 (implicit authorisation).[63] However, the intervention was also based

[58] Pérez-Prat Durbán (2004), p. 21. Medina Ortega refers to the risks of the United Nations becomes an instance of legitimations of the actions of the power states. Medina Ortega (2005), p. 910.

[59] UN General Assembly, Note [transmitting report of the High-level Panel on Threats, Challenges and Change, entitled "A more secure world: our shared responsibility"], 2 December 2004, A/59/565.

[60] Ibid. p. 63; See Corten (2010), p. 427.

[61] UN General Assembly, In larger freedom: towards development, security and human rights for all: report of the Secretary-General, 21 March 2005, A/59/2005.

[62] Corten (2010), pp. 426–435; Henderson (2018), p. 291.

[63] See Simpson (2008), p. 206; Corten (2010), p. 440; Sands (2012), pp. 36 *et seq.*; Gray (2014), p. 639.

on a case of pre-emptive self-defence given that, according to the United States, Iraq possessed weapons of mass destruction and intended to use them.[64] This operation demonstrated the risks of pre-emptive self-defence since there were ultimately no weapons of mass destruction.[65]

On the other hand, the lack of any condemnation by the Security Council,[66] together with the United Nations' participation, and the Security Council's approval of the rebuilding of the country by the occupying forces were understood as a confirmation of the legality of the coalition's actions. Does this mean that the Security Council's mere absence of pronunciation entails approval?

Given the composition of the Security Council in which the United States has a permanent seat and a right of veto, and taking into account its practice, the absence of a Security Council's resolution condemning the actions cannot be regarded as conclusive. The resolution would need the United States' vote in favour, and it would be rather naive to expect the state to engage in self-condemnation.[67] In addition, as the Permanent Court of International Justice stated in the *Danube* case, toleration does not give rise to a legal right or the acceptance of a right.[68] Therefore, toleration by the Security Council cannot be understood as a confirmation of a legal practice.

6.2.3 State Practice and Pre-Emptive Self-Defence

Finally, those attempting to give a legal umbrella to pre-emptive self-defence have used the practice of the states, the main subjects of international law, as their main source of justification.

The analysis of this practice has considered not only the situations in which states have used force pre-emptively, but also the declarations, national rules or documents. In this latter case, the 2002 US National Security Strategy[69] can be regarded as the key document on the matter. It established that:

> The United States has long maintained the option of preemptive actions to counter a sufficient threat to our national security. The greater the threat, the greater is the risk of inaction—and the more compelling the case for taking anticipatory action to defend ourselves, even if uncertainty remains as to the time and place of the enemy's attack. To forestall

[64] Henderson (2018), p. 288; Gray (2014), p. 639; Corten (2010), p. 440.

[65] Duelfer (2018), p. 2.

[66] See Andrés Saenz de Santamaria (2012), p. 556.

[67] As Torrecuadrada García-Lozano stated, the right of veto is to be expected to be used in order to avoid the consequences of the implementation of the collective security system. Torrecuadrada García-Lozano (2018).

[68] PCJI, Jurisdiction of European Commission of Danube Between Galatz and Braila, Advisory Opinion, 1927 P.C.I.J. Series B-No. 14, paras. 93–95.

[69] The National Security Strategy of the United States of America, September 2002. https://2009-2017.state.gov/documents/organization/63562.pdf

> or prevent such hostile acts by our adversaries, the United States will, if necessary, act preemptively.

This policy was later confirmed by Prime Minister Blair when he stated that 'we surely have a duty and a right to *prevent* the threat (proliferation and acquisition of weapons of mass destruction illegally) materializing'.[70] In any case, the United Kingdom seems more favourable to anticipatory self-defence than to pre-emptive self-defence since the former Attorney-General, in its legal opinion to the Prime Minister in 2003, stated that:

> in my opinion there must be some degree of imminence. I am aware that USA has been arguing for recognition of a broad doctrine right to use force to pre-empt danger in the future (. . .) this is not a doctrine which, in my opinion, exists or is recognized in international law.[71]

This doctrine of pre-emptive self-defence has not been abandoned by the United States. On the contrary, it has been concealed in the subsequent National Security Strategies and policies, as in the case of Obama's doctrine of "Necessary Force",[72] or in the Biden National Security Strategy, in which the use of force is linked to American interests without any reference to international law.

> America will not hesitate to use force when necessary to defend our national interests. But we will do so as the last resort and only when the objectives and mission are clear and achievable, consistent with our values and laws, alongside non-military tools, and the mission is undertaken with the informed consent of the American people.[73]

Regarding state activities in the field, there are only three major cases[74] in which states explicitly recognised and acted based on a right of pre-emptive self-defence. The latest, i.e., Russia's aggression, will be addressed in a separate section. The first

---

[70] 'Prime Minister warns of continuing global terror threat', Sedgefield 2004, Tony Blair (Labour). http://www.britishpoliticalspeech.org/speech-archive.htm?speech=282. See Sands (2012), p. 346.

[71] UK Government. National Archives https://webarchive.nationalarchives.gov.uk/20170831105413/http://www.iraqinquiry.org.uk/media/247743/2003-03-07-minute-goldsmith-to-prime-minister-iraq-resolution-1441.pdf, para. 3.

[72] Herderson (2010), p. 3.

[73] National Security Strategy, October 2022, p. 20. https://www.whitehouse.gov/wp-content/uploads/2022/10/Biden-Harris-Administrations-National-Security-Strategy-10.2022.pdf. While the 2017 Trump National Security Strategy did not expressly mention the pre-emptive use of force, there were some veiled references, such as: "we will pursue threat to their source, so that jihadist terrorists are stopped before they ever reach our borders", "(T)his system (missile defense system) will include the ability to defeat missile threats prior to launch" or "we will act against sanctuaries and prevent their reemergence, before they can threaten the U.S. homeland". National Security Strategy of the United States, December 2017. https://trumpwhitehouse.archives.gov/wp-content/uploads/2017/12/NSS-Final-12-18-2017-0905.pdf. In any case, support for this doctrine could be observed in practice when after the killing of General Soleimani, the US Department of Defense confirmed in a statement that "This strike was aimed at deterring future Iranian attack plans". Statement by the Department of Defense, 2 January 2020. https://www.defense.gov/News/Releases/Release/Article/2049534/statement-by-the-department-of-defense/

[74] Deeks considers that it is infrequent to base on pre-emption to initiate attack. Deeks (2015), p. 676. The others cases referred as precedents of anticipatory or pre-emptive self-defence had actually a justification on a previous attack, as the Six Days war or the attack of Iraq against Iran.

case is the aforementioned Operation Iraqi Freedom, in which the United States relied on pre-emptive self-defence.[75] The positions of other allies and third states were not so clear, however. The United Kingdom and Australia did not rely on pre-emptive self-defence to carry out the attack,[76] and the same justification was rejected by France, Germany, and Belgium as well as by the Non-Aligned Movement (125 states) together with the Islamic Conference Organisation (57 states).[77] Therefore, the United States did not find any support for its argument, ultimately relying on a Security Council authorisation through the contested interpretation of Resolution 1444.

The second case was Israeli strike on an Iraqi nuclear reactor in 1981. Israel, in a letter to the President of the Security Council, recognised that 'Under no circumstances will we allow an enemy to develop weapons of mass destruction against our people. We shall defend the citizens of Israel in time, and with all the means at our disposal'.[78] Later, during a Security Council debate, the Israeli representative stated that 'In the light of Iraqi declarations and deeds, and Iraq's refusal even to sign an armistice agreement with Israel, Israel had full legal justification to exercise its inherent right of self-defence to abort the Iraqi nuclear threat to Israel'.[79] In both cases, Israel referred to threats to Israeli people and not to an attack. It thus relied in this case on pre-emptive self-defence. Israel's action was condemned by the Security Council[80] and by the General Assembly,[81] the latter resolution being adopted with 109 votes in favour, 2 against and 34 abstentions. Therefore, the majority condemned the attack.[82]

To conclude, given that pre-emptive self-defence is not expressly included in Article 51, that it has not been approved by any international organisation, and that it has not been accepted by the majority of states, it is not possible to agree on the

[75] According to Simpson 'the existence or non-existence of WMDs was somewhat beside the point from the perspective of preemption. What counted was the possibility or probability of Iraq emerging at some point in the future as a threat to US security'. Simpson (2008), p. 204.

[76] Gray (2014), p. 639.

[77] Corten (2010), p. 440.

[78] UN Security Council, Letter dated 8 June 1981 from the Permanent Representative of Israel to the United Nations addressed to the President of the Security Council (S/14510).

[79] UN Security Council, Complaint by Iraq: Letter dated 8 June 1981 from the Charge d'affaires of the Permanent Mission of Iraq to the United Nations addressed to the President of the Security Council (S/14509), 19 June 1981, Meeting Records S/PV2288, para 79.

[80] 'Strongly condemns the military attack by Israel in clear violation of the Charter of the United Nations and the norms of international conduct'. UN Security Council, Resolution 487 (1981).

[81] 'Strongly condemns Israel for its premeditated and unprecedented act of aggression in violation of the Charter of the United Nations, and the norms of international conduct, which constitute a new and dangerous escalation in the threat to international peace and security'. UN General Assembly, *Israel's Attack on the Iraqi Nuclear Installation*, 13 November 1981, A/RES/32/27.

[82] In 2007 Israel was also considered responsible for the attack to the Al-Kibar Nuclear reactor, but it acknowledged that attack in 2018. See Heller (2018), http://opiniojuris.org/2018/04/03/why-the-al-kibar-strike-does-not-contribute-to-the-customary-jus-ad-bellum/. See also Henderson (2018), p. 290.

legality of this theory.[83] Anticipatory self-defence, however, is a different matter, as it seems to be accepted—or not completely rejected at least. Moreover, it may find some kind of justification in the interpretation of Article 51 according to its object and purpose.

6.3 The Unwilling or Unable Doctrine: International Terrorism as a Cover

The unwilling or unable doctrine has also recently drawn the attention of scholars because of its potential in the fight against international terrorism. Nonetheless, its origins can be traced back in time. As early as 1953, Cheng included the absence of lawful means of protection in the conditions governing the existence and exercise of self-defence. Such a situation could take place 'when the local sovereign has proved either unable or unwilling to afford the necessary protection'.[84] Yet, Cheng went even further back in time and referred to the Caroline incident and to a message the US President addressed to the Congress in 1841, in which he stated that '(t)he territory of the United Sates must be regarded as sacredly secure against all such invasions, until they shall voluntarily acknowledge inability to acquit themselves of their duties to others'.[85]

In contemporary international law, this inability has been applied to states used as safe havens for international terrorist groups, adding the unwilling element. In sum, according to this unwilling or unable doctrine, in order to exercise self-defence against an attack or a threat of attack by non-state actors, it is necessary to have 'the territorial state's consent to military action, except where the territorial state is unable or unwilling itself to deal with the terrorist attacks'.[86] This doctrine has been accepted and developed by other organisations such as Chatham House,[87] and scholars, such as Bethlehem, who set the 16 principles applicable to the exercise of self-defence against an imminent or actual armed attack by non-state actors.[88] In this regard, according to principle 11, it is not necessary to have the territorial state's consent when it is unwilling to restrain the armed activities of the non-state actors, and when the state is unable to restrain those activities and fails or refuses 'to agree to a reasonable and effective plan of action, and to take such action'.[89]

83 Contrary to this theory: Andrés Saenz de Santamaria (2012), p. 543, Remiro Brotons et al. (2007), p. 1067; Tomuschat (1999), p. 214 *et seq.*; Brownlie (2012), p. 733.

84 Cheng (1953), p. 96.

85 Ibidem.

86 Leiden Policy Recommendations on Counter-Terrorism and International Law (2010).

87 Wilmshurst (2005).

88 Bethlehem (2012), p. 4.

89 Ibid. 776.

Focusing on this doctrine as an element that may also lead to the erosion of the principle of the prohibition of the use of force, we are brought to explore the link between this theory and two essential issues in international law: the birth of new international actors, such as terrorist groups; and the issue of attribution, which constitutes a basic principle to establish responsibility, and is, therefore, an essential element with regard to compliance with international law.

6.3.1 The Practice of Self-Defence Against Terrorist Groups

The unwilling or unable theory has been understood to allow states to use the force in self-defence on the territory of another state against non-state actors, not against the state.[90] In this regard, it must be noted that some of the non-state actors may be nationals of the state in whose territory the use of force is taking place. Therefore, we must accept the fact that it represents an attack against part of the population of the said state and thus equates to an attack against the state. In addition, assuming that the use of force is not against the state but against non-state actors would entail a violation of the state's sovereignty and a breach of the principle of non-intervention. It would also lead to acknowledging the fiction that when a state attacks the territory of another state, it is not using force against that state.

In any case, the problem lies in the possibility, according to Article 51 of the United Nations Charter, of exercising self-defence against non-state actors, essentially against terrorist groups. Article 51 does not explicitly restrain its applicability to among states only, but this article is an exception to Article 2.4 addressed to the organisation's members: the states. Such an explicit reference to states in Article 2.4 and its relation to Article 51 has led some commentators to affirm that according to Article 51, self-defence can only be exercised against states.[91] In the same vein, the International Court of Justice has recognised that an attack by another state is a requirement for self-defence.[92]

A fair number of arguments against this position has been advanced, beginning with Security Council Resolutions 1368 and 1373,[93] adopted after 9/11, and in which the Security Council recognised the right of self-defence but without identifying the actors. According to some scholars, since Al Qaeda perpetrated the attacks, the self-defence recognised by the Security Council should be against those perpetrators, concluding that the Resolutions came to recognise the right to self-defence

[90] Cervell Hortal (2018), p. 83.

[91] Trapp (2015), p. 680; Corten (2010), pp. 162–163.

[92] ICJ, *Legal Consequences of the Construction of a Wall in the Occupied Palestinian Territory*, Advisory Opinion: I. C. J. Reports 2004, para 138; ICJ, *Armed Activities of the Territory of Congo*, Judgement of 19 December 2005: ICJ reports 2005 para. 146; See Orakhelashvili (2015), p. 171; Andrés Saenz de Santamaria (2012), p. 544; Kammerhofer (2015), p. 630.

[93] UN Security Council, Resolution 1368 (2001); UN Security Council, Resolution 1373 (2001).

against non-state actors.[94] In contrast, Corten considered that in its letter addressed to the Security Council, the United States also made the Taliban regime responsible for the attack and, therefore, the United States was exercising self-defence against the state.[95] This would justify the actions conducted in Afghanistan territory against the Taliban and Al Qaeda.

However, added to that of Afghanistan, there are further cases in which the use of force has been exercised against non-state actors on the territory of a third state. One example is the 2006 Israeli attacks against Hezbollah in Lebanon.[96] In this case, the right of self-defence was recognised by certain members of the Security Council[97] but was criticised by the League of Arab States and the Non-Aligned Movement.[98] Recently, the unwilling or unable theory was first referred to by the Unites States in its letter to the Security Council during the intervention against the Islamic State[99] in Syria:

> States must be able to defend themselves, in accordance with the inherent right of individual and collective self-defence, as reflected in Article 51 of the Charter of the United Nations, when, as is the case here, the government of the State where the threat is located is unwilling or unable to prevent the use of its territory for such attacks. The Syrian regime has shown that it cannot and will not confront these safe havens effectively itself.[100]

Later, following the terrorist attacks in Paris, President François Hollande declared in his speech at the National Assembly that:

> (l)es actes commis vendredi soir à Paris et près du Stade de France, sont des actes de guerre (. . .) Ils sont le fait d'une armée djihadiste, le groupe Daech (. . .) Les actes de guerre de vendredi ont été décidés, planifiés en Syrie, préparés. (. . .) D'ici là, la France intensifiera ses opérations en Syrie (. . .) notre ennemi en Syrie, c'est Daech.[101]

---

[94] Bethlehem (2012), p. 772; Trapp (2015), p. 690; Kammerhofer (2015), p. 636. See also Alcaide Fernández (2001), p. 9; Andrés Saenz de Santamaria (2012), p. 550. See also UN Security Council Arria-formula meeting: 'Upholding the collective Security System of the UN Charter: the Use of Force in International law, non-state actors and legitimate self-defense'. Statement by D. Fiona Webster, Deputy Permanent Representative of Australia to the United Nations, 24 February 2021. S/2021/247. Belgium considers that after these resolutions the states have initiated a practice. UN Security Council Arria-formula meeting: 'Upholding the collective Security System of the UN Charter: the Use of Force in International law, non-state actors and legitimate self-defense'. Statement by H.E. Ambassador Karen Van Vlierberge, Deputy Permanent Representative of Belgium to the United Nations. S/2021/247.

[95] Corten (2010), pp. 179–180. See also Tladi (2017), p. 4; González Vega (2001), pp. 1–2.

[96] See Gray (2014), p. 633.

[97] Deeks (2015), p. 691.

[98] Corten (2015), p. 869.

[99] See Pozo Serrano (2016).

[100] UN Security Council, Letter dated 23 September 2014 from the Permanent Representative of the United States of America to the United Nations addressed to the Secretary-General. S/2014/695.

[101] Déclaration de M. François Hollande, Président de la République, devant le Parlement réuni en Congrès à la suite des attaques terroristes perpétrées à Paris et en Seine-Saint-Denis, Versailles le 16 novembre 2015. https://www.vie-publique.fr/discours/196856-declaration-de-m-francois-hollande-president-de-la-republique-devant

According to this declaration, France had been the victim of an armed attack conducted by a terrorist group, and France's intention was to fight that terrorist group on Syrian territory,[102] therefore using self-defence against a non-state actor. This self-defence action was confirmed by France's Permanent Representative at the United Nations during the debates for the adoption of Resolution 2249 (2015):

> As I said, the events of 13 November were an armed aggression against France. Our military action, of which we informed the Security Council from the outset and which was justified as legitimate collective self-defence, can now also be characterized as individual self-defence, in accordance with Article 51 of the Charter of the United Nations.[103]

Moreover, we must mention the widespread use of drones by certain states to fight international terrorism in third states, such as in Somalia, Pakistan, or Yemen.[104]

These are examples of individual self-defence against non-state actors. However, in the case of Syria, collective self-defence was also raised because of Iraq's request for assistance to fight Daesh, not only on Iraqi territory, but also in Syria.[105]

Therefore, the use of force against non-state actors can be established as a recent and significant practice. And considering that Article 51 does not expressly refer to the use of force against a state, it would be easy to accept this broad interpretation. This practice adds a new dimension to the status of a non-state actor as it is subject to the application of Art. 51 of the UN Charter. In this case, Corten considered that this would entail the absurd recognition of terrorist groups as subjects of international law,[106] yet we must note, nonetheless, that terrorist groups are already the addressees of obligations regarding humanitarian law, human rights law, or Security Council resolutions, without being recognised as subjects of international law.

---

[102] Previously France had used the force in Syria against Daesh as an action of collective self-defence to help Iraq. Pozo Serrano (2016), pp. 171–172.

[103] Security Council—Adoption of Resolution 2249—Explanation of vote by Mr. François Delattre, Permanent Representative of France to the United Nations—20 November 2015 https://onu.delegfrance.org/Against-Daesh-we-have-our-common-humanity. The military action of France was contested by a group of professors through the manifest: Contre une invocation abusive de la légitime défense pour faire face au défi du terrorisme—A plea against the abusive invocation of self-defence as a response to terrorism. https://cdi.ulb.ac.be/contre-invocation-abusive-de-legitime-defense-faire-face-defi-terrorisme/

[104] See Gómez Isa (2015), p. 1; Kramer (2011), p. 2.

[105] Pozo Serrano (2016), pp. 168 et seq.; See Coalition website https://theglobalcoalition.org/en/. See also UN Security Council, Letter dated 20 September 2014 from the Permanent Representative of Iraq to the United Nations addressed to the President of *the* Security Council. S/2014/691.

[106] Corten (2010), pp. 172–174.

6.3.2 A Legal Practice?

The existence of an international practice does not entail its legality and, in the case of the unwilling or unable theory, legalisation rests on the question of the attribution of responsibility to the territorial state for the terrorist attacks.

Once a terrorist group conducts an attack, the exercise of the use of force in self-defence requires a territorial space in which to launch the response against the non-state actor. Despite the attempts to create a fiction according to which the state is using force against a non-state actor and not against the territorial state,[107] the use of force is in fact taking place within a state territory, so the state is victim of a violation of Article 2.4 of the Charter. As established in the report of the International Law Association: 'using force within the territory of another state—even if the forcible measures are limited to strikes against a non-state actor—must be considered as within the notion of force as it exists in Article 2(4) of the Charter'.[108]

Two options have been put forward to justify such actions in violation of Article 2.4. The first is to hold the state responsible for the attacks owing to the support it is giving to non-state actors by allowing or not preventing them from using its territory to organise attacks. This justification is not supported by the theory of attribution since, as clearly stated in the Nicaragua case by the International Court of Justice, to hold a state responsible for the action of a non-state actor, it is necessary to have effective control over that group. Therefore, actions such as financing, organising, training, supplying, equipping, selecting military or paramilitary targets, or planning the entire operation are insufficient to attribute the group's acts to the state. Then, the actions of harbouring or supporting the attackers will not be sufficient to hold the host state responsible for the terrorist group's acts.

The second option has been to rely on necessity. According to Bethlehem, 'the extent of the responsibility of the state for aiding or assisting the non-sate actor in its armed activities may be relevant to considerations of the necessity to act in self-defence'.[109] This concept of necessity has been interpreted by Deeks as a bridge between Article 51 and Article 2.4 of the Charter, allowing the use of force on the territory of the host state even though the host state is not responsible for the attack. In other words, necessity may allow attributing the attack to the host state. The flaw of this theory lies in the misinterpretation of the concept of necessity, because necessity is an element and a requirement to consider in order exercise the use of force in application of Article 51.[110] It does not represent a principle that serves to interpret Article 2.4 and the concept of attribution. Therefore, necessity cannot be

[107] Cervell Hortal (2018), p. 84–87.

[108] International Law Association, Draft Report on Aggression and the Use of Force (May 2016). Johannesburg Conference 2016, p. 12.

[109] Deeks (2015), p. 776.

[110] See Andrés Saenz de Santamaria (2012), p. 540; Trapp (2015), p. 695; Corten (2010), p. 862.

used to justify the violation of Article 2.4, which is a *jus cogens* norm,[111] nor to attribute an illegal act or an armed attack committed by a non-state actor to the host state.

Coming back to state practice, a state of affairs can be inferred from the Security Council's Arria formula meeting on the use of force against non-state actors and legitimate self-defence.[112] A total of 34 states participated in this meeting which was held in February 2021. During the meeting, the states adopted a variety of positions making it impossible to conclude that this new theory is widely accepted. While states such as the Unites States, Belgium, Australia, the Netherlands, the United Kingdom, Turkey, Estonia or Azerbaijan expressed their support for an expansive view regarding self-defence against non-states actors, all of them, except the United States, considered that the existence of an imminent attack originating in the host state territory was necessary, that state being unwilling or unable to prevent it. For its part, the Unites States considered on the contrary that the existence of a previous attack and the non-termination of hostilities was sufficient to resort to force in self-defence.[113] Contrary to this expansive view of self-defence, other states including Brazil, Mexico, Sri Lanka, and China[114] manifested their opposition to the use of force against non-state actors without the consent of the concerned state. Other states did not give a clear opinion on the issue. For example, Russia believed that it was necessary to ask for the host's cooperation in cases where the state is willing to collaborate, but gave no answer in cases where the state refuses to cooperate.[115] And France confirmed that the military actions taken after the Paris terrorist attacks were

[111] Article 26 ARSIWA establishes that 'Nothing in this chapter precludes the wrongfulness of any act of a State which is not in conformity with an obligation arising under a peremptory norm of general international law'. Therefore it is not possible to justify the violation of the use of force on grounds of necessity. UN General Assembly, *Responsibility of States for internationally wrongful acts*: Resolution, 8 January 2008, A/RES/62/61.

[112] UN General Assembly and UN Security Council, *Strengthening of the United Nations system*. Letter dated 8 March 2021 from the Permanent Representative of Mexico to the United Nations addressed to the President of the Security Council, 16 March 2021. Annex I to the letter dated 8 March 2021 from the Permanent Representative of Mexico to the United Nations addressed to the President of the Security Council Chair's summary of the Arria-formula meeting of the Security Council on the theme "Upholding the collective security system of the Charter of the United Nations: the use of force in international law, non-State actors and legitimate self-defence", held on 24 February 2021, A/75/993; S/2021/247. See also Arria Formula Meeting, 24 February 2021: https://www.unmultimedia.org/avlibrary/asset/2604/2604457/

[113] Hague (2021), p. 3, https://www.justsecurity.org/57223/self-defense-self-defense-syria/. Arria Formula Meeting, 24 February 2021: https://www.unmultimedia.org/avlibrary/asset/2604/2604457/

[114] Arria Formula Meeting, 24 February 2021: https://www.unmultimedia.org/avlibrary/asset/2604/2604457/. China has come, in any case, to recognize the possibility of the use of force abroad as part of its counterterrorism policy. Patey (2016), p. 5; see also Duchâtel (2016), p. 6.

[115] UN Security Council Arria-formula meeting: 'Upholding the collective Security System of the UN Charter: the Use of Force in International law, non-state actors and legitimate self-defense'. Statement by Vassily Nebenzia, Permanent Representative of Russia to the United Nations at the UN SC Members Arria formula meeting 'Upholding the collective Security System of the UN

justified as collective and individual self-defence, without giving an express opinion on the issue.[116] Other states refused to express any opinion whatsoever.[117]

To conclude, the cases mentioned above—in which the states used force in a third state's territory against non-state actors, relying on the right of self-defence—do not have any legal bases in international law. We can affirm that state practice has led to an interpretation of Article 51 allowing the exercise of self-defence against non-state actors, since it has been demonstrated that according to Article 51, their attacks can amount to an armed attack.[118] Self-defence, however, needs to be exercised on a third state's territory, yet international law does not allow the use of force on the territory of another state without its consent. In fact, such an exercise is even problematic when consent is given, as analysed in previous sections. Despite the option of fighting terrorism in a third state has gained ground, as demonstrated in the Arriaga Formula meeting, there is no common practice or opinion on the matter and, therefore, such uses of force must be considered a breach of international law. The unwilling or unable theory calls not only for Article 51 to be changed, but also the concept of the prohibition of the use of force. The theory assumes the use of force against a state that has not carried out an attack, and falls outside the justification of Article 51. These actions become even more difficult to accept considering the *jus cogens* status of the prohibition of the use of force, at least regarding aggression.

6.4 Western Expansionist Theories on the Use of Force: A Backfire? The Russian Aggression Against Ukraine

The Russian aggression against Ukraine has been rightly qualified as the greatest shock to the global order since World War II.[119] It has brought us to rethink or review international laws on the prohibition of the use of force, and in most cases to reaffirm its existence and value despite such flagrant disregard.

However, as examined in the previous sections and chapters, the prohibition of the use of force has been breached over the years since the adoption of the United Nations Charter and its Article 2.4. This situation has an impact not on the existence of the norm, but on its compliance.[120] In this regard, Western states have pushed the

---

Charter: the Use of Force in International law, non-state actors and legitimate self-defense', 24 February 2021. S/2021/247.

[116] Arria Formula Meeting, 24 February 2021. https://www.unmultimedia.org/avlibrary/asset/2604/2604457/

[117] Ahmad (2021), p. 9. https://www.justsecurity.org/75487/self-defense-against-non-state-actors-all-over-the-map/

[118] It must be noted that in order to qualify such attack as an armed attack, the position of the Security Council regarding those groups must be taken into account, as well as any Security Council resolution considering those groups or the attacks as a threat to the peace or a breach of peace.

[119] Bunk and Hakimi (2022), p. 688.

[120] O'Connell (2018), p. 861.

use of force forward or have directly violated its prohibition and intervened in internal affairs of the states,[121] creating the image that, the mentioned and analysed doctrines of humanitarian intervention, expansive self-defence or intervention by invitation "were developed for the use of certain leaders of certain states, not leaders such as Putin, Trump or LePen".[122]

President Putin referred to all these previous Western violations of the use of force in his egregious speech announcing the launching of his 'special operation' in Ukraine.[123] In that speech, he referred to Kosovo, Iraq, Libya, or Syria, which constitute well-known cases of violation of the prohibition of the use of force and examples of its expanded use and interpretation.

There have been attempts to differentiate between those uses of force and the aggression against Ukraine. It has been pointed out, for example, that in the case of Iraq, a Security Council Resolution had recognised that Iraq posed a threat to international peace and security and was in material breach of its obligations.[124] In the case of Syria, the government had made use of chemical weapons, and in the case of Kosovo, there was a humanitarian crisis.[125] However, as the authors rightly recognise, not all these reasons constitute legal justifications for the use of force because they do not fulfil the requirements. On the contrary, these interpretations and justifications have become useful precedents and theories for Russian aggression. The difference is that in the case of Ukraine, there is no evidence that the same acts and situations mentioned above took place. Therefore, we can affirm that "years and years of using military force has been costly in many respects and largely counter-productive".[126]

As in the case of Western countries, Russia has also used its own narrative to justify its aggression against Ukraine, as well as its previous acts of use of force in the former Soviet republics, the 'near abroad',[127] in order to maintain its realm of influence. In this way, Russia's legal justifications in the case of Ukraine were previously tested in Georgia in 2008 or Crimea in 2014, both in the aftermath of Kosovo. The latter also seems to represent a critical point in Russia's confrontation with the West regarding the use of force, and the starting point of a new narrative.[128]

[121] Bunk and Hakimi (2022), p. 689.

[122] O'Connell (2018), p. 871.

[123] Address by the President of the Russian Federation. 24 February 2022. http://en.kremlin.ru/events/president/news/67843

[124] UN Security Council, Resolution 1441 (2002).

[125] Bunk and Hakimi (2022), pp. 690–691.

[126] O'Connell (2018), p. 872.

[127] See Toal (2017); O'Loughlina et al. (2016), 6.

[128] See Pupcenocks and Seltzer (2021), p. 4. It is also worth noting that in a Letter from the Permanent Representatives of China and Russia to the United Nations addressed to the Secretary-General on 15 May 1997, both countries called for a new international order based on a multipolar world, therefore challenging the world order established at that moment. UN Security Council, Letter dated 15 May 1997 from the Permanent Representatives of China and the Russian Federation to the United Nations addressed to the Secretary-General. (S/1997/384)

In any case, as has been stated, Russia seems to apply a dual normative order: one for the former Soviet republics, and another for the countries that are not part of its 'near abroad', that is, a regional order and a global order. The defence of state sovereignty or integrity is thus analysed and interpreted in different ways depending on the country at stake.[129]

The way Russia has employed Western expansive theories on the use of force can be clearly observed in the case of Ukraine in Putin's 24 February address to the nation.[130] We can infer three major justifications that had been previously used by Western countries for the use of force: pre-emptive self-defence, intervention by request, and humanitarian intervention. Together with these justifications, a reference to the protection of nationals abroad and to the self-determination of the people of the self-proclaimed republics of Luhansk and Donetsk can be added to Russia's myriad unfounded justifications for its flagrant violation of the principle of the prohibition of the use of force.

6.4.1 *Self-Defence Against Who?*

Self-defence constitutes Russia's main grounds of justification, together with the most relevant Western theories. In this regard, Russia's appeal for self-defence is linked to the theory of pre-emptive self-defence but without referring to that concept. The country is therefore using the language but not the terms.

In his 24 February speech, Putin refers to Iraq as a remarkable example of violation of the prohibition of use for force by the United States—who lied about the existence of weapons of mass destruction—affirming that there were no legal grounds for the said intervention. As mentioned earlier, allegations of weapons of mass destruction were part of the United States' strategy of pre-emptive self-defence, as they considered that those weapons entailed a future threat to the state. However, focusing on Russia's reaction to that military action and justification, we can infer that the pre-emptive issue was not the problem. The problem was rather the falsehood regarding the existence of weapons of mass destruction. During the Security Council's debates after the aggression against Iraq, the Russian Minister of Foreign Affairs, Sergey Lavrov, stated:

> The military action undertaken by the United States and the United Kingdom just at that moment — in violation of Security Council resolutions — cannot be justified in any way. In fact, those countries were unable to provide any proof to support their allegations regarding Iraq's possession of weapons of mass destruction and Baghdad's support for international

[129] Ibid, p. 758.

[130] Address by the President of the Russian Federation. 24 February 2022. http://en.kremlin.ru/events/president/news/67843

> terrorism — or with regard to a threat to the countries of the region or to international security emanating from Iraq.[131]

It seems therefore, that the problem was a lack of evidence, not the use of self-defence to confront a future threat, as can also be inferred from Putin's speech. This position has ultimately been useful for Russia to justify its aggression against Ukraine.

On 24 February 2022, the Permanent Representative of the Russian Federation to the United Nations sent a letter to the Secretary General informing about the measures adopted "in accordance with Article 51 of the Charter of the United Nations in exercise of the right of self-defence".[132] Those measures were referred to in the annex to the letter, which was in fact a transcript of Putin's 24 February speech. Therefore, the official and legal Russian justifications regarding the use of force in self-defence were included in Putin's speech. This makes it necessary to analyse this political statement to determine the legal bases for the military action.

Two sources of threat to Russia can be identified in the speech: NATO and Ukraine. Putin underscores NATO at the very beginning of his speech as a fundamental threat, since it is moving its military infrastructure closer to the Russian border. According to Putin, the military presence in territories bordering Russia 'will stay for decades to come or maybe forever, creating an ever mounting and totally unacceptable threat for Russia'. Therefore, the threat that NATO poses to Russia is not an imminent threat but a future threat to the 'interests' and 'existence' of the state. In addition, the speech refers to the United States and its allies' policy focused on containing Russia and obtaining geopolitical dividends. So it is possible to infer that NATO and its members represent more of a geostrategic threat than an armed attack threat.

We can conclude that Putin actually called for pre-emptive self-defence to be applied on different grounds. First, the lack of an armed attack,[133] which is the main requirement of Article 51, and second, the lack of evidence of an imminent attack by NATO. Indeed, NATO, unlike Russia, had not deployed any troops, nor was there any evidence of plans of attack,[134] which would have led to the application of anticipatory self-defence. Finally, the application of pre-emptive self-defence is also confirmed by the reasoning laid out in Putin's speech.

The doctrine of pre-emptive self-defence, as described above, has attracted little support from states and scholars. In this regard, we must also note that in the *Armed Activities* case, the International Court of Justice established that preventive security

[131] United Nations Security Council. *The situation between Iraq and Kuwait*. S/PV.4726 (Resumption 1), pp. 26–27.

[132] UN Security Council, Letter dated 24 February 2022 from the Permanent Representative of the Russian Federation to the United Nations addressed to the Secretary-General (S/2022/154).

[133] As Gill has also stated, early uses of force by NATO member do no constitute a cumulative amount of armed attack, and it must be added that those uses of forces were not against Russia. Gill (2022), p. 122.

[134] Grzebyk (2021), p. 147; Green et al. (2002), pp. 10–12, Gill (2022), p. 123.

needs, such as those referred to in Putin's speech, are not covered by self-defence, and the use of force to achieve them constitutes a violation of international law.[135] In this case, Uganda stated that the aim was to 'ensure that the political vacuum does not adversely affect Uganda, to prevent attacks from "genocidal elements", to be in a position to safeguard Uganda from irresponsible threats of invasion, to "deny the Sudan the opportunity to use the territory of the DRC to destabilize Uganda"'.[136] These preventative security needs can also be inferred from Putin's speech when he refers to NATO's and Western states' control of the territories adjacent to Russia. Or when commenting on how NATO and Western policies are trying to contain Russia, placing armed forces in adjacent territories for a future attack. He goes on to compare the situation with that of Nazi Germany and the final attack on Russia. In sum, Russia's foreign policy preferences were used to justify a preventive war.[137]

Nevertheless, among the most controversial issues regarding the exercise of self-defence against NATO threats is that the response is taking place against a state that is a non-NATO member and has no NATO armed forces in its territory. We previously analysed the legal problems posed by the fight against terrorism in third state territories regarding the attribution of acts to the state, responsibility, and self-defence. But in this case, the situation even became rather irrational: Russian pleas were to act in self-defence against another state in order to protect itself from a remote attack in the future, launched by an organisation with no base in the targeted state, and of which the targeted state is not a member. This means that no attribution of responsibility is possible. The whole theory is based on 'future predictables', overlooking today's principle of sovereignty—that allows choosing one's military alliances—and current international law, that outlaws the use of force to prevent a state from joining a security organisation.[138]

Russia's outrageous reasoning constitutes a grave and dangerous threat to international security and the international community, affecting the real bases of peaceful coexistence and the survival of the international legal order.

However, together with the exercise of self-defence against NATO, Russia seems to consider that Ukraine also poses a threat itself:[139] 'Russia cannot feel safe, develop, and exist while facing a permanent threat from the territory of today's Ukraine'. The speech suggests that the far-right nationalist and neo-Nazis groups in Ukraine wish to bring war to Crimea[140] and are claiming other Russian regions, waiting for the right moment to attack Russia while also aspiring to acquiring nuclear weapons. In this case, it seems that it is not Ukraine's government that poses a threat to Russia but certain national groups, bringing the situation close to the unwilling or

---

[135] ICJ, *Armed Activities of the Territory of Congo*, para. 163. See Green et al. (2002), p. 13.

[136] ICJ, *Armed Activities of the Territory of Congo*, para. 143.

[137] Gill (2022), p. 125.

[138] Grzebyk (2021), p. 150.

[139] Green et al. (2002), pp. 13 et seq.

[140] Russia considers Crimea part of the its territory after its illegal annexation in 2014. See O'Connell (2018).

unable theory. In this regard, the speech also links this threat to previous actions against terrorist groups to those of the Caucasus or Syria. Therefore, Russia is again using a broad interpretation of the use of force in self-defence as grounds for intervention, in this case against non-state actors based in a third state.

In the Security Council's above-cited 2021 Arria Formula meeting on the use of force against non-state actors and legitimate self-defence, Russia stated that it was necessary to comply with two requirements to invoke self-defence against terrorist attacks: (1) an armed attack has to be fulfilled; and (2), an assessment of the position from which the armed attack has taken place, determining whether the government is directly supporting that armed attack or is otherwise fighting terrorist groups and is open to receiving help from other states. In the latter case, it would be necessary to request the government's consent to intervene. In addition, Russia criticised the use of force in Syria's territory against Islamic State (ISIL) without any Security Council authorisation and without requesting Syria's consent to act on its territory, as Syria was also fighting against ISIL.[141]

In the case of Ukraine, Russia disregarded its previous statements, acting mainly without any armed attack having taken place against Russia by far-right nationalist or neo-Nazi groups. It did not have any proof either of imminent attacks by those groups that could justify anticipatory self-defence. Hence, if the first requirement is not fulfilled, there is no need to take the second into consideration. It could be argued that Russia again twisted expansive theories on the use of force and self-defence, applying the unable and unwilling theory preventively, that is, connecting the said theory to the pre-emptive self-defence doctrine.

Finally, Russia's last plea regarding self-defence was linked to collective self-defence. Following the declaration of independence of Donetsk and Luhansk, the two secessionist territories, and their recognition as independent states by Russia,[142] treaties of friendship and mutual assistance were signed between Russia and the said territories.[143] Article 4 of both treaties establishes the following:

> The Contracting Parties shall jointly take all measures within their power to remove threats to peace and breaches of the peace and to counter acts of aggression perpetrated against them by any State or group of States, and shall afford one another the necessary assistance,

---

[141] UN General Assembly and UN Security Council, *Strengthening of the United Nations system.* Letter dated 8 March 2021 from the Permanent Representative of Mexico to the United Nations addressed to the President of the Security Council, 16 March 2021. Arria-formula meeting. Statement by Vassily Nebenzia, Permanent Representative of Russia to the United Nations, pp. 66–67.

[142] Signing of documents recognising Donetsk and Lugansk People's Republics. February 21, 2022. http://kremlin.ru/events/president/news/67829

[143] Treaty of Friendship, Cooperation and Mutual Assistance between the Russian Federation and the Donetsk People's Republic; and Treaty of Friendship, Cooperation and Mutual Assistance between the Russian Federation and the Lugansk People's Republic. Source: UN General Assembly and UN Security Council, Right of peoples to self-determination. Letter dated 3 March 2022 from the Permanent Representative of the Russian Federation to the United Nations addressed to the Secretary-General. A/76/740–S/2022/179.

> including military assistance, in the exercise of the right of individual or collective self-defence in accordance with Article 51 of the Charter of the United Nations.

This article, together with Article 51 of the Charter, may provide grounds for acting in collective self-defence, but the problem is the very existence of these territories as states, permitting the application of Article 51.

Article 51 was adopted to guarantee the self-defence of states; therefore it can only be invoked for those subjects of international law. Recognising those territories as states does not turn them into real states.[144] In fact, the republics can be understood as a fiction created by Russia that are under Russian control.[145] In addition, the recognition was considered by the General Assembly as a violation of Ukraine's sovereignty and integrity.[146] Therefore, the plea of collective self-defence has no legal grounds, despite: (a) the existence of the friendship and mutual assistance treaties; (b), the request for assistance of the two territories to face the 'aggression of Ukraine'; and (c), the sending of both letters of information to the Secretary General, one with the content of the treaties and the assistance request,[147] and a second informing about the launching of the military operation in order to comply with the requirement of Article 51.[148] As Russia stated in the Arria Formula:

> circulation of article 51 notifications in the Security Council and the lack of immediate reactions from States does not and should not mean that actions taken in accordance with them gained legality or that such conduct contributes to the foundation of a new norm of law.[149]

6.4.2 The Humanitarian Intervention Wild Card

Introducing the situation in the Donbas, Putin's 24 February speech stated:

[144] Grzebyk (2021), p. 150; Green et al. (2002), p. 18.

[145] Miklasová (2022). https://voelkerrechtsblog.org/russias-recognition-of-the-dpr-and-lpr-as-illegal-acts-under-international-law/; Weller (2022).

[146] UN General Assembly, Aggression against Ukraine, 2 March 2022. ES-1171.

[147] UN General Assembly and UN Security Council, Right of peoples to self-determination. Letter dated 3 March 2022 from the Permanent Representative of the Russian Federation to the United Nations addressed to the Secretary-General. A/76/740–S/2022/179.

[148] UN Security Council, Letter dated 24 February 2022 from the Permanent Representative of the Russian Federation to the United Nations addressed to the Secretary-General. (S/2022/154).

[149] UN Security Council Arria-formula meeting. Statement by Vassily Nebenzia, Permanent Representative of Russia to the United Nations. In this regard it must be notice that in the case of the Russian aggression there were immediate reactions from the states. Among other reactions, see UN Security Council, Letter dated 28 February 2014 from the Permanent Representative of Ukraine to the United Nations addressed to the President of the Security Council (S/2014/136). Meeting Minutes. S/PV.8979.

> you cannot look without compassion at what is happening there. It became impossible to tolerate it. We had to stop that atrocity, that genocide of the millions of people who live there.

And after declaring Russia's decision to execute a 'special military operation', Putin affirmed that 'the purpose of this operation is to protect people who, for eight years now, have been facing humiliation and genocide perpetrated by the Kiev regime'.

Those declarations have led to understanding humanitarian intervention as another source of justification for the use of force against Ukraine. However, we must remember that later, Russia rejected this argument when alleging that the International Court of Justice lacked jurisdiction in the case instituted by Ukraine against Russia on *Allegations of Genocide*.[150] In this case, Russia declared that the special operation was grounded in self-defence and in Article 51 of the Charter.

Surprisingly, to defend that position before the Court, Russia referred to the letter of 24 February 2022 sent to the Secretary General, to which, as mentioned earlier, was annexed Putin's 21 February speech with the legal bases for the intervention. That speech clearly established, along with the reference to self-defence, that the purpose of the operation was to protect people.

Humanitarian intervention constitutes one of the most controversial justifications for the use of force in international law.[151] Its main recent instance was NATO's intervention in Kosovo without any authorisation by the United Nations Security Council, attracting a drove of criticisms[152] by states and scholars. It also gained, however, stances of support based on the legitimacy of the intervention rather than its legality.[153]

Among the States that manifested their opposition to the intervention in Kosovo was Russia. In a letter addressed to the President of the Security Council on 24 March 1999,[154] the state affirmed that:

> Russia is profoundly outraged by NATO's military action against sovereign Yugoslavia, which is nothing less than an act of open aggression.
>
> Only the Security Council can decide on what measures, including the use of force, should be taken to maintain or restore international peace and security. The Security Council did not take such decisions with regard to Yugoslavia.

---

[150] ICJ, *Allegations of Genocide under the Convention on the Prevention and Punishment of the Crime of Genocide* (Ukraine v. Russian Federation: 32 States intervening). Document (with annexes) from the Russian Federation setting out its position regarding the alleged 'lack of jurisdiction' of the Court in the case. 7 March 2022.

[151] See among others: Richmond (2016), p. 2; Chesterman (2001); Pattison (2010); Cassese (1999), p. 4; Rodley (2015); Coady et al. (2018); Kohen (2012), p. 1; Prandler (2008).

[152] Burri (2010), p. 8; Jacobs and Radi (2011), p. 2; Kohen and Del Mar (2011), p. 2; Peters (2011), p. 2; Jiménez Piernas (2011), p. 1.

[153] Cassese (1999); Roberts (2009).

[154] UN Security Council, Letter dated 24 March 1999 from the Permanent Representative of the Russian Federation to the United Nations addressed to the President of the Security Council (S/1999/320). Minutes of Meeting, S/PV.3988.

In addition, Sergey Lavrov, Russia's representative at the security Council, declared in the convened meeting to discuss the letter that:

> Attempts to justify the NATO strikes with arguments about preventing a humanitarian catastrophe in Kosovo are completely untenable. Not only are these attempts in no way based on the Charter or other generally recognized rules of international law (. . .).[155]

Two days later, Russia and Belarus passed a draft Security Council Resolution condemning the use of force by NATO without the Security Council's authorisation and affirming that it constituted a violation of Article 2.4 of the Charter.[156] The draft Resolution only obtained three votes in favour: those of China, Namibia, and the Russian Federation.

As previously stated, the intervention in Kosovo constituted a turning point in Russian relations with NATO, leading Russia to review its relationship with the organization.[157] However, NATO strikes also gave Russia a precedent to apply the same policy in its 'near abroad', the case of Georgia[158] being the most significant until Ukraine. It is worth mentioning that Lavrov had already advanced the risks of that unilateral intervention, stating that it will have "long-term harmful consequences (. . .) for the stability of the entire modern multi-polar system of international relations".[159]

The situation seemed to enter a new phase when the 2011 Security Council Resolution authorised the intervention in Libya to protect the population[160] based on the new concept of Responsibility to Protect. This concept was the result of the work of the International Commission on Intervention and State Sovereignty created by Canada to study the idea of humanitarian intervention. The resulting document[161] embraced the possibility of the use of force on the territory of a third state when loss of life has taken place on a large scale with genocidal intent or not, or ethnic cleansing has taken place on a large scale, but always with the Security Council's authorisation.[162] The same position was adopted later, in 2005, in the United Nations World Summit Outcome Document.[163]

---

[155] Ibidem

[156] Security Council, Draft Resolution S/1999/328 of 26 March 1999.

[157] UN Security Council, Letter dated 24 March 1999 from the Permanent Representative of the Russian Federation to the United Nations addressed to the President of the Security Council (S/1999/320). Minutes of Meeting, S/PV.3988.

[158] See Pupcenocks and Seltzer (2021), pp. 763–768. Gray (2018)

[159] UN Security Council, Letter dated 24 March 1999 from the Permanent Representative of the Russian Federation to the United Nations addressed to the President of the Security Council (S/1999/320). Minutes of Meeting, S/PV.3988.

[160] UN Security Council, Resolution 1973 (2011).

[161] International Commission on Intervention and State Sovereignty (2001) Report: Responsibility to Protect. p. 32.

[162] Ibid. p. 50

[163] UN General Assembly, 2005 World Summit Outcome: Resolution, 24 October 2005, A/RES/60/ 1.

However, while the Libya Resolution could have brought about a new era of cooperation to end gross human rights violations, NATO overstepped the power given by the Security Council and its intervention resulted in a change of government, with accusations of *ultra vires* action.[164] This intervention was rejected by Russia, which has since blocked any Security Council resolution authorising the use of force to protect populations facing gross human rights violations, especially in Syria.

Some of the consequences of those illegal interventions, mainly that of Kosovo's, can be linked to today's illegal intervention in Ukraine, but also to previous interventions in Georgia and Crimea.[165] In the same vein, Kosovo was clearly used as a legal precedent by representatives of the Donbas territories when they requested Russia's military assistance.[166] In all these cases, Russia used the humanitarian intervention arguments but without referring to the concept of humanitarian intervention or the Responsibility to Protect, probably due to the lack of a Security Council resolution authorising the use of force.

In this regard, the principle of humanitarian intervention requires the commission of mass atrocities, such as genocide or ethnic cleansing, and although the Russians allege that genocide and other mass atrocities have been committed in the Donbass, there was no evidence of such crimes. Neither the Organization for Security and Co-operation in Europe (OSCE), nor the United Nations, or any Non-Governmental Organization (NGO) have reported genocide.[167]

It is also worth noting that the International Court of Justice never pronounced itself regarding the legality of the humanitarian intervention. In the case of *Allegations of Genocide*, however, in its order on provisional measures, the Court 'observes that is not in possession of evidence substantiating the allegation of the Russian Federation that genocide has been committed on Ukrainian territory', affirming that in any case, it is doubtful that the Convention would authorise the unilateral use of force to prevent or punish genocide.[168] Russia's legal arguments supporting its humanitarian intervention in Donbas thus seem to fall apart.

In any event, regarding humanitarian intervention, it is also necessary to refer to the concept of remedial secession, to which the former is closely linked.

Russia's recognition of the Donesk and Lugansk republics was grounded in the concept of remedial secession, as can be inferred from the 24 February speech and its

[164] Address by the president of Russia Federation. 21 February 2022. http://en.kremlin.ru/events/president/news/67828

[165] Ingimundarson (2022).

[166] O'Connell (2018), p. 867.

[167] Green et al. (2002), p. 22; Grzebyk (2021), p. 151; Gill (2022), p. 123.

[168] ICJ, *Allegations of Genocide under the Convention on the Prevention and Punishment of the Crime of Genocide*. Request for indication of provisional measures. Order of 16 March 2022, para 59.

reference to the feelings and pain of the Donbas people as a reason for recognition.[169]

We must remember that even though Russia rejected NATO's airstrikes in Kosovo, it did not uphold any similar strong opposition to the concept of remedial secession. The latter was used to justify Kosovo's independence, and the International Court of Justice expressed its doubts on the matter considering the 'radically different views' of those states intervening in the proceeding.[170]

Russia was one of those intervening States, and it advanced its views on remedial secession. According to Russia, remedial secession can be exercised in 'truly extreme circumstances, such as an outright armed attack by the parent State, threatening the very existence of the people in question'.[171] It must be noted that this position was put forward in 2009, after the recognition Abkhazia and South Ossetia in 2008 as 'the only possibility to save human lives'.[172]

The remedial secession was also the grounds of Crimea's independence, which concluded with its annexation by Russia. Russia's representative at the Security Council recognised again that secession was an extraordinary measure, but that it was the only solution to face the consequences of the coup in Ukraine.[173]

However, Putin's speech on Crimea's annexation at the Duma in 2014[174] twisted once again international law and the Court's Opinion on Kosovo. According to Putin, Kosovo was a precedent accepted by Western countries and by the Court, as it confirmed that declarations of independence did not violate international law. Based on this precedent, Crimea's declaration of independence did not therefore violate international law. Since Kosovars separated from Serbia, the 'Russians, Ukrainians and Crimean Tatars in Crimea' should have the same right to separate from Ukraine.

In this statement, Putin seems to abandon the theory of remedial secession, since he holds that Western countries had considered Kosovo a special case, which, owing to the large number of human casualties, was not applicable to Crimea. According to Putin, this justification had no legal bases, since the Court did not mention this issue or requirement, and therefore, there was no need for bloodshed to secede. Nonetheless, the Court ruling was criticised, as mentioned earlier, for not examining the

[169] '(T)he feelings and pain of these people that were the main motivating force behind our decision to recognise the independence of the Donbass people's republics'. Address by the President of the Russian Federation. 24 February 2022. http://en.kremlin.ru/events/president/news/67843

[170] ICJ, *Accordance with international law of the unilateral declaration of independence in respect of Kosovo*, Advisory Opinion of 22 July 2010: I.C.J. Reports 2010, para. 82.

[171] ICJ, *Accordance with international law of the unilateral declaration of independence in respect of Kosovo,* Written Statement of the Russian Federation, 16 April 2009, paras. 87–88.

[172] Statement by President of Russia Dmitry Medvedev. 26 August 2008. http://en.kremlin.ru/events/president/transcripts/1222

[173] United Nations Security Council, Letter dated 28 February 2014 from the Permanent Representative of Ukraine to the United Nations addressed to the President of the Security Council (S/2014/136). Minutes Meeting, S/PV.7134.

[174] Address by President of the Russian Federation, 18 March 2014. http://en.kremlin.ru/events/president/news/20603

legality of the consequences of the declaration of independence.[175] It merely conducted a formal analysis of the declaration in which there was no room for the existence of human casualties and therefore no link to remedial secession.

Therefore, as in the case of Kosovo, Russia has supported the exercise of secession or remedial secession in its 'near abroad' and has focused on the territorial integrity of the states outside that area.[176] In this case, while recognising the theory of remedial secession, Russia concluded that the situation in Kosovo in 2008, when the declaration of independence was adopted, did not call for the application of remedial secession. Indeed, according to Russia, when NATO intervened in Kosovo in 1999, it did not refer to self-determination or secession, despite accusations of genocide and ethnic cleansing. Thus, if the situation in 1999 did not require remedial secession, neither would the situation in 2008 following Security Council Resolution 1244.[177]

Remedial secession also came into play in the case of Donbas, where, following Russian reasoning—given its written statement on the Kosovo case—it was linked to humanitarian intervention. According to that reasoning, in cases where a state commits genocide or ethnic cleansing against its population, the population has the right to self-determination in the form of secession, and a third state may help that population to implement and guarantee that right to save them from atrocities. What we can infer from Russia's practice and policy in Kosovo's aftermath, is that Russia applied the doctrine of humanitarian intervention without expressly relying on it. It did so during the intervention in Georgia,[178] recognising Abkhazia and South Ossetia just a few days later. And it did so again in Donbas. In this latter case, Russia began by recognising the independence of those republics as a solution to Ukrainian atrocities in the region and in application of the right of self-determination expressed through referendum. Later, it decided to use force, among other reasons, to save the population from the genocide being committed by nationalists and neo-Nazi groups.

6.4.3 Bogus Military Assistance on Request

The elements allowing to determine the existence of collective self-defence can also be analysed in relation to the theory of intervention by request or military assistance

[175] Supra note 152.

[176] Pupcenocks and Seltzer (2021), p. 758.

[177] ICJ, *Accordance with international law of the unilateral declaration of independence in respect of Kosovo*, Written Statement of the Russian Federation, 16 April 2009, paras 98–101.

[178] In Georgia the intervention to protect the population was done under the guise of peacekeeping and peace-enforcement. Pupcenocks and Seltzer (2021), pp. 763–764.

on request when involving the 'sending of armed forces by one State to another State upon the latter's request'.[179]

According to Putin's 24 February speech, the representatives of those self-proclaimed republics requested Russian help to fight Ukraine. Nevertheless, this request was also the justification to evoke collective self-defence, together with the reference to Article 51 of the Charter. It has also been argued[180] that Putin may have been invoking both military assistance on request and collective self-defence. A slight distinction, however, can be made considering the alleged aggressors: the Ukrainian state or the ultra-nationalist and neo-Nazi groups and militias operating in the Donbas. Military assistance on request concerns the internal disturbances or tensions that fall below the threshold of an international armed conflict.[181] Once the threshold has been passed and a state has suffered an armed attack, it can plead collective self-defence. Therefore, military assistance on request would apply to the fight against the non-state actors, such as the far-right nationalist or neo-Nazis groups or militias.

Intervention by request was already tested in Ukraine in the case of Crimea, when deposed President Yanukovich fled to Moscow and requested assistance from Russia.[182] In this case, the requirements for military assistance were not fulfilled, added to the former president's request withdrawal or at least his regret.[183] Despite the controversies regarding the legality of the request for military assistance, the analysis of this doctrine has led to the identification of a number of elements that must be considered to determine its lawfulness. And one of them is the validity of the consent. Among other requirements,[184] consent must be given by an authority that represents the State, therefore by a government in control of most of the territory or that has been in control and has a chance to recover it.[185] Yanukovich did not fulfil this requirement. Therefore, Russia's intervention in Crimea had no legal grounds based on the theory of military assistance on request.

---

[179] Institut de Droit International (2011); Green et al. (2002), pp. 21–23; Gill (2022), p. 125.

[180] Green et al. (2002), p. 22.

[181] Article 2. Institut de Droit International (2011).

[182] In a letter addressed to the president of Russia Yanukovich called 'on President Vladimir Vladimirovich Putin of Russia to use the armed forces of the Russian Federation to establish legitimacy, peace, law and order and stability in defence of the people of Ukraine'. UN Security council. Letter dated 28 February 2014 from the Permanent Representative of Ukraine to the United Nations addressed to the President of the Security Council (S/2014/136). Meeting Minutes, S/PV.7125. See O'Connell (2018), p. 864; Vermeer (2014); Byrne (2016), p. 109; Buchan and Tsagourias (2017)p. 183. On the contrary, Pupcenoks and Seltzer consider that the intention of Yanukovich was not to request assistance to Russia. Pupcenocks and Seltzer (2021), p. 769.

[183] O'Connell (2018), p. 866.

[184] The consent must be validly given, clearly established and freely. See International Law Association, Final Report on Aggression and the Use of Force. Sidney Conference 2018, pp. 18 et seq.

[185] O'Connell (2018), p. 865.

Russia's intervention in the Donbas might constitute a second attempt to use the theory of military assistance on request, this time based on a request by the representatives of the two secessionist territories.

As in the case of self-defence, however, the problem is the very existence of those states. The two states were created with Russia's support in violation of Art 2.4 of the Charter. Indeed, by the end of August 2014, Russian forces had already crossed the eastern border under the guise of 'humanitarian convoys' and participated in hostilities against Ukrainian forces, defeating them in September.[186] Therefore, the control exercise over those territories was obtained through a Russian armed intervention,[187] which invalidates[188] any government request arising from that action.

Added to the problem of recognising those states, we must remember that, as in the case of collective self-defence, a state does not exist merely based on the recognition of a few states.[189] Despite the adoption of constitutive or declaratory statehood theories, it is accepted that states must comply with the Montevideo requirements for statehood[190] and the Donbas republics did not fulfil them. In addition, even though they are not under the control of Ukraine, their existence depends on Russia, which provides economic, financial, political, and military support:[191] their independent existence is thus fictional. In this regard, the fourth criteria of the Montevideo Convention, that is, the capacity to enter into legal relations with States, has been linked with independence, both factual and legal independence, i.e., the "ability to govern a territory without taking direction from another State" and "no other valid claims by other States to govern that territory".[192] Given this situation, the territories were still part of Ukraine, and therefore, any military intervention not requested by the Ukrainian government entails a violation of international law.

The state's controversial existence also affects the authority[193] requirement of consent. Indeed, consent to Russian intervention was given by representatives who

---

186 Pupcenocks and Seltzer (2021), p. 767.

187 Weller (2022)

188 O'Connell (2018), p. 866; According to Article 41.2 of the Articles on Responsibility of States for international Wrongful acts: 'No State shall recognize as lawful a situation created by a serious breach within the meaning of article 40, nor render aid or assistance in maintaining that situation'.

189 The Republics have been recognized by Russia, Syria and North Korea. See https://www.sana.sy/en/?p=264314; https://www.lemonde.fr/en/international/article/2022/07/19/north-korea-recognizes-independence-of-pro-russian-territories-in-eastern-ukraine_5990644_4.html

190 Convention on Rights and Duties of States adopted by the Seventh International Conference of American States. Montevideo 26 December 1933. Recueil des Treaties, vol. CLXV, 1936.

191 Miklasová (2022); According to the Committee of Legal affairs and Human Rights of the Parliamentary Assembly of the Council of Europe: 'There can be no doubt that the "DPR" and "LPR" are wholly dependent on Russia'. Committee of Legal affairs and Human Rights (2016), para. 5.6.

192 Akande (2013).

193 The question of the authority to consent is one the most controversial regarding military assistance on request. See among others: Lieblich (2020), p. 1; Lo Giacco (2019). De Wet (2020).

do not control the whole territory, who are in power owing to a violation of Article 2.4 of the Charter, have no international recognition, and whose territory is disputed and lacks established international borders. To consider that in those circumstances, the representatives of those territories have consent authority regarding a foreign military intervention entails a breach or a misinterpretation at least of the doctrine of military intervention by request based on national interests, disregarding again the risks that those expansive interpretations of uses of force pose for the international community.

6.5 Does the European Union Have a Role in Protecting This Principle Against the New Interpretations?

The European Union has always declared its commitment to international law and the principles of the United Nations Charter, as set out in Article 3 TEU. The European Union must therefore respect the prohibition of the use of force, an obligation that must be understood as promoting peace. In line with this objective, the European Union should be rather reluctant to interpret anticipatory or pre-emptive self-defence or the theory of unwilling or unable, as it may affect the content and core of one of the fundamental principles of international law.

In this regard, the European Union's Global Strategy[194] can serve to illustrate the different approaches taken by the European Union and the United States in the fight against international terrorism—at least on paper. The European Strategy focuses on the cooperation between agencies and Member states, which can be considered an internal aspect of these activities. But when it refers to third states, the Strategy calls for cooperation to combat and prevent terrorism.[195] In addition, the Strategy also includes references to the fight against terrorism when addressing the role of the European Union in relation to international and non-international conflicts, and 'full respect for international law'[196] appears to be a basis for its actions. In the same vein, the EU Strategy against the proliferation of weapons of mass destruction[197] refers to the use of force and establishes that those measures must be taken 'under Chapter VII of the UN Charter and international law', the UN Security Council playing a key role.[198]

If we now focus on the content of the TEU and the European Union's competences, Article 41 TEU establishes that the Union may use civilian and military

[194]European Union Global Strategy. Shared Vision, Common Action: A Stronger Europe, June 2016,

[195]Ibid, p. 21.

[196]Ibid., p. 30.

[197]Council of the European Union. EU Strategy against proliferation of weapons of mass destruction, 10 December 2003, 154,085/03.

[198]Ibid.

assets 'on missions outside the Union for peace-keeping, conflict prevention and strengthening international security in accordance with the principles of the United Nations Charter'. The latter option can be rather broad and it may include the kinds of missions referred to above when considering the various self-defence theories. However, Article 42 shapes these capabilities by providing a list of the types of missions that can be deployed by the European Union: joint disarmament operations, humanitarian and rescue tasks, military advice and assistance tasks, conflict prevention and peace-keeping tasks, and tasks of combat forces in crisis management, including peace-making and post-conflict stabilisation. Within these missions, Article 42.7 TEU includes the exercise of collective self-defence in cases where a member state is a victim of an armed attack—but it should be exercised according to Article 51 of the United Nations Charter.

The cases of uses of force analysed that tend to erode the principle of the prohibition of the use of force are based on an alleged right to legitimate self-defence against states or terrorist groups. Therefore, the EU has perhaps established its position regarding the theories of anticipatory and preventive self-defence, as well as the theory of unwilling or unable, to use force based on the implementation of Article 42(7). In any event, the EU's approach is also reflected in its declarations regarding the use of force by other states.

6.5.1 The Position of the European Union Regarding the Use of Force Against Terrorist Groups

Before moving on to European Union practice, we must note that this is an area in which the European Council as well as the Council have the main role. The positions of member states are thus essential. It has been commented in this regard that: 'the national interests of the Member States related to conflict in Europe's near abroad can be substantial and diverge profoundly (...)'. Therefore, 'the extent to which the political positions of key Member States can be aligned on a given conflict is a key variable for EU institutional foreign policy effectiveness'.[199]

Coming back to practice, we will briefly refer to two cases in which some states have made use of force grounded in the theories mentioned above and which were analysed in the previous sections: the armed interventions in Afghanistan and Syria.

In this regard, the European Union backed the military operations of the United States and the United Kingdom in Afghanistan after 9/11. On 7 October 2011, in a Declaration of the EU Presidency, the European Union considered that the United States' response was legitimate based on Security Council Resolution 1368.[200] This operation has been examined earlier regarding the right of self-defence against

[199] Van Veen et al. (2021), p. 12.

[200] Military Operations in Afghanistan - Declaration by the EU Presidency; October 7, 2001, https://avalon.law.yale.edu/sept11/eu_006.asp. See also González Vega (2001), p. 12.

non-state actors on the territory of third states and, as set out, the United States based its military operation against Afghanistan on the responsibility of the Taliban government and Al Qaeda. Therefore, it is difficult to infer from that declaration whether the European Union's support entailed a recognition of the right of self-defence against non-state actors, or simply the recognition of the right of self-defence against a state, in this case, Afghanistan and its Taliban government. In addition, the EU Presidency resolution established that the military operations were 'part of a larger campaign against international terrorism which has mobilised the international community since 11 September'. Moreover, without mentioning Afghanistan, the resolution advanced that this was not a campaign 'against Islam, or against the Arab and Muslim world'. Does this mean that they were merely using force against a terrorist group?

Later, on 19 October 2001, in a Declaration by the Heads of State or Government of the European Union and the President of the Commission, the European Council confirmed 'the staunchest support for the military operations which began on 7 October and which are legitimate under the terms of the United Nations Charter and of Resolution 1368 of the United Nations Security Council'.[201] In this statement, the European Council confirmed that the main objective of these military missions was the elimination of Al Qaeda, which was considered to be responsible for the 9/11 terrorist attacks. However, the declaration also referred to the Taliban government, which had not handed the leaders of Al Qaeda over and stood for a change in government. According to the statement: 'We must now, under the aegis of the United Nations, work towards the emergence of a stable, legitimate and representative government for the whole of the Afghan people'. It was therefore not only a war against a terrorist group but also against the Taliban government, which has recently proved to be a total failure.

The European Union's position regarding the right of self-defence against non-state actors was perhaps confirmed in 2015 with France's invocation of Article 42.7 of the TEU:

> If a Member State is the victim of armed aggression on its territory, the other Member States shall have towards it an obligation of aid and assistance by all the means in their power, in accordance with Article 51 of the United Nations Charter. This shall not prejudice the specific character of the security and defence policy of certain Member States.

The European Union had not previously manifested any common position regarding the use of force in Syria. In this regard, France and the United Kingdom were

[201] Declaration by the heads of State or Government of the European Union and the President of the Commission Follow-Up to the September 11 Attacks and the Fight Against Terrorism, Brussels, 19 October 2001 SN 4296/2/01 REV 2.

favourable[202] towards an armed intervention following the use of chemical weapons by the Assad regime,[203] but Germany did not support such an intervention.

After the Paris terrorist attacks, President François Hollande, in the above—mentioned speech at the National Assembly, stated '*J'ai demandé au ministre de la Défense de saisir dès demain ses homologues européens au titre de l'article 42–7 du traité de l'Union'*,[204] and therefore requested the application of collective self-defence against a non-state actor. Even though the member states did not implement the article in full, when analysing the invocation of Article 42.7 in a meeting held on 16 and 17 November 2015, they 'expressed their unanimous and full support to France and their readiness to provide all the necessary aid and assistance'.[205]

France's invocation of Article 42.7 also gave rise to different reactions at the European Parliament. The 14 January 2016 motion for the resolution on the mutual defence clause was tabled. It included the rejection of France's invocation of Article 42.7 in the following terms:

> Strongly disagrees with the interpretation of the Article as an obligation to support France militarily, in military operations, or to justify and legitimise ongoing or already planned military actions; further rejects the presentation of the attacks in Paris as acts of war in order to legitimise a military response, and stresses that according to international law the so-called 'Islamic State / Daesh' is not a state.[206]

This resolution was rejected, and some days later, on 21 January, a resolution was passed acknowledging and welcoming 'the unanimous support given to France by all EU Member States; welcomes the readiness of all Member States to provide the full necessary aid and assistance'.[207]

We must remember at any rate that the UN Security Council Resolution 2249 (2015)[208] authorised the use of all necessary means on the territory under ISIL control to prevent and suppress terrorist acts. This Resolution was adopted on 20 November, following the European Council meeting in which the member states expressed their support to France in accordance with Article 42.7. However, even

---

[202] Irfan et al. (2014).

[203] UN Secretary General, 'Report of the United Nations Mission to Investigate Allegations of the Use of Chemical Weapons in the Syrian Arab Republic on the alleged use of chemical weapons in the Ghouta area of Damascus on 21 August 2013: note / by the Secretary-General'. A/67/997.

[204] Irfan et al. (2014).

[205] European Council, Foreign Affairs Council, 16–17 November 2015. https://www.consilium.europa.eu/en/meetings/fac/2015/11/16-17/. See Pozo Serrano (2016), p. 171; Cervell Hortal (2018), p. 93.

[206] European Parliament resolution on the mutual defence clause (Article 42(7) TEU) (2015/3034 (RSP)), B8–0057/2016. https://www.europarl.europa.eu/doceo/document/B-8-2016-0057_EN.html

[207] European Parliament resolution of 21 January 2016 on the mutual defence clause (Article 42(7) TEU) (2015/3034(RSP)), P8_TA(2016)0019. https://www.europarl.europa.eu/doceo/document/TA-8-2016-0019_EN.html

[208] Resolution 2249 (2015) Adopted by the Security Council at its 7565th meeting, on 20 November 2015. S/RES/2249 (2015)

though the Resolution referred to 'all necessary means', it was adopted under Chapter VI and therefore did not authorise the use of force.[209]

Finally, we can conclude that through its support to the French request for collective self-defence, the European Union eventually recognised, first, the applicability of self-defence against non-state actors, and second, the use of force against supporting or harbouring states.[210]

6.5.2 *Military Assistance on Request and the European Union: Practice in the Field*

To date, the European Union has deployed a significant number of civilian and military missions in third countries.[211] Analysing the mandate and capabilities of these missions, we could conclude that some of their activities clearly involve the traditional use of force on the territory in which they are deployed. Other missions, for their part, may correspond to other instances of the use of force identified by the International Court of Justice in the Nicaragua case, such as logistical support and the provision of arms and training.[212] All of these would fall in any case under the concept of military assistance on request.

In this regard, Article 42.1 TEU states that missions must be conducted in accordance with the principles of the United Nations Charter, which forms an integral part of Union law,[213] entailing the respect of the principle of non-intervention and the prohibition of the use of force. Therefore, to determine the legality of these military missions, we must consider the concept of military assistance on request.

When examining the international mandate of these types of missions, we assume that the host state's authorisation, or the Security Council's authorisation or endorsement constitutes a source of legal intervention, thus fulfilling the requirements demanded by international law.[214] Therefore, from a theoretical viewpoint, a host state's authorisation is regarded as the sole and sufficient source for the deployment of a military mission.[215]

---

[209] Urrea Corres (2016), p. 27.

[210] See Contre une invocation abusive de la légitime défense pour faire face au défi du terrorisme—A plea against the abusive invocation of self-defence as a response to terrorism. https://cdi.ulb.ac.be/contre-invocation-abusive-de-legitime-defense-faire-face-defi-terrorisme/

[211] See https://www.eeas.europa.eu/eeas/missions-and-operations_en

[212] ICJ, Military and Paramilitary Activities in and against Nicaragua, paras 195 and 228.

[213] See Van Vooren and Wessel (2014), pp. 221–222. On the problem of the autonomy of EU law see De Burca (2009), p. 1.

[214] Naert (2010), p. 233. According to Wolff, it would also lend legitimacy to the missions. Wolff (2018), p. 55

[215] Naert (2008), p. 377; Hadden (2009), p. 67.

However, the Union's practice entails a different result. Indeed, it is the Council that authorises the deployment of missions in third states, and the Council Decisions, or Joint Actions at the time, relating to the deployment of military missions, refer to the authorisation or at least the endorsement of the Security Council[216]—not only the state's authorisation.

While it seems to be widely accepted that valid state authorisation is sufficient to conduct an armed intervention or to provide military assistance within the Union, opinions differ in fact. Countries such as Finland, France and Ireland consider it important and necessary to obtain the Security Council's authorisation, while others, such as the United Kingdom, do not consider it necessary to deploy such missions.[217] The European Union's position is thus not clear on this matter. However, we can infer from practice that the Security Council's authorisation, or its endorsement at least is necessary.

We are not, however, before a complete lack of explicit assertion on this issue. Indeed, in the case of EUFOR RCA, for example, the European Union addressed a letter to the Security Council written by the High Representative pointing out that:

> A mandate by the Security Council is necessary to allow for the adoption of a decision to establish an operation by the Council of the European Union and therefore the deployment of the European Union force. I would therefore be grateful if the Security Council could adopt a resolution providing the European Union force with an appropriate mandate and including a provision authorizing it to use all necessary means to accomplish its mandate[218]

This mission in CAR seems to clearly indicate the Union's practice and position regarding the deployment of missions in third states, the Security Council backing being considered necessary. In any event, we can infer a position shift based on more recent decisions, since the Union seems to accept both the Security Council and State authorisation. In the SOPHIA operation, the Council established that it could intervene in the waters and territory of third States with Security Council or State

[216]Council Decision 2003/202/CFSP of 18 March 2003 relating to the launch of the EU military operation in the Former Yugoslav Republic of Macedonia, OJ L 76, 22/3/2003; Council Decision 2003/432/CFSP of 12 June 2003 on the launching of the European Union military operation in the Democratic Republic of Congo, OJ L 147, 14.06.2003; Council Decision 2008/101/CFSP of 28 January 2008 on the launching of the European Union military operation in the Republic of Chad and in the Central African Republic (Operation EUFOR Tchad/RCA), OJ L, 34, 8.2.2008; Council Joint Action 2004/570/CFSP of 12 July 2004 on the European Union military operation in Bosnia and Herzegovina, OJ L 252, 28.07.2004 Council Decision 2008/918/CFSP of 8 December 2008 on the launch of a European Union military operation to contribute to the deterrence, prevention and repression of acts of piracy and armed robbery off the Somali coast (Atalanta), OJ L 330, 09.12.2008; Council Decision 2010/96/CFSP of 15 February 2010 on a European Union military mission to contribute to the training of Somali security forces. *OJ* L 44, 19.2.2010; Council Decision 2013/34/CFSP of 17 January 2013 on a European Union military mission to contribute to the training of the Malian Armed Forces (EUTM Mali), OJ L 14, 18.01.2013.

[217]Wagner (2005), p. 27–28.

[218]UN Security Council, Letter dated 25 February 2014 from the Secretary General addressed to the President of the Security Council, S/2014/45.

authorisation.[219] In the same way, in the Decision on operation Irini, the Council considered the possibility of extending the mission with the authorisation of the Libyan authorities.[220] This change was confirmed by the Decision on the deployment of a military mission in Mozambique which only refers to the President of Mozambique's welcoming of the mission.[221] It was also confirmed by the Decision on the deployment of a military mission in Niger in which the EU accepted the invitation of the Minister for Foreign Affairs and Cooperation of the Republic of Niger as a legal basis for the deployment.[222]

The need to obtain a Security Council endorsement may also stem from the difficulties of ensuring that the consent given by states meets the requirements of valid consent. Indeed, some of those missions are deployed in the course of internal armed conflicts or have been authorised by transitional governments accused of human rights violations. Therefore, it would be in cases where the consent is clearly valid that the European Union could dispense with the Security Council's backing. In any case, we cannot deny that the European Union's latest practices have evolved and may lead to overlooking the requirement of a Security Council backing.

References

Abass A (2004) Regional organisations and the development of collective security. Beyond chapter VIII of the UN Charter. Hart Publishing, London

Abellán Honrubia V (2005) Sobre el método y los conceptos en Derecho Internacional Público. In: Urritia VG et al (eds) Soberanía del Estado y Derecho Internacional: Homenaje al Profesor Juan Antonio Carrillo Salcedo. Universidad de Córdoba, Córdoba, Universidad de Sevilla, Sevilla, Universidad de Málaga, Málaga

Ahmad A (2021) Self-defense against non-state actors: all over the map. Just Security

Akande D (2013) The importance of legal criteria for statehood: A response to Jure Vidmar. EJIL: Talk!

Alcaide Fernández J (2001) La "Guerra Contra el Terrorismo": ¿una "Opa Hostil" al Derecho de la Comunidad International? Rev Esp Derecho Int 32:1

Andrés Saenz de Santamaria P (2012) Sistema de Derecho Internacional Público. Civitas, Madrid

Bethlehem D (2012) Self-defense against an imminent or actual armed attack by nonstate actors. Am J Int Law 106(4):770

Bowet W (1986) The use of force for the protection of nationals abroad. In: Cassese A (ed) The current legal regulation of the use of force. Martinus Nijhoff Publishers, Leiden

Bowett DW (1994) Self-defence in international law. Manchester University Press, Manchester

Brownlie I (2012) Principles of public international law. Oxford University Press, Oxford

---

[219] Council Decision (CFSP) 2015/778 of 18 May 2015 on a European Union military operation in the Southern Central Mediterranean (EUNAVFOR MED), OJ L 122, 19.5.2015.

[220] Council Decision (CFSP) 2015/778 of 18 May 2015 on a European Union military operation in the Southern Central Mediterranean (EUNAVFOR MED, OJ L, 122 de 19.05.2015.

[221] Council Decision (CFSP) 2021/1143 of 12 July 2021 on a European Union Military Training Mission in Mozambique (EUTM Mozambique), OJ L 247, 13.7.2021.

[222] Council Decision (CFSP) 2022/2444 of 12 December 2022 on a European Union military partnership mission in Niger (EUMPM Niger), OJ L 319, 13.12.2022.

Buchan R, Tsagourias N (2017) The crisis in Crimea and the principle of non-intervention. Int Comm Law Rev 19(2–3):165
Bunk IW, Hakimi M (2022) Russia, Ukraine, and the future world order. Am J Int Law 116:687
Burri T (2010) The Kosovo opinion and secession: the sounds of silence and missing links. Ger Law J Int Law 11(8):881
Byrne M (2016) Consent and the use of force: an examination of ‘intervention by invitation’ as a basis for US drone strikes in Pakistan, Somalia and Yemen. J Use Force Int Law 97(1):109
Cassese A (1999) A follow-up: forcible humanitarian countermeasures and opinio necessitatis. Eur J Int Law 10(4):791
Cassese A (2005) International law. Oxford University Press, Oxford
Cervell Hortal MJ (2018) Sobre la doctrina “unwilling or unable State”, (¿podría el fin justificar los medios?). Rev Esp Derecho Int 70(1):77
Cheng B (1953) General principles of law as applied by international courts and tribunals. Cambridge University Press, Cambridge
Chesterman S (2001) Just war or just peace? Humanitarian intervention and international law. Oxford University Press, Oxford
Coady CAJ, Dobos N, Sanyal S (eds) (2018) Challenges for humanitarian intervention. Oxford University Press, Oxford
Committee of Legal affairs and Human Rights (2016) Legal remedies for human rights violations on the Ukrainian territories outside the control of the Ukrainian authorities
Corten O (2010) The law against war. The prohibition on the use of force in Contemporary International Law. Hart Publishing, London
Corten O (2015) Necessity. In: Weller M (ed) The Oxford handbook of the use of force in international law. Oxford University Press, Oxford
Crawford J, Nicholson R (2015) The continued relevance of established rules and institutions relating to the use of force. In: Weller M (ed) The Oxford handbook of the use of force in international law. Oxford University Press, Oxford
De Burca G (2009) The EU, the European Court of Justice and the International Legal Order after Kadi. Harv Int Law J 51:1
De Wet E (2020) Military assistance on request and the use of force. Oxford University Press, Oxford
Deeks A (2015) Taming the doctrine of pre-emption. In: Weller M (ed) The Oxford handbook of the use of force in international law. Oxford University Press, Oxford
Duchâtel M (2016) Terror overseas: understanding China’s evolving counter-terror strategy. European Council on Foreign Relations, Policy Brief
Duelfer CA (2018) The Iraq Survey Group and the search for WMD (U). Int Stud 49:2
Forteau M (2015) Rescuing nationals abroad. In: Weller M (ed) The Oxford handbook of the use of force in international law. Oxford University Press, Oxford
Ghilès F (2023) Global South does not buy western stance on Ukraine. CIDOB Opinion 765, May
Gill FD (2022) The Jus ad bellum and Russia’s “special military operation” in Ukraine. J Int Peacekeep 25:122
Glennon MJ (2015) The limitations of traditional rules and institutions related to the use of force. In: Weller M (ed) The Oxford handbook of the use of force in international law. Oxford University Press, Oxford
Gómez Isa F (2015) Los Ataques Armados con Drones en Derecho Internacional. Rev Esp Derecho Int 67:61
González Vega JA (2001) Los atentados del 11 de septiembre, la operación «libertad duradera» y el derecho de legítima defensa. Rev Esp Derecho Int 53(1–2):247
Gray C (2014) The use of force and the international legal order. In: Evans MD (ed) International law. Oxford University Press, Oxford
Gray C (2018) The conflict in Georgia – 2008. In: Ruys T, Corten O, Hofer A (eds) The use of force in international law: a case-based approach. Oxford University Press, Oxford

Green JA (2015) Questioning the peremptory status of the prohibition of use the force. Mich J Int Law 32(2):215
Green JA, Henderson C, Ruys T (2002) Russia's attack on Ukraine and the Jus ad Bellum. J Use Force Int Law 9(1):4–30
Grotious H (1625) The Iure Belli ac Pacis. Liber Primus, Caput I
Grzebyk P (2021) Escalation of the conflict between Russia and Ukraine in 2022 in light of the law on the use of force and International Humanitarian Law. Polish Yearb Int Law XLI:147
Hadden T (2009) A responsibility to assist: human rights policy and practice in european union crisis management. Hart Publishing, London
Hague AA (2021) Self-defense against self-defense, in Syria and beyond. Just Security
Heller KJ (2018) Why Al-Kibar does not contribute to pre-emptive self-defence. Opinion Juris
Henderson C (2018) The use of force and International Law. Cambridge University Press, Cambridge
Herderson C (2010) The 2010 National Security Strategy of the United States and the Obama Doctrine of 'Necessary Force'. J Conflict Sec Law 15(3):1467
Higgins R (1994) Problems and Process: International Law and how we used it. Oxford University Press, Oxford
Ingimundarson V (2022) The 'Kosovo Precedent': Russia's justification of military interventions and territorial revisions in Georgia and Ukraine. Strategic update. LSE! Ideas
Institut de Droit International (2011) Present problems of the use of force in International Law. Sub-Group C – Military assistance on request. Gerhard Hafner Rapporteur, Session Rodhes
Irfan M, Sánchez A, Margalef H and Soler E (2014) Dossier: Syria in conflict. International Reactions. CIDOB (1)
Jacobs D, Radi Y (2011) Waiting for Godot: an analysis of the advisory opinion on Kosovo. Leiden J Int Law 24(2):331
Jiménez de Aréchaga E (1978) International Law in the past third of a century. Recueil des Cours. In: Collected Courses of The Hague Academy of International Law, vol 159
Jiménez Piernas C (2011) Los principios de soberanía e integridad territorial y de autodeterminación de los pueblos en la Opinión consultiva sobre Kosovo: una oportunidad perdida. Rev Esp Derecho Int 63(1):29
Kammerhofer J (2015) The resilience of the restrictive rules on self-defence. In: Weller M (ed) The Oxford handbook of the use of force in international law. Oxford University Press, Oxford
Kohen M (2012) The principle of non-intervention 25 years after the Nicaragua Judgment. Leiden J Int Law 25(1):157
Kohen M, Del Mar K (2011) The Kosovo Opinion and UNSCR 1244 (1999): a declaration of independence from International Law ? Leiden J Int Law 24(2):109
Kramer C (2011) The legality of targeted drone attacks as US policy. Santa Clara J Int Law 9(2):375
Lieblich E (2020) Why can't we agree on when governments can consent to external intervention? A theoretical inquiry. J Use Force Int Law 7(1):5–25
Lo Giacco L (2019) "Intervention by invitation" and the construction of the authority of the effective control test in legal argumentation. Heidelb J Int Law 79:663
Medina Ortega M (2005) La prohibición de la fuerza en el siglo XXI. In: Urritia VG et al (eds) Soberanía del Estado y Derecho Internacional: Homenaje al Profesor Juan Antonio Carrillo Salcedo. Universidad de Córdoba, Córdoba, Universidad de Sevilla, Sevilla, Universidad de Málaga, Málaga
Miklasová J (2022) Russia's recognition of the DPR and LPR as illegal acts under International Law. Völkerrechtsblog, 24.02.2022
Millán Moro L (2007-2008) La interpretación de los tratados. Cursos Euromediterranéos Bancaja de Derecho Internacional, XI/XII
Naert F (2008) Accountability for violations of human rights law by EU forces. In: Blockmans S (ed) The European Union and crisis management. T.C.M. Asser Press, The Hague
Naert F (2010) International Law aspects of the EU's security and defence policy, with a particular focus on the law of armed conflict and human rights. Intersentia, Antwerp

O'Connell ME (2018) The crisis in Ukraine – 2104. In: Ruys T, Corten O, Hofer A (eds) The use of force in International Law: a case-based approach. Oxford University Press, Oxford
O'Loughlina J, Toalb G, Kolosovc V (2016) Who identifies with the "Russian World"? Geopolitical attitudes in southeastern Ukraine, Crimea, Abkhazia, South Ossetia, and Transnistria. Eurasian Geogr Econ 57:6
Orakhelashvili A (2015) Changing Jus Cogens through state practice? The case of the prohibition of the use of force and its exceptions. In: Weller M (ed) The Oxford handbook of the use of force in international law. Oxford University Press, Oxford
Patey L (2016) China, the Syrian Conflict, and the threat of terrorism: geopolitics and non-western intervention in Syria. Danish Institute for International Studies
Pattison J (2010) Humanitarian intervention and the responsibility to protect: who should intervene? Oxford University Press, Oxford
Pérez-Prat Durbán L (2004) La provincia en el Derecho Internacional. Dykinson, Madrid
Peters A (2011) Does Kosovo Lie in the Lotus-Land of Freedom? Leiden J Int Law 24(2):95
Pozo Serrano P (2016) El uso de la fuerza contra el Estado Islámico en Irak y Siria: problemas de fundamentación jurídica. Anuario Español de Derecho Internacional 32:141
Prandler A (2008) The concept of 'responsibility to protect' as an emerging norm versus 'humanitarian intervention. In: International Law between Universalism and Fragmentation. Festschrift in Honour of Gerhard Hafner. Brill/Nijhoff, Leiden
Pupcenocks J, Seltzer EJ (2021) Russian strategic narratives on R2P in the 'near abroad'. Natl Pap 49(4):757
Remiro Brotons A et al (2007) Derecho Internacional. Tirant Lo Blanch, Valencia
Richmond S (2016) Why is humanitarian intervention so divisive? Revisiting the debate over the 1999 Kosovo intervention. J Use Force Int Law 3(2):234
Roberts A (2009) Legality vs legitimacy: can uses of force be illegal but justified? In: Alston P, Macdonalds E (eds) Human rights, intervention and the use of force. Oxford University Press, Oxford
Rodley N (2015) Humanitarian intervention. In: Weller M (ed) The Oxford handbook of the use of force in international law. Oxford University Press, Oxford
Ronzitti N (1986) Use of force, Jus Cogens and State Consent. In: Cassese A (ed) The current legal regulation of the use of force. Martinus Nijhoff Publishers, Leiden
Sands P (2012) Operationalizing the UN charter rules on the use of force. In: Cassese A (ed) Realizing Utopia. The future of international law. Oxford University Press, Oxford
Schmidt M (2003) Preemptive Strategies in International Law. Mich J Int Law 24(2):521
Schrijver N, Van Den Herik L (2010) Leiden policy recommendations on counter-terrorism and International Law. Neth Int Law Rev 57(3):531–550
Simpson G (2008) Law and force in the twenty-first century. In: Armstrong D et al (eds) Routledge handbook of international law. Routledge, London
Tladi D (2017) The nonconsenting innocent state: the problem with Bethlehem's Principle 12. Am J Int Law 107(3):570
Toal G (2017) Near abroad: Putin, the West and the contest over Ukraine and the Caucasus. Oxford University Press, Oxford
Tomuschat C (1999) International Law: ensuring the survival of mankind on the eve of a new century. In: Recueil des Cours. Collected Courses of The Hague Academy of International Law, vol 281
Torrecuadrada García-Lozano S (2018) El Consejo de (¿qué?) Seguridad. In: Diez-Hochleitner Rodríguez J (ed) Principios y justicia en el derecho internacional libro homenaje al profesor Antonio Remiro Brotóns. Dykinson, Madrid
Trapp K (2015) Can non-state actors mount an armed attack? In: Weller M (ed) The Oxford handbook of the use of force in international law. Oxford University Press, Oxford
Urrea Corres M (2016) Las cláusulas de asistencia mutua y solidaridad tras los atentados de París: la respuesta europea frente al terrorismo internacional. Rev Esp Derecho Eur 57:13

Van Veen E, Di Pietrantonio PA, Ezzeddine N, Napolitano P (2021) Band-aids, not bullets: EU policies and interventions in the Syrian and Iraqi civil wars. Clingendael, CRU Report
Van Vooren B, Wessel RA (2014) EU external relations law. Cambridge University Press, Cambridge
Vermeer Z (2014) Intervention with the consent of a deposed (but legitimate) government? Playing the Sierra Leone card. EJIL: Talk!
Wagner W (2005) The democratic legitimacy of European security and defence policy. Inst Sec Stud Occas Pap 57:27–28
Weller M (2022) Russia's Recognition of the 'Separatist Republics' in Ukraine was Manifestly Unlawful. EJIL Tlak!
Wilmshurst E (2005) Principles of International Law on the use of force by states in self-defence. Chatham House. ILP WP 05/01
Wolff AT (2018) Invitations to Intervene and the Legitimacy of EU and NATO Civilian and Military Operations. Int Peacekeep 25(1):55

Chapter 7
Epilogue: Will the International Community and Its Principles Endure?

Today, the future of the world order is uncertain, owing not only to the Russian aggression but also to certain state practices and the consequent weakening of the fundamental principles of international law. Nevertheless, we can still consider that an international community exists on the grounds of common principles and values that still stand. When we refer to an international community, we are not suggesting that positions are shared across the board: not all members always have exactly the same interests. Members are not equal and interests may vary, but the principles and values remain.

In such a scenario, distinct interests may lead to different interpretations of the principles of international law or even directly to a violation of those principles. And the latter can arise if the principles are contradictory in some specific situations, if their content is not clear, or if their interpretation is contested.

The question is whether we can find a core element in these principles that will make them last over time and across different contexts. This central component may shield the principles against attempts of erosion or obliteration resulting from certain state practices. Moreover, the core element will make it possible to determine whether the majority of states defend a certain interpretation that may favour the continuity of these common principles and, consequently, the continuity of the international community.

Among the fundamental principles of international law, sovereignty constitutes an essential precept: it enables peaceful cooperation. However, sovereignty is not absolute, as it entails obligations vis-à-vis third states. Moreover, the evolution of the international community and the international system has led to further restricting state sovereignty to ensure coexistence and cooperation. It may seem contradictory, but state sovereignty needs to be strengthened as much as it needs to be limited.

International organizations have been portrayed as the main constrainers of sovereignty, since their unrelenting acquisition of new competences tends to greatly limit state sovereignty. In this sense, the European Union extended its competences to domains such as external relations. The organisation has thus shown how states

G. Fernández Arribas, *Contemporary Challenges to the Fundamental Principles of International Law and EU Interaction*, European Union and its Neighbours in a Globalized World 19, https://doi.org/10.1007/978-3-031-75453-1_7

may witness further limits to their sovereignty in realms that they had not foreseen when they decided to join. The European Union is nevertheless understood to play an essential part in achieving common objectives and in defending the interests of member states in a globalised world. In such a world, partnerships and common actions seem to be the best formula, leading perhaps some states to have 'mixed feelings' about the EU's extended competences.

This conception of sovereignty and international organizations seems to have led states to pursue new directions that can meet both sovereignty preservation concerns and the real need to cooperate in the international system through a stable institution. The result has been institutions such as treaty organs. The latter have almost all the same features and functioning as international organizations, but they are not attributed any legal status. This way, they are prevented from falling into the expansionist eagerness of competences that characterise international organizations.

Therefore, state sovereignty remains in state hands as a pivotal principle of the international community. States can revert the cession of sovereignty and review the cooperation system. But states have also acknowledged that in some domains, sovereignty loss may be necessary to achieve common objectives, and in most cases, it is up to the states to decide on the transfer of competences. This confirms that sovereignty is today essential, especially to make states feel inviolable and to maintain their status as the main international subjects.

A major triumph of a system based on community interests was the recognition of the right to self-determination, which empowered the peoples that had been under oppression for many years. However, the implementation of this right did cost the lives of many individuals, despite its international recognition, and remains to be fully realised. In this regard, the United Nations agenda still includes the list of non-self-governing territories and peoples living under occupation.

The fact that the right to self-determination originates and has its *raison d'être* in the decolonization process has not prevented it from gaining value over time. The content of the right to self-determination is broader than the guarantee of the colonial peoples' right to decide, since it also implies securing the freedom of those who are under subjugation, domination, and foreign exploitation. This latter situation is suffered by various peoples today.

The system of guaranteeing the right to self-determination under the auspices of the United Nations has not succeeded at resolving the situation of some peoples, despite the World Court's recognition of their right to self-determination. Western Sahara and the Chagos Archipelago are examples of failed decolonization processes, which have continued into the twenty-first century. Moreover, these cases show how states can abandon the interests of the international community and their commitment to the implementation of international law in favour of individual interests. However, the case of Palestine, which can be described as foreign occupation and subjugation, has attracted a lot of attention. Various solutions have been proposed, but they do not seem to have taken into account the fact that the solution lies in the hands of two parties that are asymmetrical, thus hindering a real and viable solution.

Following decolonisation, the broad interpretation of this right has brought it closer to the problem of secession. This right has been used by separatist movements to claim a right of secession in many regions, remedial secession being one of its most controversial manifestations. But secessionist claims have also taken place within the European Union. The existence of separatist movements in an integration organization, with the aim of eventually becoming part of it, has given rise to numerous controversies. Secessionist movements are part of a state's internal affairs, and territorial issues do not fall within the competence of the European Union. Yet the EU's stability also depends on the stability and strength of its individual members states, and these movements are a major threat. Moreover, the movements have manifested their intention to apply for membership or to remain as a member. Although this situation has not occurred yet, it has led the European Union to make statements that have made it look as if it has taken sides in the controversy.

For its part, the principle of non-intervention plays an essential role in guaranteeing state sovereignty. This principle has been the object of contradictory state practices, probably due to the lack of a clear and widely accepted definition and content. Nevertheless, the progress of human rights has probably brought about a shift in the interpretation of the principle, weakening it in order to enhance the pre-eminence of values, leading at times to flagrant violations of the principle for the purposes of a hidden agenda.

States' attempts to justify interventions in third states on the basis of human rights has led to the invocation of doctrines such as humanitarian intervention. According to the latter, on the grounds of the protection of human rights, states decide to intervene using the force in third state territory. Although this intervention may be justified as necessary to protect the population, the use of force outside the system established by the Charter has no legal justification. The international community, which is based on common values and principles—notable among which the respect for human rights—must therefore face the perplexing situation of choosing between two of them: non-intervention or the protection of human rights. Worthy of note, the place given to human rights in this dilemma is of great significance for the concept of the international community.

The European Union has also faced that dilemma and, leaving the question of the use of force out of the picture, it seems that the Union's position has been the defence and protection of human rights, despite a possible accusation of intervention in internal affairs. In this regard, the criticism and peaceful actions adopted to promote and to guarantee respect for human rights has until now been agreed upon by the majority of the members of the international community.

In the same vein, invitation has been used by states to justify interventions. In these cases, the main problem, setting aside the requirements for the invitation to be legal, has been that Resolution 2625 (XXV) clearly establishes the prohibition of intervention in internal armed conflicts. One attempt to reconcile the intervention by invitation and the prohibition of intervention has been based on state practice. The birth of a customary law on this topic has been assumed. However, upon analysis of that construction, it does not include a major element of custom: the *opinion iuris*. In this sense, when states have intervened in internal armed conflicts, they have never recognised that they do so based only on state invitation, the key justification is always different such as fighting terrorism, the defence of the right to self-determination or a counter intervention. This situation illustrates how strong the sovereignty principle still is. Indeed, even though the states are in fact intervening in third states, and can therefore create a new practice and thus a new customary law, they refrain from recognising such a right to intervention.

In addition, the digital world has created new sovereignty challenges that states are not ready to cope with and for which international law does not yet have clear solutions.

The potential offered by the cyber world to intervene in the internal affairs of states has been demonstrated by foreign interventions in the democratic process. While the way in which foreign states intervene may not be new and resemble past propaganda, the methods employed and the objectives have evolved. Today, cyberspace allows spreading the effect of the intervention, making it more effective and dangerous. In addition, the objectives of those interventions seem to go beyond weakening a state and attacking the whole system on which the target state rests.

The capacity of international law to cope with this challenge is affected by the space in which the activities take place. The inability to clearly determine a violation of the non-intervention principle owing to the spreading of disinformation during democratic elections originates in the definition of non-intervention itself. The definition was conceived for an analogical world. It was hard to imagine at the time how a group of messages could possibly affect the results of the national elections in a country of over 300 million inhabitants. It is also difficult to demonstrate such an effect, as there is little evidence allowing the targeted states to launch a response.

In any case, a modern interpretation of the traditional elements of non-intervention may serve as a temporary solution while we wait for international law to evolve and meet these challenges. The law lags behind the community it serves, but this slowness should not create a vacuum that puts the peaceful coexistence and cooperation of the community and its principles at risk.

Finally, the principle of the prohibition of the use of force is one of the most controversial fundamental principles of international law, as well as the most necessary to preserve. Indeed, its violation entails the violation of other fundamental principles at the same time. State practice has demonstrated that the prohibition of aggression as a *jus cogens* norm is largely accepted, and such positions differ when referring to other uses of force.

In any event, that understanding of the prohibition of aggression as a *jus cogens* norm has not prevented some states from breaching it. They have attempted to justify their actions by elaborating new theories that have led for example to new interpretations of the concept of self-defence included in Article 51 of the Charter. These new theories have sought to erode the principle of the prohibition of the use of force in order to accommodate the will of some states and not the interest of the international community. Those theories, nonetheless, are not accepted by a large part of the international community.

Pre-emptive self-defence is a clear example of the fact that, despite attempts to justify this theory based on customary law, United Nations endorsement, or State practice, the theory has no place in the international legal order and has not been adopted by the majority of states. The theory poses one of the greatest risks to peaceful coexistence, as it allows states to use armed force based solely on an internal assessment of a remote threat, thus taking state security out of the equation and, consequently, affecting international peace and security. This position confirms that the international community intends to limit and restrict the use of force and thus establishes the value of this fundamental principle for the peaceful relations and the survival of the international community.

The same applies to the unwilling or unable theory. Indeed, though one could infer the recognition of the use of force against non-state actors from state practice, use of force requires a geographical territory in which to conduct the attacks, and this is where the theory shows its drawbacks. Attempts to justify the use of force on another state's territory without its consent have not fit into any international norm. The failure of this theory and the tragic consequences for populations were visible in Afghanistan, where the United States referred to the Taliban government's refusal to prevent terrorism in order to intervene without the state's consent and with the objective of preventing future attacks. The lack of support from the intervened state transformed the intervention into a long war, not only against the terrorists but also against the state itself.

Therefore, we can affirm that the new 'war on terror' has had a real impact on the core of the principle of prohibition of the use of force, a cornerstone precept of the international system to guarantee peace and security. The principle is undergoing flexible interpretations along with an extended right to self-defence, making the following scenarios possible: attacking a state that has not conducted any previous attack; breaking legal certainty in international law; and expanding the use of force to unknown limits. The enlargement of this doctrine may have consequences on the concept of an international community. Indeed, this fundamental principle which was adopted to guarantee its survival and to generate security and trust has been weakened and modelled to the interests of some states to accommodate their solutions to fight international terrorism. In sum, it seems that the major powers have opted, as Charon's boat in Patinir's painting, for the short, fast and therefore, dangerous path.

The danger of such expansive interpretations of the use of force, which were anticipated, has been confirmed by Russia's aggression against Ukraine. Western states have regarded it as a threat to the international world order, and an open defiance of the prohibition of the use of force. Russia has used all the theories once created by Western powers to justify the illegal use of force. In this regard, Russia referred to previous illegal uses of force, mainly by the United States, and subsequently, veiledly used the same arguments, though not the same concepts. Putin referred to the need to exercise self-defence against a remote threat posed by NATO and Ukraine, as the USA did in Iraq. Russia also referred to the necessity of saving the population from a massacre and recognised the secessionist territories as NATO and Western states did in Kosovo—though not in the same order. Finally, Russia also cited the fight against terrorism, as Western states had already done in Afghanistan or Iraq.

The facts that led Western powers to the use of force differ from those in the case of Ukraine. But all of them entailed a breach of international law regarding the use of force. These uses of force have given Russia fuel to circumvent the law, use the force and jeopardise the international rule-based system.

Regrettably, despite the European Union rejecting Russia's illegal use of force in strong terms, it eventually approved some of these theories in specific situations.

In the case of military assistance by request, the practice of the European Union was to act with the Security Council's backing. By proceeding in this way, though not stating it expressly, the European Union seemed to accept the Security Council's main role with respect to the maintenance of international peace and security, as well as regarding the authorisation of the use of force. The last missions, however, were launched based only on the state request. This may be perhaps because the legitimacy and validity of the request were not in doubt, or because the European Union is changing its position, getting closer to state practice in the field. In any event, to respect the principle of non-intervention and prohibition of the use of force, the most appropriate option would be to obtain the Security Council's explicit authorisation. The latter would leave no doubt as to the legitimacy and legality of the missions deployed in third states.

In addition, the European Union has recently backed uses of force against non-state actors in the territory of third states. This seems to be the case in Afghanistan, but undoubtedly also the case of the French strikes in Syria as a response to the Paris terrorist attacks. This position of the European Union, based on fear and the inability to uphold international law even in the most difficult situations, has the consequence of moving away from the perception of being a valued actor fully respectful of international law and values, towards those states that are the object of criticism and lack of trust.

Bearing this EU position shift in mind, together with recent threats to Europe's values, we should perhaps remember María Zambrano's description of Europe before World War II:

> The betrayal began long ago. Europe was gradually hiding its face behind the fog, its axes behind a thicket. Its principles and even its appearance were hidden behind an inconsistent wall where we felt ourselves sinking little by little as we went in search of it.[1]

We can conclude that the principles on which the international community has based its existence still stand. In this regard, they have been repeatedly acknowledged by international institutions and certain states, such as in the Millennium Declaration[2] and the Declaration on the commemoration of the seventy-fifth anniversary of the United Nations.[3] This suggests that the international community intends to uphold the values they enshrined. These documents, moreover, call for the expansion of the

---

[1] 'La traición comenzó hace tiempo. Europa iba poco a poco ocultando su rostro detrás de la niebla, sus ejes detrás de una espesura. Se escondían sus principios y aún su apariencia detrás de un muro inconsistente donde nos sentíamos hundir poco a poco al ir a buscarla'. Zambrano M (1945) *La Agonía de Europa*, reedited by Trotta (2000) Madrid.

[2] UN General Assembly, United Nations Millennium Declaration 18 September 2000, A/RES/55/2.

[3] UN General Assembly, Declaration on the commemoration of the seventy-fifth anniversary of the United Nations, A/RES/75/1.

principles. For example, the Millennium Declaration refers to the respect for human rights and fundamental freedoms, the respect for the equal rights of all without distinction as to race, sex, language or religion. It also advocates the identification of what could be considered global publics goods,[4] which are also essential for the survival of the international community, such as the protection of the environment.

However, even though the inspiring of those documents, the core international principles are being contested and threatened by recent and past state practices. State powers, and mainly those that shaped the system after World War II, have interpreted, adapted or twisted international norms and principles. They have found appropriate words in every case, thus covering up their illegal actions and giving them a legal appearance. In so doing, they have failed to address the damage they have caused to international peace and security and to the international community's stability and endurance.

The way states will decide to proceed after the Russian aggression remains to be seen: Will they return to the principles that led to the adoption of the United Nations Charter? Or will they opt to further defend individual interests, putting them before the interests of the international community?

[4] United Nations Secretary-General's Report, "Our Common Agenda". United Nations, 2021.

The manufacturer's authorised representative in the EU is Springer Nature Customer Service Centre GmbH, Europaplatz 3, 69115 Heidelberg, Germany. If you have any concerns regarding our products, please contact ProductSafety@springernature.com

Printed and bound by CPI Group (UK) Ltd, Croydon, CR0 4YY
01/10/2026
02225876-0020